Producing Written and Oral Business Reports

Producing Written and Oral Business Reports

Formatting, Illustrating, and Presenting

Dorinda Clippinger

BEP BUSINESS EXPERT PRESS

Producing Written and Oral Business Reports: Formatting, Illustrating, and Presenting

Copyright © Business Expert Press, LLC, 2017.

All rights reserved. No part of this publication may be reproduced, stored in a retrieval system, or transmitted in any form or by any means—electronic, mechanical, photocopy, recording, or any other except for brief quotations, not to exceed 400 words, without the prior permission of the publisher.

First published in 2017 by
Business Expert Press, LLC
222 East 46th Street, New York, NY 10017
www.businessexpertpress.com

ISBN-13: 978-1-63157-415-3 (paperback)
ISBN-13: 978-1-63157-416-0 (e-book)

Business Expert Press Corporate Communication Collection

Collection ISSN: 2156-8162 (print)
Collection ISSN: 2156-8170 (electronic)

Cover and interior design by Exeter Premedia Services Private Ltd., Chennai, India

First edition: 2017

10 9 8 7 6 5 4 3 2 1

Printed in the United States of America.

Abstract

Producing Written and Oral Business Reports: Formatting, Illustrating, and Presenting emphasizes efficient, cost-effective methods for producing reports that will do what you, the writer or presenter, want them to do. This book is for you if you are:

- A business manager or other professional who must convey objective and organized information to others, in and outside your organization.
- An MBA candidate or an upper-level student in any professional field.

The following list highlights some of the book's content:

- Gives the steps for planning written and oral reports (presentations) by individuals and teams.
- Shows the steps and stages for preparing reports on those occasions when the first draft is not the final one.
- Discusses various ways to package, or format, reports that entice readers and lead them effortlessly through information.
- Provides guidelines for choosing and constructing traditional charts and graphs, tables, maps, and photographs, and questions a few data visualization practices.
- Shows a comprehensive analytical report with visuals and discusses the report body section by section as well as the report preliminaries and supplements.
- Offers guides for rehearsing a presentation, including the management of:
  - Speaker notes and speech anxiety symptoms;
  - Vocal and verbal aspects, including accent reduction;
  - Presentation aids in face-to-face and webinar settings;
  - Nonverbal aspects, including gesturing and walking;
  - Background conversations (Twitter backchannel and others); and
  - Question-and-answer sessions.

- Provides a checklist for revising, or re-seeing, reports from the readers' viewpoint and a checklist for evaluating a final draft.
- Includes basic formatting guides in addition to specific guides for e-mail, memo, letter, manuscript, web page, report deck, and infographics formats.
- Examines big data and data visualization trends and cites visualization authorities.
- Identifies and demonstrates frequently occurring writing lapses, or FOWLs.
- Offers guidelines for producing printed newsletters, which consumers prefer over e-mail and online newsletters.
- Draws attention to a range of online resources for producing written and oral reports.

Numerous examples, helpful illustrations, and a concise writing style let you acquire vital information rapidly; and each chapter ends with at least one convenient checklist. In *Producing Written and Oral Business Reports* you have a how-to guide for reports you generate throughout your career!

Keywords

accent, backchannel, bar graph, data visualization, deck, draft, edit, e-mail, format, FOWLs (frequently occurring writing lapses), infographics, letter, line graph, manuscript, maps, memo, newsletter, nonverbal, PDF, photos, pie chart, planning, preliminaries, presentation, question-and-answer, rehearsal, reports, revise, slides, table, team, texting, visuals, web page, webinar, writing

Contents

Preface ix
Acknowledgments xi

Chapter 1 First Draft to Final Draft 1
Chapter 2 Formatting Reports 29
Chapter 3 Illustrating Reports 81
Chapter 4 Reporting Business Research 137
Chapter 5 Presenting an Oral Report 193

Notes 235
References 239
Index 249

Preface

Producing Written and Oral Business Reports: Formatting, Illustrating, and Presenting is designed to help business managers, MBA candidates, and upper-level college students develop business reporting skills. Think of reports as organized, objective presentations of facts, experiences, or observations used in the decision-making process. Some reports are short, simple e-mail messages; others are much longer and more complex. This book is the ideal tool for mastering all kinds.

The main purpose of *Producing Written and Oral Business Reports* is to enable readers to approach report production systematically and confidently. This book provides guidelines for all aspects of oral report presentation in addition to guides for drafting, formatting, and illustrating written reports—including research-based analytical reports. Guides are also given for completing those procedures in collaboration with team members. The guidelines aim for efficiency in report production by taking advantage of current technologies.

In the book's five chapters, readers receive practical solutions to the reporting problems they deal with regularly. A chapter-by-chapter review follows:

- Chapter 1 shows you how to decide on a report writing style; then, describes drafting reports in steps and stages. It recommends revising and editing techniques that let you get those jobs done in short order. Special tips for collaborative writers offer to streamline your teamwork.
- Chapter 2 gives basic formatting guides that you can use for all your written reports. It also depicts and describes seven report formats—traditional and leading-edge—and gives you specific guides for each format. Also, it includes information for producing printed newsletters, starting with reasons for putting your newsletters on paper rather than in e-mail or online.

- Chapter 3 highlights why visuals are necessary in your reports and what sets effective visuals apart from ineffective ones. The focus is on aiding you in choosing the right visual in each situation and then giving you pointers for constructing those visuals.
- Chapter 4 dissects an analytical research report, exposing separate parts of the report body. It takes apart report supplements and prelims (preliminary parts), too. Guides aid you in deciding which parts you need in a given situation and then assist you in creating each part. Other guides focus on teamwork in producing research reports.
- Chapter 5 emphasizes planning and outlining oral reports; preparing presentation aids, including slide decks; and rehearsing presentations. It offers tips for dealing with nervousness and a foreign or regional accent if it detracts from the presenter's message. You will get how-to information for all nonverbal aspects of presenting, including ways to enhance your oral reports by walking and gesturing as you speak.

Producing Written and Oral Business Reports: Formatting, Illustrating, and Presenting is intended to be your go-to guidebook, now and later. Just reading through it in a few hours, you can pick up plenty of new, valuable information to apply immediately. Then keep the book handy for future reference as the need arises for you.

Please send your suggestions for improving future editions of *Producing Written and Oral Business Reports*.

Acknowledgments

I owe a huge debt to Dr. Shirley Kuiper, who laid groundwork for this book years ago. And I appreciate Dr. Debbie DuFrene's editorial expertise in transforming my drafts into this highly useful publication. My husband, William Jewell, deserves thanks for his enduring support. During my 50 years of teaching, publishing, research, and business ownership, many colleagues and students influenced my thinking about communication and education for business. And they earned my enduring gratitude.

CHAPTER 1

First Draft to Final Draft

Good reports start out with careful planning. Your plan will start with articulating your purpose and what it is you want to accomplish. What is your general purpose: production, innovation, goodwill, what? Then, specifically, what do you want the receiver(s) of your report to do?

Next, you will need to analyze your audiences—both your immediate reader and possible others who might be brought into the thought process—and what they want and need from the report. Another important element in your planning is to consider the context, or overall circumstances, in which you are writing and whether the writing style should be formal or informal.

Then, you will decide on the content needed, how to organize the report, and how to deliver it. From there you will outline the report, either informally (list of keywords, phrases, or both) or formally (structured numbering system).

With your outline in hand, you are ready to create the first draft.[1] In simple reporting situations, the first draft often is also the final draft. In more complex situations, you may need to revise and edit the draft several times before it is finally produced and delivered. Each successive draft should bring you closer in style to what your audience needs and expects.

Style can be thought of as a distinctive manner of expression or a technique by which something is done or created. Empathy, accuracy, completeness, conciseness, and clarity are qualities that should be demonstrated in all reports—long or short, simple, or complex. To achieve these qualities, you must decide purposefully on a writing style instead of just letting it happen. Ideally, writing style decisions are made before you begin writing your first draft.

Decide on a Writing Style

In choosing a writing style for a particular report, empathize with your readers. Consider their needs—both information needs and ego needs. Information needs are the data that will enable your audience to understand and fulfill the objectives of your report. Ego needs are desires for recognition and acknowledgment of worth. A report may provide all the information a receiver needs; but unless the report also satisfies ego needs, it may not motivate that person to act.

The content, context, and desired outcomes for simple and complex reports may differ considerably. The overall style of simple, relatively short reports (such as a trip report, a production report, or minutes of a meeting) differs from the style of complex specialized reports (such as a business plan or a business research report). Then, the decisions you make about report tone, level of formality, and objectivity will further define your writing style.

Choose Report Tone

Tone is evidence of your attitude toward your message and the receiver. Some descriptors of tone are personal, impersonal; formal, informal; positive, negative; courteous, curt; passive, forceful; and conciliatory, defensive. In written reports, tone is conveyed by word choice and message structure. In oral reports, tone also may be conveyed by vocal pitch and emphasis, posture, and gestures.

The following examples demonstrate how you might plan to accommodate a receiver's needs by carefully selecting your tone, structure, and delivery medium, in addition to content. Notice that your objective in both cases is to get the receiver to act.

Style for a Simple, Informal Report

> *Sender's objective:* A bank teller will move to a station that will enable more effective customer service.
> *Receiver's needs:* Information needs—to know when to move, where to move. Ego needs—to be respected as a valued member of the organization.

Report structure: Direct—main point followed by brief explanation, if any.
Report tone: Courteous, informal.
Delivery medium: Face-to-face, with this e-mail follow-up.
Example: As we discussed this morning, Juan, please close your teller window and take over the drive-up window every Friday from 1 p.m. until closing time. Cars back up out there on Friday afternoons.

Style for a Relatively Complex Report

Sender's objective: Upper management will move the store to a new location so that profits may increase.
Receiver's needs: Information needs—justification for, likely benefits of, and estimated costs of moving the store. Ego needs—recognition of status and decision-making authority; respect for value of reader's time.
Report structure: Direct—recommendation to move the store to a new location followed by supporting details: profitability of current location, problems associated with current location, goals for store, cost of move to new location, and benefits of move.
Report tone: Formal and respectful, yet forceful and confident.
Delivery medium: Written report, supplemented by oral presentation; both enhanced by visual aids.

Choose Degree of Formality

When you draft a report, you must choose the degree of formality you want to convey. Formality is conveyed by language and by inclusion or exclusion of certain parts of a report. You can decide what formal parts to include with your report after you have written the report body. You must, however, decide about the formality of language before you draft the report body.

Some contexts may justify informality, a style that is most often reserved for situations in which you know the primary reader well or frequently work with that person. Even under those circumstances, however, an informal style may not be appropriate because secondary readers must also be considered. If a report is likely to pass among many readers, some of whom you may not even know, a formal style is generally preferable. Similarly, when the primary reader files the report for future use by other people, a formal style is often preferred.

Assume, for example, that two cities are trying to annex a residential area known as Winslow Hills. You are a member of the Winslow Hills Homeowners Association, and its officers have asked you to determine the homeowners' attitudes and preferences with respect to annexation. The officers will circulate the summary of your final report to all homeowners and will present the full report to the competing city councils. In such a situation, an informal style is appropriate for a progress report to the officers of the homeowners' association, whom you know well and with whom you share common concerns. The final report, however, would likely be written in a formal style, which would show respect for the elected officials while emphasizing the seriousness of the annexation issue.

No sharp distinction exists between formality and informality in reports. Consequently, no one can define exactly what constitutes formal or informal language. The major difference between formal and informal language is the presence or absence of words that suggest how well the writer and reader (speaker and listener) are acquainted. The language we use with peers or individuals whom we know well—informal language—is often characterized by frequent use of first names, contractions, and first- and second-person pronouns: *I, me, my, mine, we, us, our, ours, you, your, yours*. In addition, colloquial expressions—words and phrases commonly used in conversations—connote informality. Examples include *OK, thumbs up, go-ahead* as equivalents for *agreement, approval*. Other colloquial expressions are unique to certain regions, *such as "crack the window"* for *"open the window" and "cut on the light"* for *"turn on the light."*

Despite the popularity of text messaging and its increasing use in business, the conventions of those messages—numerous abbreviations and emoji, sentence fragments, and missing capitalization, punctuation, and vowels—are generally too informal for business reporting. Most texters are young professionals.[2] Although able to decipher and send personal text messages, older professionals may be offended by such informality for business reports.

For several other reasons, even simple, direct reports should probably be delivered by e-mail or phone, not by text message. Texts can give the impression that the message is not important. Unlike e-mail, texting leaves no digital paper trail.[3] Use of a voice-to-text application only complicates matters. As the sender, you cannot be sure whose voice your phone picked up—maybe a nearby conversation or song lyrics from another device near you.[4]

In contrast, the language we tend to use with someone who holds a high-status position or individuals whom we do not know well represents formal language. Absence of first- and second-person pronouns, use of courtesy or position titles with full names or last names, and avoidance of contractions and colloquial expressions characterize formal style.

Formality, however, does not equate to wordiness, unwieldy sentences, or overuse of passive verbs. Even formal writing can be concise, clear, and vigorous. The following examples contrast features of informal and formal writing.

First- and Second-Person Pronouns

> *Informal:* I interviewed your information technology managers and technicians. Your IT crew is eager to have a tai chi class offered on your premises during the lunch hour.
> *Formal:* Interviews with information technology managers and technicians revealed their readiness to participate in an on-site tai chi class aimed at stress reduction.
> *Informal:* Your IT employees are stressed-out; you should have a good turnout if you offer a tai chi class during lunch hour.
> *Formal:* Information technology personnel have strong motivation to support an on-site tai chi class.

Names and Titles

> *Informal:* Jean said that IT support increased 12 percent in February.
> *Formal:* Ms. Jean Herriot, IT support coordinator, reported a 12 percent increase in support requests during February.

Informal: If you need additional information, Alex, please let me know.

Formal: If you need additional information, Mr. Padgett, please let me know.

Contractions

Informal: What's your reaction? I'm eager to hear from you. Call me at 555-8765.

Formal: Please direct questions or comments about this proposal to Ms. Marlow at 555-7654, Extension 109.

Informal: Your IT guys said they're swamped with support requests.

Formal: Information technology managers and technicians expressed concern about the volume of support requests.

Colloquialisms

Informal: We have to get on the ball and tackle the financial stress problem of our employees. Let's find out what companies like ours are offering for financial fitness and figure out how we can handle another employee benefit.

Formal: We must consider seriously the issues of financial stress and financial fitness for our employees. We should study what companies similar to ours are offering and whether we can fund another employee benefit.

Informal: Let's look at the numbers. The bottom line is that our employees need help managing and investing their money, and we can afford to provide four personal finance seminars if we reduce vacation allowances. Some employees said they wouldn't be able to afford a vacation anyway due to money problems.

Formal: The data show two important facts:

1. Washtenaw Electric employees want resources to help them manage their finances.

> 2. Some Washtenaw Electric employees prefer a financial education plan over a generous vacation allowance.
>
> Washtenaw Electric can afford to provide four seminars, led by certified financial planners, if it also reduces vacation allowances.

To summarize, informal reports project a personal tone, using first- and second-person pronouns and near-conversational wording. Figure 1.1 depicts a feasibility study involving seven reports. Notice that the two informal reports represent people accustomed to communicating and interacting regularly with the report reader (sales associate with sales manager and research director with research staff).

Sender	Receiver (Audience)	Report Content	Delivery Medium and Degree of Formality
A&P sales associate	A&P sales manager	Consumers in Brazil enjoy grilled meats; most use charcoal. Brazil is a potential market for A&P gas grills	Face-to-face; informal
Sales manager	Vice president, marketing	Expanding consumer market in Brazil is attracting many U.S. companies; few of A&P's competitors are selling gas grills in South America	Written; semiformal; supplemented by oral (face-to-face) summary
Vice president, marketing	Market research director	Summary of previous reports; request to study feasibility of entering South American market	Written; semiformal
Market research director	Research staff	Summary of vice president's reports; request for research proposal	Informal presentation in weekly staff meeting
Research staff	Market research director	Proposed plan for feasibility study	Written; formal research proposal
Research staff	Market research director	Findings, conclusions, recommendations of feasibility study	Formal; written; likely supplemented by formal oral presentation
Research staff and market research director	Management committee	Background; summary of preliminary studies; findings, conclusions, recommendations of feasibility study	Formal oral presentation including visuals; written summary of key findings and recommendations

Figure 1.1 Differing degrees of report formality

In contrast to informal reports, a formal report typically uses impersonal language and tone. Although formal reports may be written in memo format (internal reports) or letter format (external reports), they are often presented in manuscript form. The format frequently includes headings to guide the reader through the report content; and, if presented in manuscript format, the report usually includes a title page and perhaps a transmittal message. As report length increases, other preliminary pages may be included to accommodate reader needs, such as a table of contents and an executive summary. Some lengthy formal reports also contain supplements such as a source list and an appendix or several appendices.

The feasibility report that ends Figure 1.1 would likely be prepared as a formal report because it would go not only to the research staff's immediate supervisor (Director of Management Research) but also to upper-level management (Management Committee). In addition, the report will contain much technical market information, requiring a table of contents, a source list, and perhaps some appendices. The writer may also provide an executive summary to give readers a concise preview of the report content.

Some situations call for a combination of formal and informal styles. For example, a lengthy, complex analysis of a business problem may be presented in formal style and format, but it may be accompanied by a transmittal message that is written in an informal tone and supplemented by a semiformal oral summary.

Whether you choose a formal style, an informal style, or a combination of the two, all information must be presented objectively, not emotionally.

Write Objectively and Confidently

Objectivity requires that all available, relevant data is presented and that you focus on the data, not on what you think or feel about the situation. Each step in data analysis—presenting data, interpreting data, drawing conclusions, and making recommendations—takes you further from the original facts, experiences, or observations. To maintain credibility, discipline yourself to keep the analysis free of your biases or emotions and express your conclusions and recommendations in objective language.

For example, a bank loan officer may observe that the number of applications for home equity loans increased substantially in late December and early January. But to conclude that borrowers use home equity loans to pay for debts incurred buying winter holiday gifts is an improper conclusion. Such a conclusion may be drawn only if information obtained from customers consistently shows that they intend to use the equity loan to pay for holiday purchases. Likewise, to conclude that borrowing on home equity is irresponsible financial management is the expression of an opinion based on the writer's values, not an objective conclusion.

The following examples contrast emotional language with objective language.

> *Emotional:* I was not surprised to find that the vast majority of your clients strongly favored that you move your office to a new location. The current office is in a seedy part of town, and clients are afraid they may be mugged when they leave their cars to come into your office. Therefore, you need to find a new site now or lose your clients.
>
> *Objective:* Eighty-five percent of the clients surveyed said they are reluctant to come to your office in person. The crime level in this neighborhood is a deterrent. Therefore, I recommend that you immediately begin a search for an office in a safer area.

Although your writing should not contain unjustifiable expressions of opinion or emotion, you should demonstrate confidence in your findings, conclusions, and recommendations. Expressing yourself with confidence does not mean being brash or impudent. Instead, it means that when the data are sufficient, you do not hesitate to state your objective findings, conclusions, and recommendations, even if they are contrary to the outcome your reader might have preferred. If, on the other hand, the data are insufficient to support any logical and objective conclusions and recommendations, you also state that fact confidently.

To demonstrate confidence, many writers use imperative sentences—beginning with an action verb—like a command—when stating recommendations that are clearly supported by the data. The following examples contrast impudent, hesitant, and confident styles.

Impudent: This agency has obviously neglected to consider the safety of its clients. That error can be corrected simply by doing two things:

1. Install better exterior lighting at the current location.
2. Begin an immediate search for an office in a safer area of the city.

Hesitant: The agency might want to consider looking for an office in a safer part of town. In the meantime, the agency could probably also install better exterior lighting at the current location.

Confident: Our recommendations to Family Counseling:

1. Install better exterior lighting at the current location.
2. Begin an immediate search for an office in a safer area of the city.

Unjustifiably confident: Approximately 50% of the Family Services Board of Directors are eager to relocate the office. With their enthusiasm, you'll probably see them moving to a new facility within a month.

Justifiably hesitant: Approximately 50% of the Family Services Board of Directors expressed reluctance to relocate the office. Relocation at this time appears to be unwise. Further study to determine how to overcome objections to relocation may be necessary to ensure the eventual success of a plan to move to a new facility.

Drafting in Steps and Stages

Some, but not all, reports begin with a rough, or preliminary, draft. Others begin with a fairly well-organized, appropriately styled draft, ready for someone to review it.

The steps and stages for preparing multiple-draft reports are diagrammed in Figure 1.2. Begin drafting at the appropriate stage and repeat the steps through Stage 3.

Creating a Preliminary (Stage 1) Draft

As Figure 1.2 indicates, steps in the writing process differ, depending on the complexity of the report and relationship of the parties involved. For example, if you were asked to prepare a complex report, such as a study

	Stage 1 Preliminary draft	Stage 2 Review draft	Stage 3 Near-final draft
Step 1: Create a draft.	This initial draft helps you: • Discover what you still need to find out • Organize ideas • Experiment with format Preliminary draft is not ready for review or editing because writer still needs to do a major revision. Start here if you: • Find drafting to be difficult; • Have not written a similar report; • Do not yet know what material to include; • Cannot outline the report; or • Do not know your manager's preferences and expectations.	This well-organized draft is ready to be reviewed for content and organization. Review draft is not ready for editing because writer may still change content greatly. Start here if you: • Understand your manager's expectations and preferences; • Have made good strategic decisions about content and organization; and • Can create a good, defensible outline of your report.	This near-final draft is ready for editing and should not be reworked in major ways unless it has major omissions. Start here if you: • Are writing something simple or familiar; or • Have planned the report well and are under great time pressure.
Step 2: Review your own draft.	• Use revision checklist (Figure 1.3). • Revise before showing to a reader. • List questions to ask a colleague or project manager, to help you control that conversation.	• Use revision checklist (Figure 1.3) and revise as needed. • Then give report to a colleague or project manager to review.	• Use revision checklist (Figure 1.3). • Use Editing Checklist (Figure 1.4). • Then give report to a colleague or project manager to review.
Step 3: Get a reader review.	Reader should: • Tell writer what is confusing and what questions need to be answered; and • Return report to writer for revision.	Reader should: • Check draft using revision checklist (Figure 1.3); and • Return report to writer for revision.	Reader should: • Check draft using revision checklist (Figure 1.3); • Check draft using editing checklist (Figure 1.4); • Correct minor problems; and • Point out major style problems to report writer.

Figure 1.2 Report draft stages and steps[5]

of the feasibility of moving your office to a new location, and you did not yet know all that should be included, you would begin at Stage 1 (Preliminary Draft), Step 1. The preliminary draft will be a tool for you as the report writer. It will help you organize (or reorganize) your ideas, make evident any serious gaps in information, and let you experiment with format, including visuals.

With your outline as a guide, you can draft any report by major sections. However, you need not draft the report in the sequence in which it will finally appear. Attempting to write the report from beginning to end as indicated by the outline may create writing barriers that delay production of the report.

A key to successful drafting is to recognize writing barriers and develop strategies for overcoming them. The following list suggests such strategies. Use of a particular strategy is a matter of personal preference.

- Begin by drafting the easiest sections of the report. This technique provides a sense of accomplishment and stimulates the writer to move on to the more difficult sections.
- Conversely, begin with the sections that you think will be most difficult to draft. Thus, you will feel less pressured toward the end of the writing process.
- Move among sections of the document. When you have difficulty with one part of the report, work on another section. After some time has passed, you will often find that you have subconsciously removed the writing block and can think more clearly and write more easily about the difficult topic.
- Prepare all visuals—tables, charts, graphs—before writing the report narrative. Your primary writing task then is to explain those illustrations. After writing the explanatory narrative, your next task is to write the transitions between parts of the report. Your final task is to write introductory and summary sections.

After writing and reviewing the preliminary draft, you should be prepared to discuss with a colleague or manager any questions that arose as you wrote it (Stage 1, Steps 2 and 3). Following such a conversation, you would be ready to move to Stage 2 (Review Draft).

Creating a Review (Stage 2) Draft

Figure 1.2 demonstrates, however, that not all reports need to begin at Stage 1, Step 1. A report presenting your comparative evaluation of three properties considered for the new office location could well begin at Step 1 of Stage 2 (Review Draft). If you have already collected and analyzed your data, have prepared a comprehensive outline—and perhaps even had the outline approved—you should be able to begin here. In this stage you prepare a draft that you will review thoroughly for accuracy, completeness, clarity, and structure. When you think you have done your best job, give the report to someone else—a colleague or a manager—for review. When doing so, be sure the reviewer knows not to rewrite (revise) or edit your draft. That person may suggest additions, deletions, or other modifications and return the draft to you, leading you to Step 1 of Stage 3 (Near-final Draft).

Creating a Near-Final (Stage 3) Draft

Figure 1.2 further shows that for some reports you may be able to begin at Stage 3, Step 1. This draft is ready for possible revisions in style and final editing. A simple report announcing that the office will be closed next Monday so that commercial movers can move all furniture and equipment to the new location is an example of such a report. For this report, you could easily write a near-final draft after consulting your informal outline.

Revising and Editing Drafts

Before preparing a final draft, read your report carefully to evaluate all aspects: content, structure, diction (choice of words), tone, overall style, and impact. The drafting guide shown in Figure 1.2 encourages you to review your draft carefully (Step 2 of each stage) and to subject your work to another person's critical review (Step 3 of each stage).

Revise Methodically

Revising a report involves re-seeing it from the receiver's point of view. Thus, revision also consists of rewriting sentences, paragraphs, or entire sections of a report or moving them to different locations. Adding or deleting information may also be part of the revision process. Figure 1.3 provides a systematic guide that you and your reviewers can use as you prepare the specific parts of your report.

As Figure 1.3 suggests, you should evaluate the power of the introduction and ending, the accuracy and completeness of the report's content, and the report's organization.

As you finish revising your draft, it should flow smoothly from start to finish, whether drafted by an individual or a team. The reader should

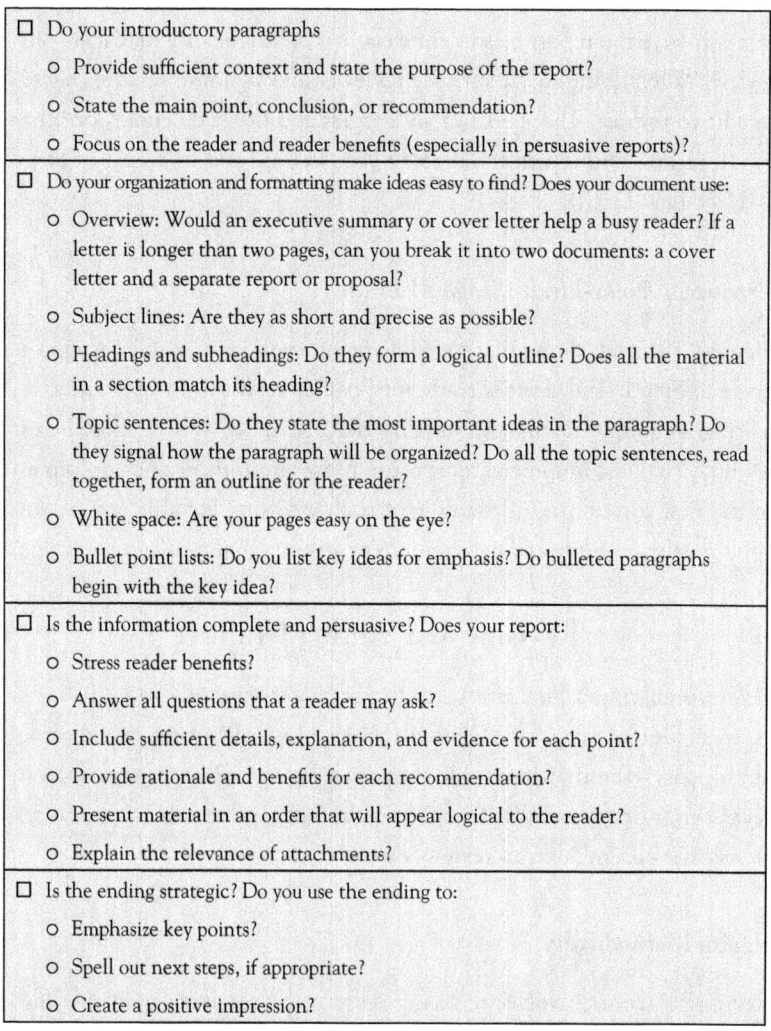

☐ Do your introductory paragraphs
o Provide sufficient context and state the purpose of the report?
o State the main point, conclusion, or recommendation?
o Focus on the reader and reader benefits (especially in persuasive reports)?
☐ Do your organization and formatting make ideas easy to find? Does your document use:
o Overview: Would an executive summary or cover letter help a busy reader? If a letter is longer than two pages, can you break it into two documents: a cover letter and a separate report or proposal?
o Subject lines: Are they as short and precise as possible?
o Headings and subheadings: Do they form a logical outline? Does all the material in a section match its heading?
o Topic sentences: Do they state the most important ideas in the paragraph? Do they signal how the paragraph will be organized? Do all the topic sentences, read together, form an outline for the reader?
o White space: Are your pages easy on the eye?
o Bullet point lists: Do you list key ideas for emphasis? Do bulleted paragraphs begin with the key idea?
☐ Is the information complete and persuasive? Does your report:
o Stress reader benefits?
o Answer all questions that a reader may ask?
o Include sufficient details, explanation, and evidence for each point?
o Provide rationale and benefits for each recommendation?
o Present material in an order that will appear logical to the reader?
o Explain the relevance of attachments?
☐ Is the ending strategic? Do you use the ending to:
o Emphasize key points?
o Spell out next steps, if appropriate?
o Create a positive impression?

Figure 1.3 Report revision checklist[6]

get a sense of forward movement when reading the final draft. And your summaries and transitions should help the reader understand the relevance of what has been said and anticipate what will be said next. Vague references such as this, that, and it without a clear antecedent disrupt the forward flow. Similarly, comprehensive references like as stated earlier or the previously mentioned facts often require readers to move backward in the document to be sure they understand the reference.

The following examples contrast a style that moves forward with a style that disrupts the message flow. The first example disrupts the flow by requiring readers to return to previous sections of the document if they do not recall the criteria. In the second example, the writer briefly recalls previous information as a transition to a discussion of empathy, thereby moving the reader forward in the document.

> *Disrupted Flow*: In addition to the characteristics already discussed, your reports should demonstrate empathy for the reader.
> *Forward Flow*: Accuracy, clarity, and conciseness will help the reader understand your message. In addition, your writing should demonstrate empathy for the reader.

After moving through all the steps in Stage 3 (Figure 1.2), you are ready to format the report. Chapter 2 presents guides for document design and commonly used report formats.

Edit Thoroughly

Editing consists of locating and correcting errors at the paragraph, sentence, and word levels and includes these categories of errors: content, format, grammatical, mechanical, and usage (word choice).[7] Attention to these details helps you communicate effectively and builds your credibility in the business community. Harvard Business Review blogger Keith Wiens posted "I Won't Hire People Who Use Poor Grammar. Here's Why."[8] According to Wiens, people who confuse their, there, and they're "deserve to be passed over for a job—even if they are otherwise qualified for the position." Wiens went on to state that grammar is relevant for all companies and that in his experience "people who make fewer mistakes on a grammar test (which he administers to every job applicant) also make fewer mistakes when they are doing something completely unrelated to writing."

In a related article, Brad Hoover concluded from his research that good grammar is a predictor of professional success. Professionals with fewer grammar errors in their LinkedIn profiles achieved higher positions in their first 10 years of employment; received promotions more frequently during that period; and also changed jobs more often. Grammar skills as such may not cause career success but may be linked to contributing attributes, such as attention to detail, critical thinking, and intellectual aptitude.[9]

Wiens' reactions and Hoover's findings demonstrate the importance of correcting the most common errors to best represent yourself, your work, and your employer.

Identify Frequently Occurring Writing Lapses (FOWLs)

The following list describes common types of writing lapses you will want to overcome:

- *Content lapses* include incorrect or missing details, such as dates and days of the week, locations and times of events, lists of items, and spelling of names (people and places). Confirm these data extra carefully for accuracy and completeness. Ask the person who reviews your report draft to point out content lapses; then proof the draft yourself.
- *Format lapses* are variations in report design. Examples include misaligned bullets, multiple bullet styles, bullets instead of numbers when ranking and order matter, and overuse of ALL CAPS. Additional examples involve inconsistent fonts, font sizes, and font styles; inconstant heading styles; and a mix of blocked and indented paragraphs. Format lapses also take in extra or missing spaces between words and sentences and erratic spacing between lines of text. In Chapter 2, we will look more closely at problems related to report formatting.

- *Grammatical lapses* include violations of punctuation rules and sentence structure errors. Lapses in the punctuation grouping include omitting needed apostrophes and commas, inserting unnecessary apostrophes and commas, and joining two sentences with a comma (comma splice). Omitting or misusing the colon and semicolon are also in this category, along with overuse of parentheses or parenthetical expressions.[10] Three common sentence structure flaws are sentence fragments; fused sentences (comma splice or run-on); and faulty sentences (nonparallel construction, mixed construction, or dangling and misplaced modifiers).[11]

The following examples illustrate faulty sentences.

FOWL: Nonparallel construction

1. The company's net income differed from its projections because of random events, ignoring relevant assumptions, and when interest rates fluctuated.
2. This job requires skills in accounting, management, and the ability to communicate well.
3. An employee manual should be revised when:
   New laws are enacted.
   The company changes benefit plans.
   There are new company policies.
   Changes in company goals and philosophies.

Parallelism indicates equality of ideas. To achieve parallelism, balance nouns with nouns, adjectives with adjectives, verbs with verbs, adverbs with adverbs, prepositions with prepositions, conjunctions with conjunctions, and verbals with verbals.

Corrections

1. The company's net income differed from its projections because of random events, omission of relevant assumptions, and fluctuations of interest rates.

2. This job requires skills in accounting, management, and communication.
3. An employee manual should be revised when changes occur in:
Laws
Company benefits
Company policies
Company goals and philosophies.

FOWL: Mixed construction

1. By attending the research conference as a company representative rather than as an instructor was a new experience for Cynthia.
2. Drake realized that during the team meeting how inattentive he had been.
3. Because the area between Charleston Harbor and King Street receives the greatest impact from cruise ships in the harbor explains why the analysis was limited to that area.

Mixed construction usually causes an awkward sentence, as parts of the sentence are mismatched. In general, mixed construction happens when a sentence begins with one grammatical structure and shifts to another grammatical form. Specifically, in a mixed construction the subject of the sentence does not match the verb or the verb does not match the object.

Corrections

1. Attending the research conference as a company representative rather than as an instructor was a new experience for Cynthia.
2. Drake realized that he had been inattentive during the team meeting. Or Drake realized that during the team meeting he had been inattentive.
3. Because the area between Charleston Harbor and King Street receives the greatest impact from cruise ships in the harbor, the team's analysis was limited to that area.

FOWL: Misplaced and dangling modifiers

> 1. After completing the audit, *a* report *was prepared for the client.*
> 2. Raising EPS to $5.79, the *annual report* shows diversification has paid off.
> 3. For a family of four with a teenage driver, *which drives 15,000 miles per year,* the CR-V is a more economical vehicle than the Suburban.

A modifier must be structurally and logically related to a word or clause in the sentence. Dangling and misplaced modifiers frequently occur when the writer begins a sentence with a verbal phrase and follows the phrase with a noun that the phrase cannot logically modify. Misplaced modifiers frequently occur when a sentence contains too many modifying words and phrases.

Corrections

> 1. After completing the audit, the accountant prepared a report for the client.
> 2. The annual report shows that diversification has paid off, raising EPS to $5.79.
> 3. For a four-member family that drives 15,000 miles per year, the CR-V is a more economical vehicle than the Suburban.

- *Mechanical lapses* include typographical errors and errors in spelling, punctuation, number expression, capitalization, and abbreviations.

  Typographical lapses are typing errors (typos), such as duplications and transposed letters. In word processing programs, the autocorrect feature and spelling checkers may fix or find typos, but they may not find all of them. If you type the word *from* instead of *form*, the spelling checker will not likely identify the word as incorrect—because both words are in the spelling checker's dictionary.

  Check for typos in numbers, including addresses, money amounts, and phone numbers.

Spelling lapses often involve confusion of sound-alike words (accept and except, its and it's) and similar sounding words (adapt, adept, and adopt; precedent and president) and misuse of the hyphen in compound words. When in doubt about the spelling of any word, look it up. If your word-processing software includes a thesaurus, enter a synonym of the word in question. The problematic word may appear in the results.
- *Usage lapses* result from confusion of similar words, such as among and between, economic and economical, farther and further, fewer and less, infer and imply, lay and lie, passed and past, perspective and prospective, precede and proceed, than and then, and who and whom. Usage lapses are hardest to find when proofing alone because you chose the incorrect word in the first place.

Guides to Effective, Efficient Editing

The following techniques can help you find errors in content, format, grammar, mechanics, and usage:[12]

- *Let your near-final draft rest for at least a few hours* after writing. Do tasks unrelated to your report draft. When you return to the draft, you can edit from a fresh viewpoint.
- *Check for content lapses first.* When in doubt about facts, search the Internet if doing so makes sense. Use two or three reputable websites to cross-reference information, avoiding overreliance on Wikipedia. In reports that will be posted and read online, check that all your links work and that e-mail addresses are accurate.
- *Look for the kinds of errors you are most apt to make.* If, for example, you often misuse apostrophes, proof your draft once just for apostrophes. If you tend to use the word myself in place of the word me or the phrase for he and his family instead of for him and his family, find and eliminate these problems as you begin revising. In most instances, you can use the find or search feature in your word-processing software to target these lapses.

- *Read your near-final draft aloud.* Doing so accomplishes several goals. Reading audibly causes you to read more slowly and forces the brain to see mistakes and gaps that are glossed over during silent reading. And if your voice falters, you have probably found something you need to change.
- *Read your near-final draft backwards,* starting with the last paragraph and ending with the first. This disruption of the flow in your draft, forces you to pay close attention to details. Where accuracy is critical—in a new contract, for example—read each sentence backward.
- *Check your near-final draft in a different format.* For example, make a paper copy and note edits on it; convert your text to HTML (web page); or simply change the font or font color temporarily. Increase the font size temporarily so you can see details—distinguish between commas and periods for example.
- *Proof your text multiple times.* If you try to find all lapses in a single reading, you will likely miss some. Instead, narrow each scan to a particular kind(s) of lapse—one for content errors, one for capitalization and punctuation mistakes, one for grammar lapses, one for spelling errors and typos, and a final one for format inconsistencies.
- *Run spelling, grammar, and other checkers* at the end, because you will make changes as you proofread. This guide comes with a caveat: Proofing or checker technology is limited, with error detection rates generally in the 20% to 50% range.

Naturally, ignore absurd suggestions from your checker software. For those occasions when you are unsure about a suggested correction, keep an office reference manual handy, such as The Gregg Reference Manual, 11th edition, which is available in print and online (highered.mheducation.com).

For maximum effect, use three or more checkers on one piece of writing, starting with the tools included in your word processing software. A few other online checker options include the following:[13]

22   PRODUCING WRITTEN AND ORAL BUSINESS REPORTS

- o After the Deadline (www.polishmywriting.com)
- o Ginger Grammar Checker (www.gingersoftware.com)
- o Grammarly (www.grammarly.com)
- o Language Tool (www.languagetool.org)
- o Online Correction (www.onlinecorrection.com)
• *Edit a passage again* if you changed it significantly while editing.

The checklist in Figure 1.4 can aid you as you evaluate your edited draft.

Although writers sometimes underrate the importance of the matters discussed in this chapter, mastering this content may ultimately make or break your career, as is shown in the following anecdote.

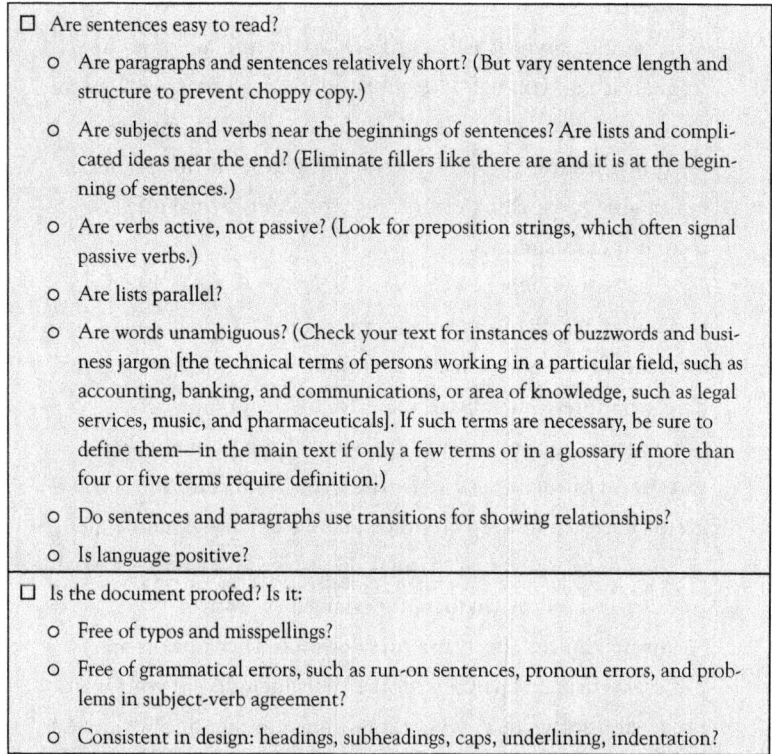

☐ Are sentences easy to read?
  o Are paragraphs and sentences relatively short? (But vary sentence length and structure to prevent choppy copy.)
  o Are subjects and verbs near the beginnings of sentences? Are lists and complicated ideas near the end? (Eliminate fillers like there are and it is at the beginning of sentences.)
  o Are verbs active, not passive? (Look for preposition strings, which often signal passive verbs.)
  o Are lists parallel?
  o Are words unambiguous? (Check your text for instances of buzzwords and business jargon [the technical terms of persons working in a particular field, such as accounting, banking, and communications, or area of knowledge, such as legal services, music, and pharmaceuticals]. If such terms are necessary, be sure to define them—in the main text if only a few terms or in a glossary if more than four or five terms require definition.)
  o Do sentences and paragraphs use transitions for showing relationships?
  o Is language positive?
☐ Is the document proofed? Is it:
  o Free of typos and misspellings?
  o Free of grammatical errors, such as run-on sentences, pronoun errors, and problems in subject-verb agreement?
  o Consistent in design: headings, subheadings, caps, underlining, indentation?

Figure 1.4 Report editing checklist[14]

An MBA graduate returned to reminisce with his former report writing professor. He related his experience in a highly competitive training program. The program required each trainee to give five presentations; a single lapse, including the kinds presented in this chapter, would result in a failing assessment for that report. Three failures would result in expulsion from the program.

How did this man pass the test? He remembered his professor urging students to know their weaknesses and to submit all writing to a trusted critic before releasing it to the ultimate audience. In this instance, the audience included readers and listeners who could make or break his future with the company. The MBA graduate in this story demonstrated appropriate awareness of his strengths and weaknesses and the wisdom to use a strategy to overcome the weaknesses.

Collaborative Report Writing

Many report projects are completed by teams of workers rather than by a single writer. Such collaborative projects require coordination and agreement on various strategic and stylistic issues. While drafting such a report, team members may first work independently as each person drafts the parts of the report for which he or she is responsible. Since most collaborative reports are relatively complex, each writer would likely begin at Stage 1 (Preliminary Draft), Step 1 (see Figure 1.2).

Ideally, each person's preliminary text file would be shared with each of the other report writers, who would act as reviewers. You might share files with one another in any of the following ways:

- Transmitting your files as e-mail attachments and use the review features in your word processor to provide feedback in other writers' files. Microsoft Word, for example, includes features for writing comments in the margins and for tracking changes made to a draft. Of course, when your draft is sent back to you, you can delete any comments after reading them and accept or reject any changes.
- Using an online office suite, such as Google Docs (www.google.com/intl/en-GB/docs/about), Dropbox Paper (www.dropbox.

com/paper), or Zoho Docs (www.zoho.com/docs). These document management software tools include presentation and spreadsheet applications as well as word processing.
- Using a more advanced software tool for reports containing sensitive information. A virtual data room (VDR), such as SecureDocs (www.securedocs.com), iDeals (www.idealsvdr.com), or Firmex (www.firmex.com), offers more data security and control of access than online office suites.
- Using an online collaboration (project management) service such as Wrike (www.wrike.com), Slack (slack.com), or AceProject (www.aceproject.com).

After writing and sharing the preliminary drafts of their report sections, the team should discuss any questions that remain (Stage 1, Steps 2 and 3). Depending on the proximity of team members, this discussion may take place in an actual face-to-face meeting or in a virtual meeting via audio conferencing or video conferencing. Or teams may be able to discuss their report drafts using teleconferencing capabilities or the instant messaging (chat) function of their collaboration software. Following this discussion, each writer would be ready to move to Stage 2 (Review Draft) in their respective parts of the report.

Once individuals have written their review drafts (Stage 2, Step 1), the group would review each other's work. As reviewers, team members should provide constructive criticism, and the team should give individual authors directions for the near-final draft. The individual writers should continually evaluate the suggestions of the group and incorporate the best of their advice into the report file. Individual responsibilities also include editing one's own text.

Ideally, all writers participate in production of the team's final draft, assisting with merging their near-final drafts, preparing and placing visuals, and spotting errors and inconsistencies. Then one team member should serve as coordinator-editor, making the final draft a seamless product in which readers are unable to distinguish one writer's work from another's.

Summary

After planning a report, you are ready to write a draft, which you may need to revise and edit several times. For simple reports, however, your first draft may be your final draft. To save time and effort when drafting and revising, decide on a writing style before you draft. Always empathize with readers, considering their information needs and ego needs, and keep the context and your purpose in mind. Your writing style will be further defined by three attributes:

- ☐ *Tone* refers to the attitude the writer conveys about the message and the reader. For example, a report may be appeasing or defensive, passive or persuasive, personal or impersonal, polite or peremptory, and positive or negative.
- ☐ *Degree of formality* refers to wording that conveys how well the writer and reader are acquainted. Use of first names; contractions; first- and second-person pronouns, such as *I, me, we, us, and you;* and colloquial expressions characterize informal style. The absence of these elements denotes formal style.
- ☐ *Objectivity* involves reporting all relevant data—even if the reader would have preferred a different outcome. The word also includes expressing your conclusions and recommendations without bias or emotion—but with suitable confidence.

Generally, you will draft in three stages—preliminary draft, reviewer draft, and near-final draft. Other times you may begin with a well-organized, well-written reviewer draft, ready for a reader to give you feedback. And sometimes, your first draft will become your near-final or final draft with little or no additional work. These guides will help you determine whether you need to begin at Stage 1, 2, or 3.

- ☐ Stage 1 Preliminary draft. Start at Stage 1 if:
  - o Drafting is difficult;
  - o You have not written a similar report;
  - o You do not yet know what material to include;

- o You cannot outline the report; or
- o You do not know your manager's expectations.
- ☐ Stage 2 Review draft. Start at Stage 2 if:
  - o You know what your manager expects;
  - o You already know what information to include and how to organize it; and
  - o You can make a solid outline of the report.
- ☐ Stage 3 Near-final draft. Start at Stage 3 if:
  - o You are writing a simple report or familiar material; or
  - o You have planned well and need to finish the report straightaway.

At each of these stages, drafting a report involves three steps:

- ☐ Step 1—creating a draft
- ☐ Step 2—reviewing your own draft
- ☐ Step 3—getting a colleague or manager to review your draft.

When creating a preliminary draft, find ways to overcome writing barriers. Some common techniques include:

- ☐ Drafting the easiest sections first for a sense of accomplishment early in the project;
- ☐ Drafting the most challenging sections first to reduce pressure at the end;
- ☐ Moving among the sections to ensure continuous progress on the report; and
- ☐ Preparing illustrations first then drafting text to explain those visuals.

Unless you begin at Stage 3 (Near-Final draft), expect to revise your draft. Revision involves adding information, deleting information, reorganizing paragraphs, and rewording sentences to achieve the objectivity, degree of formality, and tone you aimed for. Use the revision checklist provided (Figure 1.3) to:

- ☐ Assess the strength of the report introduction and ending;
- ☐ Ensure that report content is accurate, complete, and organized for easy reading; and
- ☐ Confirm that your draft flows smoothly from beginning to end, giving a sense of forward motion.

How carefully you edit affects your credibility as a communicator and business person. Editing—done after making all revisions—consists of finding and correcting errors in content, format, grammar, mechanics, and usage. Become aware of the common lapses in each of these five categories. Then use these techniques for proofing your text:

- ☐ Before editing, let your draft rest for at least a few hours (up to three days) after writing it.
- ☐ First, check for content errors; then look for the kinds of errors you are prone to make.
- ☐ Read aloud from your draft, which causes you to slow down and notice details. To slow down even more, read the draft from end to beginning.
- ☐ Change the appearance of your text in one or more ways during editing; increasing the font size is especially helpful.
- ☐ Go over your draft several times, looking for a specific kind of error each time.
- ☐ Run grammar and spelling and style checkers last. Besides the checker tools in your word processing software, use additional online checkers, such as Grammarly and Polish My Writing.

The editing checklist provided in Figure 1.4 may be used to evaluate your final draft.

When drafting collaboratively, team members should alternate between working independently and collectively.

- ☐ Each writer drafts his or her assigned section.
- ☐ Writers share their drafts with the other writers by means of e-mail attachments, an online office suite, like Google Docs;

a virtual data room such as SecureDocs (for reports containing sensitive information); or an online collaboration service, such as Slack.
- ☐ The team meets—actually or virtually—to deal with questions and concerns.
- ☐ Writers independently create their reviewer drafts and then review each other's work.
- ☐ Individuals evaluate others' suggestions and incorporate the best ones in their respective sections, along with editing those sections.
- ☐ Working together, team members merge report sections, place visuals, and edit the draft.
- ☐ One team member acts as coordinator and editor to eliminate any remaining inconsistencies and ensure a seamless report.

Using the draft process to produce successively better versions of your report will lead to better outcomes for you and your audience. Mastering the content of this chapter could make or break your career.

CHAPTER 2

Formatting Reports

After planning, drafting, revising, and editing your report, you may feel confident that you have prepared an effective message. However, you must also consider how to package that product. An effective format will entice the receiver to read the report; lead the reader effortlessly through the information presented; maintain the reader's interest; and, ideally, stimulate the reader to respond to the report as you had hoped.

You can produce professionally formatted reports by (1) following guides for designing documents; (2) knowing traditional formats (memo, letter, and manuscript); and (3) mastering newer formats (e-mail, web page, report decks, and infographics). We will explore each of these important components in this chapter.

Basic Formatting Guides

To maintain a consistent image, companies often adopt standards for reports and other documents and require that all employees adhere to those specifications. Such a policy helps assure consistency and a common appearance across documents. Applying the following guides will help your reader scan your report, quickly determine its content, and focus attention on specific information. Whether you choose memo, letter, or manuscript format, apply the following basic guides.

Spacing

Most printed business reports omit blank lines between text lines. Therefore, this kind of spacing, called single spacing, is customary for memo and letter reports. The trend is to use single spacing for manuscript reports, too, although some organizations use double spacing (blank line between text lines).

Actually, multiple spacing is often used in place of strict single spacing because Multiple is the default setting in Microsoft Word. Multiple spacing puts a tiny space between text lines, making text more open and easier to read. In Word 2016, the default spacing is Multiple 1.08; in Word 2010 and 2013, Multiple 1.15. In everyday usage, these default settings are still referred to as single spacing. (Instead of using default settings automatically, determine the preferences of your readers (your employer or other readers); and change the settings to meet their expectations.

A small amount of blank space roughly equivalent to a line of text separates paragraphs of single-spaced reports. Generally, single-spaced paragraphs have no paragraph indentations but should always have one or more blank lines below each paragraph. Double-spaced reports have no extra blank space between paragraphs but have a paragraph indentation, typically one-half inch.

Fonts

Your selection of typography—font, font style, and font size—affects the appearance and readability of your report. The primary goal of typography is to create a document that is consistent, harmonious, and balanced. Too much variety can be distracting to a reader.

Font refers to the shape or design of letters and characters. As the fonts shown in Figure 2.1 demonstrate, some fonts are considerably more intricate—and often less readable—than others.

Serif Fonts	Sans Serif Fonts
Cambria, 12-point, regular **Cambria, 14-point, bold** *Cambria, 16-point, italics*	Calibri, 12-point, regular **Calibri, 14-point, bold** *Calibri, 16-point, italics*
Times New Roman, 12-point, regular **Times New Roman, 14-point, bold** *Times New Roman, 16-point, italics*	Tahoma, 12-point, regular **Tahoma, 14-point, bold** *Tahoma, 16-point, italics*
Palatino Linotype, 12-point, regular **Palatino Linotype, 14-point, bold** *Palatino Linotype, 16-point, italics*	Verdana, 12-point, regular **Verdana, 14-point, bold** *Verdana, 16-point, italics*

Figure 2.1 Comparative fonts, font styles, and font sizes

Fonts are also identified as serif or sans serif. Serif refers to the fine lines that cross the bottom and top of a letter. (Notice the lines at the bottom of *f, k, l, m, n,* and *r* in the previous sentence.) Sans serif fonts do not have lines at the bottom and top of letters.

A third way to classify fonts is by spacing characteristics. Monospaced fonts allocate equal space to each letter and resemble text produced on typewriters a few decades ago. Examples of monospaced fonts include Consolas and Lucida Console (sans serif) and Courier New and Monotype Corsiva (serif).

Most popular fonts are proportionally spaced, meaning the fonts allocate more space to wide letters, such as W, and less space to narrow letters, such as l.

Along with choosing a font, you must consider font style and size. Most of your report text should be produced in regular or plain style. Bold, italic, bold-italic, and underlining may be used sparingly for emphasis or to clarify the text. For example, bold is often used for headings and subheadings and italics for names of publications or other emphasis. Limit underlining to subheadings, if you like underlined subheadings, and a few words in paragraphs. Readers recognize words by their shapes; underlining tends to obscure the descending portions of letters such as g, j, p, and y as shown here: g, j, p, y.

Font size is measured in points (1 inch = 72 points) from the top of the characters' ascenders (letters such as d and k) to the bottom of its descenders (letters such as p and q). Font size for report text should be 10 to 14 points. Size 10 may be too small for some readers, but you might occasionally use it when you want to limit the pages in a report or shrink a report to one page. Any size larger than 14 points is considered a display font and should be reserved for headings. Using anything larger than 12 points for the main text may give the impression that you are trying to pad your report. In e-mail, memos, and letters, use one size font only. In manuscripts, you may use a hierarchy of sizes, with headings always larger than the text.

Again, check the default font in your word processing program. For example, Microsoft Word 2016 uses Calibri, a sans serif font, as the default setting. Traditionally serif fonts, such as Times New Roman or Century Schoolbook, have been used for the main text of printed reports because the serifs create a line to lead a reader's eye from left to right. Thus, serif text is easier to read on the printed page. If the default setting in your software does not correspond with the standards set by your employer, change the default settings to meet expectations.

Emphasis Techniques

When you want to emphasize certain information in a report, you may use one of several emphasis techniques, such as full capitalization (ALL CAPS), bold style, italics style, bulleted lists, numbered lists, and shading. The following list will guide you in using these emphasis techniques:

- Use ALL-CAPS in short spans, such as a main heading or a few key words in a long paragraph. LONG STRINGS OF CAPITALIZED TEXT ARE HARD TO READ. Additionally, using all uppercase letters has come to be equated with shouting. E-mail protocols, for example, discourage use of all capital letters except for headings or occasional emphasis within a message.
- Use bold in moderation. Apply it to a few words or phrases up to a short sentence or two that are altogether worthy of emphasis.
- Likewise, use italics sparingly. When too many things are emphasized, nothing receives appropriate attention. Besides italicizing coined words and the titles of complete published and artistic works that contain subdivisions, use italics when you want *readers to slow down and read more carefully*.

Grouping and bulleting or numbering closely related items focuses attention on that information. To group items effectively, follow these guides:

- Use an introductory sentence or phrase to unify the group. The sentence immediately preceding this list is an example of such a sentence. Include at least two or three items in your list. Logically, you cannot have a group of one.

- Write all items in parallel grammatical structure. For example, each item in this list begins with an imperative verb and is followed by additional information.
- Use bullets if order of the items is irrelevant. Use numbers if the list represents a ranking of importance or a sequence, such as the steps in a procedure.
- Choose one bullet style for all lists in a document. For a formal report, use a traditional bullet style (large, solid circle or square), reserving more exotic characters for less formal reports, such as a newsletter.
- Put the same space between bulleted or numbered items that appears between regular paragraphs.
- Align bulleted or numbered items at the paragraph point.
- Use the hanging indentation style for bulleted and numbered items. This style aligns the text 0.25 inch or 0.5 inch to the right of the bullet or number.
- Use shading selectively to separate report sections, highlight examples, set off long quotations, or draw attention to other text. Use light shading behind text and strips of medium-to-dark shading as dividers between text blocks.

Headings

Headings should represent the outline of your report and guide the reader through its content. When you use headings, their appearance must convey the relationship of report sections. All first-level headings, which indicate major divisions of the report, must be printed in uniform style; and all second-level headings, which identify subdivisions of the major divisions, must be printed in a uniform style that clearly distinguishes them from first-level or third-level divisions. One acceptable treatment for headings is shown in Figure 2.2.

In Figure 2.2, first-level headings are centered; second-level headings are placed at the left margin; and third-level headings are placed at the beginning of paragraphs. The figure also shows headings in varying styles as they might appear in a manuscript report. To enhance the appearance and readability of a report in manuscript format, you might use a sans serif font for the title and Level 1 and 2 headings and use different sizes, such as 18,

Title	Organizational Effectiveness
First Level	**Determining Criteria for Effectiveness**
	Xxxxxxxxxxxxx xxx xxxxxxxxxxxx xxxxx xxxxx xxxxxx. xxxxxx xxxx. Xxxxxxxxxxxxxx. X . . .
First Level	**Assessing Effectiveness**
	Xxxxxxxxxxxxx xxxxxxxxxx xxxxxxx xxxxxxxx . . .
Second Level	**Setting Standards**
	Xxxx xxxxxxx xxxxxxxxxx xxxxxxxx xxxxxxxx xxxxxxxx. Xxxxx xxx . . .
Second Level	**Selecting Indicators**
	Xxxxxxxxxxxxxx xxxxxx xx xxxxxxx xxx xxxx xxx xxxxx. Xxxxxxxxxxxx xxxxxx x xxxx xxxxx xxx . . .
Third Level	*Outcomes*. Xxxxxxxxxx xxxx xxxx xxxxx xx. Xxxxxxx . . .
Third Level	*Processes*. Xxxxx xxxxxxxxx xx xxxxx xxx xxxx. Xxxxxxx xxx xxxxxxxxxxxxx xxxx xxxxxx .
Third Level	*Structures*. Xxxxxxx xxx xxxxxxxxx xxx xxxx xxx. Xxxxxx
	Xxxxxx . . .
Second Level	**Selecting Samples**
	Xxxxxxxxxxxxxx xxxxx xxxx xxx. Xxxx xxx xxxxxx . . .
Second Level	**Applying Measurements**
	Xxxxxxxxx xxxxxx xx xxxxx xxxx. Xxxx xxx xx xxxxxxx. . . .
First Level	**Explaining Effectiveness**
	Xxxxxxxxx xxxxxxxxxxxx xxxxx xxxxxxxxxxxxxxxxxxx
	xxxxxxxx xxxxxxxxx xxxxxxxxx xxxx xxx xxxxx. . . .

Figure 2.2 **Heading levels in reports**

16, and 14, respectively. For Level 3 headings, use the same font and font size as the paragraphs; the use of italics (shown in Figure 2.2) is optional.

Each heading should be close to the text it covers. The space between a heading and the text to which it applies should be the same as the space between paragraphs. And if a heading appears on the last line of a page, use a page break or spacing to force it to the top of the next page. Also, insert text below every heading. For example, if the report contains Level 1 and 2 headings, a Level 2 heading should not appear immediately below a Level 1; instead the text below the Level 1 heading should introduce the Level 2 topics.

As you study the illustrations of reports in this book, note how these basic guides for spacing, fonts, headings, and emphasis are applied, or at least simulated. In addition, observe the following specific guides for reports in e-mail, memo, letter, manuscript, web page, report deck, and infographic formats.

Specific Formatting Guides

Report formatting refers to appearance and arrangement of individual elements in reports. Historically, paper-based reports involved three main formats—manuscript, memo, and letter. Each format involved conventions that most business people used in producing their reports and expected to find in the reports they received. In fact, the standards for manuscripts, memos, and letters remain largely the same today.

However, with the rise of electronic media (e-mail, slide decks, web page) for delivering reports to audiences, rigid formatting rules have given way to guidelines for producing reports in each medium. The following two guidelines apply equally, though, to all report formats:

- Choose a simple, functional design. You will impress readers most by providing just the information they need in a way that makes it easy for them to find and understand it. In any format, an overly elaborate design may give readers the impression that you did not pay enough attention to content.
- Know what formatting decisions you can or may make. Your company, for example, may already have a standard report format that everyone in the organization is supposed to use. For example, some organizations require report decks of one to three slides for certain kinds of internal reports. Others increasingly use infographics to condense reports and save readers' time.

  You may be expected to use certain templates in your word processing or presentation software so that documents in a series look alike; or if someone has adapted or created a template for reports like the one you are writing; you may be expected to use it.

> Organizations often use wikis for internal reporting, especially progress, or status, reports. In addition, companies often use blogs for reports requiring immediate written feedback from report readers, such as evaluation and recommendation reports.[1]

E-mail Format

Brief internal or external reports may be delivered by e-mail. E-mail has a couple advantages over other formats. It can be distributed and received quickly to single or multiple audiences, and e-mail reports can be filed electronically or printed and filed on paper for future reference. Figure 2.3 shows a report in e-mail format.

The format in Figure 2.3 shows standard e-mail headings: receivers' address (To heading), the topic (Subject heading), and the recipient of a courtesy copy (Cc heading). Another copy option is Bcc (blind courtesy copy), used to conceal the identity of a copy recipient. Once sent, the e-mail will show the sender's address (From heading) as well as when the message was mailed (Date and Time headings).

The subject field is vital to an e-mail report's success, so always specify the topic of your report. Following these guidelines will help you write effective subject lines:[2]

- Fill in the subject field before entering your message. Doing so keeps you from forgetting. E-mail with a blank subject field is often deleted or lost—and is always irritating to the recipient who must open it to determine its subject.
- Enter six to eight words that precisely describe your topic. Place the most important words at the beginning, omitting fillers. While a typical mailbox shows 60 characters in the subject field, a mobile device shows half that number or fewer, so keep it short. Include keywords that the recipient might use to filter and search for your report later.
- Use combined Caps and lowercase, which is easier to read at a glance than ALL CAPS.

- When you receive a reply that in turn requires a reply from you, be sure to change the subject line to match your new message.

As shown in Figure 2.3, a salutation, or greeting, above the e-mail message is appropriate. A greeting confirms for the recipient that he or she is the intended reader of the e-mail. Since e-mail is inherently informal, a greeting such as "Dear Mr. Sandberg" is too formal. Depending on how well you know your individual recipient, one of these salutations is suitable: Dear William, William Sandberg, or just William.

Figure 2.3 *Report in e-mail format*

In ongoing dialogues, you may consider deleting the greeting after the initial exchange, but if you are writing to a client or to someone in your organization who is senior to you, wait until that person omits the salutation before doing so.[3] Additional guidelines follow:

- Use content headings to show how your e-mail report is organized, as shown in Figure 2.3.
- Use a sans serif font, which, on a computer screen, is easier to read than a serif font. And use a medium-sized (about 12-point or normal) or bigger (about size 14 or large) font. The larger font shows consideration for people who read e-mail on their mobile phones. Headings can be even larger (about size 16 or huge). But do keep this point in mind: The larger the font the faster the screen fills up, leading to more scrolling for readers.[4]
- Keep the format simple: Omit paragraph indentations; allow lines of text to wrap naturally; insert a blank line below each paragraph; and aid readability with bulleted lists. If your e-mail lacks a bullet feature, create bullets using two hyphens (--).

Memo Format

Relatively brief internal reports may be written in interoffice memorandum—or memo—format. A commonly used memo format is shown in Figure 2.4.

The memo heading includes the guidewords To, From, Date, and Subject. The date may appear above the name of the recipient, if you prefer, without the word Date in front of it. Some organizations include other guidewords, such as cc (courtesy copy). Follow these guides as you prepare memo reports:

- Courtesy and professional titles (Mr., Mrs., Ms., Dr., etc.) are usually omitted in intracompany memos, but position titles (Vice President, Supervisor, etc.) are sometimes included. When beginning a new job in a large organization, showing your department affiliation is a good idea until others in the organization become acquainted with you. In any case, it is wise to check the organization's office manual or files to determine the preferences within that company.

- A memo template is a preformatted file containing placeholders and guides for completing a memo. Templates are designed to save users' time, and most word processing software offers a variety of memo templates. Online sources of memo templates include Microsoft Word Templates (www.wordtemplates.org/memo-word-templates/memorandum-template), Tidy Forms (www.tidyforms.com/business.html), and Vertex 42 (www.vertex42.com).
- Before using a template, find a design that conforms to your organization's standards. It may be necessary to adapt a template to your specifications and save it for future use.

{UbiQuiTous}

To: All Typing & Transcription Service Reps

From: Marilyn L. Hogue, Production Leader *mLh*

Date: July 16, 2017

Subject: Standard Memo Format

This report demonstrates or memo format. (The word memo comes from the original name of this document: interoffice memorandum.) Please notice these features of memo format.

1. The standard heading consists of the captions *To*, *From*, *Date*, and *Subject*. Those captions may be arranged in different ways, but either *Date* or *To* should be the first item; and *Subject* should immediately precede the memo body (message). On a memo, the date may appear as shown or in *mm/dd/yy* format.
2. The subject line must be a brief, meaningful summary of the memo's content.
3. The memo body has a blank line below the heading and below each paragraph.
4. Left and right margins should be at least one inch wide.
5. Numbering focuses the reader's attention on specific information, emphasizing items in top-to-bottom order. Numbered items also permit a reader to identify specific items for response. If a memo contains only one major point, do not number it.
6. The memo sender frequently writes her or his initials after the typed name to indicate approval of the message. Some writers sign or initial the memo at the end of the message. However, do not use a closing (such as Sincerely or Yours truly) at the end of a memo.

Figure 2.4 Report in memo format

Letter Format

External reports of one to three pages may be arranged in letter format. If the report is longer than three pages, it should be written in manuscript format, accompanied by a letter to the receiver.

Figure 2.5 shows a report in letter format. This specific format is called block because all parts of the letter are aligned on the left.

Notice that the body (message) of the letter explains features of its format. As you study Figure 2.5, notice also the following features and their sequence, which apply to all letters.

Communications Design Associates

801 JACKSON STREET, WEST TEL: 312-555-9753
CHICAGO, IL 60607-5511 FAX: 312-555-9750

August 7, 2017

Ms. Taylor Pettas
Communications Director
Pettas Fine Foods
1849 N. Halifax Ave.
Daytona Beach, FL 32018-4421

Dear Ms. Pettas

This report demonstrates letter format. In this specific format, called block, all lines begin at the left margin. No letter parts or paragraphs are indented.

This letter format is now widely used in business. Its efficiency and crisp appearance are pleasing to today's business writers.

This letter also shows open punctuation, with no punctuation mark after the salutation or the complimentary closing. Mixed punctuation, with a colon after the greeting and a comma after the closing, may be used; but use of that punctuation style is declining.

I believe this block letter format will be useful for your business reports and correspondence, Ms. Pettas. If you have other questions about report formats, I will discuss them with you and provide illustrations.

Sincerely

Jerri Martino

Jerri Martino
Staff Consultant

Figure 2.5 Report in letter format

1. *Identity of sender.* Every letter must include a letterhead or return address to identify the sender. A well-designed letterhead presents the organization favorably and provides all information needed to communicate with that organization, such as USPS address, phone and fax number(s), and e-mail and web addresses.

    Letterhead is used only for the first page of a letter. Any additional pages are printed on plain paper of the same color and quality. A heading appears at the top of these pages, including the receiver (first line of letter address), page number, and date. A second-page heading may be arranged vertically or horizontally as shown in the following examples.

Vertical heading for pages after first	Horizontal heading for pages after first
Ms. Taylor Petas Page 2 May 7, 2017	Ms. Taylor Petas 2 May 7, 2017

    If no letterhead is used, the sender's return address appears first. Depending on the length of the letter, the return address should be placed one to two inches from the top of the page. The return address *omits the writer's name*, which always appears in the signature line at the end of the letter.

2. *Date of letter.* A letter should always contain the date on which it was written or mailed. And the date should always appear in the style shown here—the month spelled out, followed by the date in cardinal (1, 3, 9, etc.), not ordinal (1st, 3rd, 9th, etc), style, a comma, and four-digit year. When letterhead is used, place a blank line or two between the letterhead and the date. But, when a return address is used, place the date immediately below that address, as shown here.

1610 Castle Drive Byron Center, MI 49315 January 11, 2018	Rt. 1, Box 50 Edgerton, MN 56128 May 18, 2018	8 Chourikharka Lukla 56010, Nepal 27 September, 2018

    Your word processor likely treats each line of an address as a separate paragraph, with extra space below it. You will need to remove this excess space between address lines.

3. *Address of receiver.* The letter address (receiver's address) is placed several lines below the date. Since messages going outside an

organization tend to be more formal than those moving within, etiquette calls for using a person's courtesy or professional title (if it is known) in a letter report. But do not include a courtesy title if you do not know the person's gender or a woman's title preference. A position title, placed after the name or on the next line, may also be included. The letter address governs the envelope address—the two must be identical.

Again, you may need to remove excess space between lines of the letter address.

4. *Greeting or salutation.* The letter address also governs the salutation. When a courtesy or professional title appears in the address, it is used in the salutation, without the individual's first name. For example, the standard greeting for a letter addressed to Ms. Kimberly Hagood is "Dear Ms. Hagood," not "Dear Kimberly Hagood." An exception to that rule is appropriate when the letter writer knows the reader very well. Then a first-name greeting, such as "Dear Kimberly" or even "Dear Kim" is appropriate. When the address has no courtesy title (for example, K. Hagood) or has only a position title (for example, Marketing Director), you must choose an alternative to the standard salutation. Popular choices include the following:

- The person's name as given in the address (Dear K. Hagood).
- The position title used in the address, when no name is given (Dear Marketing Director).
- Omitted salutation AND complimentary close (see Item 5).

Sometimes the first line of the letter address is a company name rather than an individual's name; or a letter may be addressed to an organization, followed by an attention line that names a person. Although some writers use an impersonal greeting such as "Ladies and Gentlemen" or "Gentlemen and Ladies," that language seems excessively formal for today's business writing. Considerate writers avoid "Dear Sir" or "Dear Sirs" because those words convey an exclusionary, sexist tone. Avoid, also, the excessively impersonal "To whom it may concern"; that greeting may connote that you do not care who reads the message. It also shifts the responsibility of determining an appropriate reader from you, the sender, to the receiver.

5. *Complimentary close.* The complimentary close begins the closing lines. Use a traditional complimentary close, such as "Sincerely." (This particular close is appropriate for any formality level.) Leave a blank line between the letter body and the complimentary close.
6. *Signature block.* The signature block includes the writer's name and, usually, his or her position title or department affiliation. The name and title may appear on the same line (separated by a comma) or on separate lines. Leave a couple blank lines between the complimentary close and your typed name. Sign the letter (black or blue ink) in this blank area.
7. *Envelope.* If you are not using a window envelope, then prepare an envelope for your letter. The envelope address should be identical to the letter address. The address is blocked beginning at the approximate center of the envelope. The first line should be about halfway down from the top of the envelope. Most word processing programs have an envelope addressing function that will print the letter address onto an envelope. This function also allows you to print a return address on the envelope if your envelope is not already printed with such an address.

Manuscript Format

Internal or external reports that exceed three pages are generally written in manuscript format. A cover letter or memo almost always accompanies such a report, and the report usually has a title page. Figure 2.6 shows the title page and two report pages in manuscript format.

Notice that the report in Figure 2.6 discusses and demonstrates the general guides for spacing, fonts, emphasis, and headings. In specialized reporting situations, several additional preliminary or supplementary parts are included in the manuscript, such as table of contents, list of illustrations, executive summary, list of sources, glossary, and appendix.

Manuscript reports may be distributed to a wide audience on the web once the file is in Portable Document Format (PDF). Uploading and linking a PDF to a website is recommended when:

- The audience will likely want to print all or part of the report; or
- The report is too complex to lay out well as a web page.[5]

Producing Reports in Manuscript Format

Prepared for

Mountain View Industries
13666 E. Bates Avenue
Aurora, CO 80014

Green Mountain Ski Resort

Woodland, VT 05409 (802) 555-3265

Prepared by

KC&S Communication Consultants
Suite 116, Castle Complex
1218 Fairview Road
Denver, CO 80202

(303) 555-9154

January 2018

Producing Reports in Manuscript Format

This illustration explains one commonly used format for business reports. Notice these features of the report format: title page, margins, fonts and font styles and sizes, report headings, and spacing.

Title Page

A title page may be used to orient the reader to the report and its writer. The title page should include the report title, for whom the report is written, by whom it is written, and the transmittal date. This information, arranged in four clusters, is <u>centered</u> <u>horizontally</u> and <u>vertically</u> on the page.

Informative Title

To showcase the report title, type it display size (18- to 24-point font) and place it uppermost on the page. Create a concise, informative title, as follows:

- Consider the who, what, when, where, and why factors; then include the most important factors in the title.
- If the report contains recommendations that readers will easily accept, include your main recommendation in the title.

If the title you generate is too long, divide it into a main title and secondary title. On the title page, insert line breaks at logical points. An example follows.

Not this	But this
Increasing Tourism in The Hatfield-McCoy Mountains Region of West Virginia	Increasing Tourism in The Hatfield-McCoy Mountains Region of West Virginia

Optional Items

Optional items are the company logo(s), page borders, and other design elements that suggest the report content or nature of the organization. Although a title page itself may be optional in some situations, an inventive design can create a positive first impression. Therefore, use a title page to help convey your professionalism.

Margins

Place the title 1.5 to 2 inches from the top of the first page of the report. Use a 1-inch top margin for all remaining pages. If the manuscript is unbound or stapled in the upper left corner, use a 1-inch left margin. For a left-bound manuscript, use a 1.5-inch left margin. (Staple the finished report a half inch from the left edge near the top, middle, and bottom.) Right and bottom margins should be approximately one inch on all pages.

Fonts

Use no more than two fonts in your report. This illustration, for example, uses a sans serif font (Arial) for the title and headings and a serif font (Times New Roman) for the report text. It would also be appropriate to use the same serif font for headings and report text. You may use bold and italic sparingly for emphasis. *Note:* You may need to change defaults in your word processing program to get the appearance you want.

Spacing

This single-spaced, blocked format is used extensively by contemporary business writers. All paragraphs in this example are single-spaced. To give the text a more open appearance, change the line spacing to a Multiple setting of 1.08 or 1.15 if available. Use two or three blank lines below the title, with one blank line above and below headings and between paragraphs.

Since some readers prefer a double-spaced format, always try to determine reader preference before completing the final copy of your report. If you use double spacing, tradition calls for indented paragraphs (0.5 inch) and no additional space between paragraphs.

Report Headings

Use headings in any report containing more than one major section. Headings should orient the reader to the report content.

Font style and placement must indicate the relationship of headings and subheadings. Notice that all main headings in this report have the same appearance. The subheadings are designed to distinguish them from the main headings.

Summary

Following these format guides will have two results: (1) a report that invites the receiver to read it and (2) a report that leads the reader effortlessly through its pages.

Figure 2.6 Report in manuscript format

Many word processing, spreadsheet, and presentation applications allow you to convert files from their native format to PDF. If conversion is not available in your word processing program, use one of the free online converters: CutePDF (www.cutepdf.com), Online2PDF (online2pdf.com), or PDF Converter (www.freepdfconvert.com).

An alternative to converting file formats: Create your PDF in the professional version of Adobe Acrobat. You also can use Acrobat when you want your PDFs to be secure, as the files cannot be edited by readers. Your report in PDF must be uploaded to the web. Some websites use a content management system (CMS) for this, which allows users with limited expertise to add content to the web without a webmaster's help. Otherwise, a standard file transfer protocol (FTP), such as FileZilla, would be needed to add your PDF report to the website's directories.

These days providing a link to Acrobat (PDF) Reader is unnecessary; but you can do so if you like. The following list includes do's and don'ts for posting PDF reports on the web.

- Don't exceed 60 pages or 30 to 40 kilobytes. Anything longer will take too long to download.
- Do tell readers when a web link will open a PDF. It shows consideration for your audience.
- Do compress any photographs in your report using an image optimizer program, such as Compressor.io (compressor.io), Optimizilla (optimizilla.com), or ImageOptim (imageoptim.com/mac) (also available for Linux and Windows at this site).
- Do include navigation in the PDF—a clickable table of contents, for example; forward and back buttons; and the like.
- Don't use a font size below 12.

Web Page Format

Reports on the web vary widely in kind and appearance. But all have commonality: Readers click hyperlinks or use a search function to locate specific content. Therefore, to be effective, a report in web page format— whether on the World Wide Web or a company intranet—should include its main navigation features on the first screen. These features serve as a table of contents, and readers can open any report section with a few clicks. For optimum convenience to readers, navigation features remain visible from anywhere in the report.

Figure 2.7 provides an example.

The Hershey Company's home page contains no direct link to its annual report. A search for it in the company website produced a list of 23 links, and each link led to one section of the report. But these sections were also accessible individually from multiple places on the site.

The success of a web page report depends largely on how rapidly readers can download and then read, or scan, the page. In planning your web

Figure 2.7 Report in web page format

The Hershey Company 2016. Used by permission.

page report, be aware that graphics and multimedia content lowers download speed. So include only the necessary visual elements.[6]

Since most web users scan content for only a few seconds before deciding whether to leave the page or keep reading, put the report's main point in your opening sentence. Then, to increase the chances that readers will continue reading, use very short paragraphs, captivating headings, and short pages with ample blank space.[7]

Having your report in accurate HTML code is vital. You may choose to write your own code, have someone else write it, or use a tool such as Namo Web Editor 9, Dreamweaver, or Blue Griffon to convert your word processing document to HTML. In any case, follow these guides to enhance readability of your web page reports:[8]

- Set light colors for backgrounds; then use a maximum of two or three sharply contrasting font colors.
- As a general rule, use only two fonts—a sans serif font, such as Arial or Tahoma, for text and larger, attention-grabbing fonts for headings. (Sans serif fonts are easier to read than serif fonts on computer screens—just the opposite of text on paper.)
- Control line length—about 10 to 12 words (50 to 60 characters).
- Resist any temptation to reduce letter spacing or leading (space between lines) in order to squeeze more text onto a page.
- Separate text from images with substantial blank space.
- Choose emphasis techniques carefully: Use bold and ALL CAPS sparingly. Use underlined text for links only. Use indented bullet points liberally.
- Give every page of your report the same "look and feel." Use consistent styles for each level of headings in the report.
- Omit links within paragraphs to maintain consistent navigation. If links are necessary in your report, place them at the ends of paragraphs or in a menu.

Several years ago, the World Wide Web Consortium (W3C) created the Web Accessibility Initiative (WAI). Essentially, the goal of WAI is to make the web available to people with a diverse range of hearing, movement, sight, and cognitive ability. To date, not all WAI goals have been addressed widely. The following lists include measures to make your web page reports accessible to people who have hearing or vision impairments:[9]

- Add text alternatives (alt text) for all audio and visual elements. Thus web users reading with text-to-Braille hardware or text-to-speech software can take in the graphics you include.
- Likewise, provide a text transcript for podcasts and other audio elements, making the information accessible to people who are deaf or hearing impaired.
- When your report includes a video, provide closed captions or a sign language version so that deaf and hard-of-hearing users can understand the video.
- Omit design elements, such as animation, that are unsuited for text-only browsers; include adaptive tools, such as large-print software or voice software.
- Design for colorblind readers by omitting all references to colors from navigation instructions. For example, asking readers to click the blue button would be inappropriate.

Finally, test your web page report in the following ways to maximize readers' success:[10]

- Test your web pages over a low-speed modem connection. If downloading takes more than 7 to 10 seconds, consider removing images or multimedia content.
- Test your web page report on different computer monitors, including a low-resolution monitor (800 × 600 pixels, for example).
- Test your web report in different browsers, the most popular being Google Chrome, Firefox, and Microsoft Edge.

Report Deck Format

A report deck is created with presentation software, such as Keynote or PowerPoint. But, report decks are meant to be understandable without a presenter. Usually a report deck is sent as an e-mail attachment and receivers read slide by slide from their computer screens. A report in this format includes less text—and, therefore, less detail—than most other report formats (but more text than most slide shows).[11] A report deck relies on visuals (diagrams, graphs, photos) more than text to convey information and can be used for any kind of report.

A report deck offers several advantages over other formats:[12]

- One report functions as a written report and as slides for an oral follow-up report to a small group.
- Presentation software is decidedly easier to use than word processing software for placing visual elements precisely.
- As a general rule, business people are more skilled at using presentation software than word processing software.

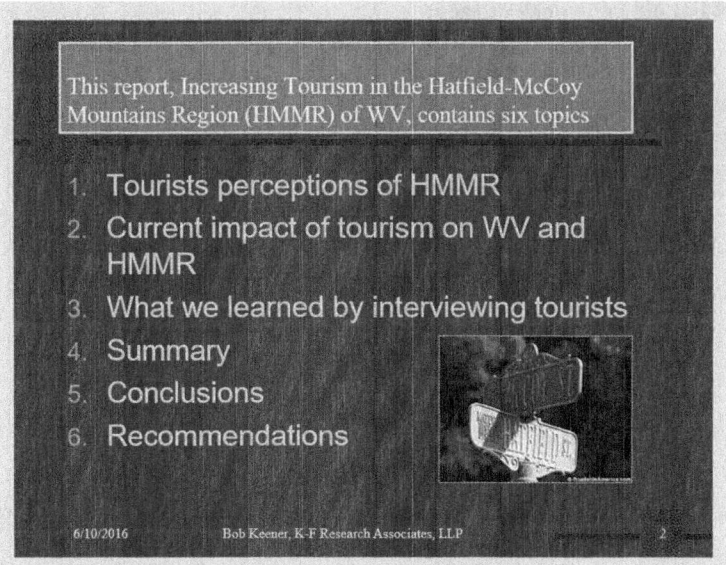

Figure 2.8(a) Page (slide) from a report deck

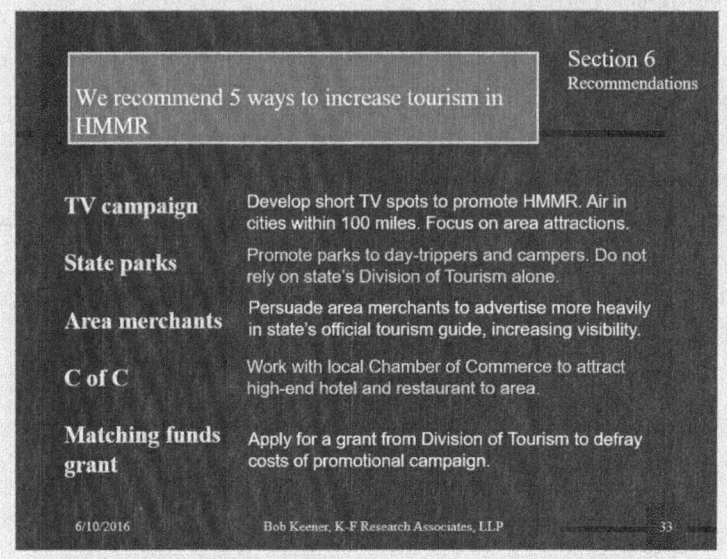

Figure 2.8(b) Report section in deck format

Naturally, to be effective, a report deck's content must be easy to grasp. Follow these content guides to aid your reader's comprehension.[13]

For effective deck content—

- Use a short-sentence headline, or title, on each page, left-aligned rather than centered. Type the headline in sentence case; that is capitalize only the first word and proper nouns. Omit a period at the end of statements, but include a question mark at the end of questions.
- Create content to reinforce the headline. Be sure that all text and visuals on the slide support the statement or answer the question in the headline. If you run out of space, create another slide with the same headline. Never try to squeeze text or visuals on a report page.
- Do not type paragraphs; instead, use concise sentences with space between them. Bullets do become monotonous, so do not use them on every slide in your deck.
- Rely on visuals as much as possible to carry your information, with text in a supporting role.

To engage your readers, a report deck must be both attractive and functional. Follow these design guides.[14]

For effective deck design—

- Create a title slide to serve as the deck's title page. Besides the report title, include the company name, author's name, and the date.
- Include a Contents slide, listing the name of each report section. If the report is long, include the starting page number for each section. Hyperlinks may be inserted in these numbers to help readers navigate the report.
- Set your design features on a master slide to ensure consistency throughout the report deck.
- Use a solid background; omit any effects that could distract readers' attention.
- Resize the headline text box so it can hold two lines of size 24 text. No text in the report deck should be smaller than size 18. *Note*: These small font sizes undermine the effectiveness of a report deck for presenting to a roomful of people. On typical presentation slides, no text should be smaller than size 24 so that the content is visible to everyone in the audience.[15]
- In one of the upper corners, place a tracker, or header, showing the section of the deck. And place a footer on each slide, including the slide number, project name, and proprietary information.

Infographics Format

Infographics (information graphics) is a relatively new report format. The infographics format largely replaces textual descriptions of data with visual representations of the data. (In fact, another name for infographics is data visualization.) The main reason for using infographics format is simple: the brain processes images faster than words. Besides, pictures inherently are more interesting than text, and scientists have confirmed that visual information is retained better and longer than textual information.[16]

54 PRODUCING WRITTEN AND ORAL BUSINESS REPORTS

Figure 2.9 shows part of a report titled "Why Visuals Actually Do Communicate Better than Words" in infographics format.

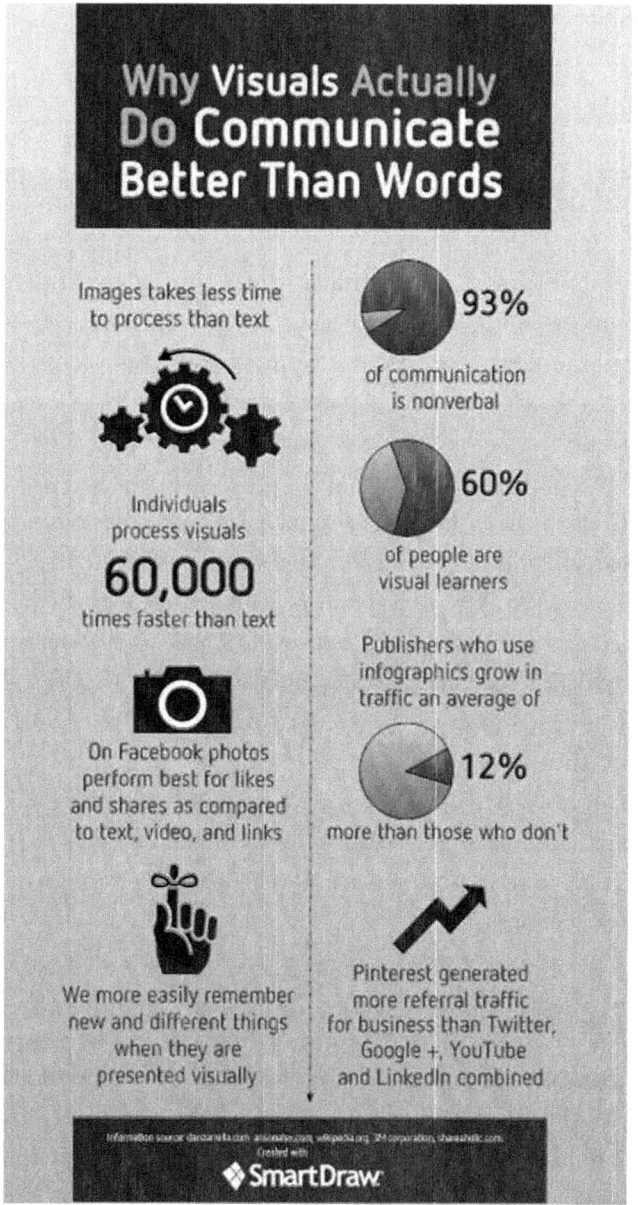

Figure 2.9 Report in infographics format

SmartDraw Software, LLC 2016. Used by permission.

People in general and business people particularly are overloaded with data, receiving the information equivalent of 174 newspapers a day. As the information available to us has grown and continues to grow, the use of art is helping us convert that information to knowledge.[17]

As a report format, infographics is used in several ways:

- *As a standalone report* with a smattering of well-chosen words calling out the images. This use is most appropriate for displaying a report poster-style at industry conventions, where people attempt to grasp quantities of new information quickly, and in magazines and similar publications where space is as limited as readers' time.
- *As enhanced illustrations* (charts, diagrams, graphs, and the like) to make a manuscript report more accessible and reader-friendly or in a slide deck to capture audience attention.
- *As executive summary* in a manuscript report, the research synopsis that immediately precedes a report body. Thus, each reader can see quickly what parts of the manuscript he or she needs to read, if any.
- *As a web-based report*, such as a company's annual report, to engage and hold readers' interest.

Initially, business people created infographics using imaging and design applications, such as Adobe PhotoShop. Today, though, they are more likely to use tools called infographics makers, many of which are available online at no cost. Some makers focus on a specific purpose. For example, the Get About application allows users to determine social media activity (track Twitter terms, hashtags, and mentions).[18] The following list names popular free online software for creating infographics:

- Easel.ly (www.easel.ly)
- Get About (www.get-about.com)
- Infogr.am (infogr.am)
- Piktochart (piktochart.com)
- Venngage (venngage.com)

For successful infographics, follow these guidelines:[19]

- *Know your data.* Since the purpose of an infographic is to tell a story, know your data extremely well. Then commit to presenting it accurately and clearly (no distortion). Identify the story your data are telling—from main point to supporting details—and let that story drive the graphic. But first, make sure that users of the infographic will learn new information.
- *Identify the take-away.* Decide what you want viewers (readers) to take away from your infographic, and give it the most visual weight (most space, most prominent placement, brightest color).
- *Start with a storyboard.* Before you start working in an infographics maker, sketch a storyboard and layout once you have decided exactly what data needs to be shown and how to show it. Organize your data-story left to right and top to bottom.
- *Limit the text.* Show readers, rather than tell them, the meaning of your data. In other words, avoid using too much text. In the infographics maker you are using, turn off the text layer to see if the infographic conveys the same message as it did with text on.
- *Use strong, but uncommon fonts.* For the text you do include as titles, headings, and labels, use strong, easy-to-read fonts; but choose fonts that are slightly unusual. For example, rather than Times New Roman, you might choose Rockwell; instead of Arial, you might choose Verdana.
- *Choose cohesive, calming colors.* Avoid dark and neon colors, and avoid a white background. Consider the rule of three: Choose three complementary colors, using the lightest one for the background. Then use the other two colors to break the graphic into sections down the page. If more colors are needed, use shades of your original three colors.
- *Test your infographic.* Ask someone without prior explanation to interpret your report.

Using a do-it-yourself infographics maker, you can produce effective art quickly and easily—if the data you depict is relatively simple and straightforward. But sometimes you may need to hire an infographics designer. Designers provide valuable insight on the front end of infographics. A designer does not simply take a client's data and do just what is asked. Designers play active, vital roles in conducting research and reporting the results. This list gives examples of designer services:[20]

- Gathering additional data related to clients' research from widely scattered sources.
- Identifying the narrative, or story, a data set tells; recognizing gaps in clients' data that weaken the narrative; and collaborating with clients to build consensus about the narrative.
- Defining the unique purpose an infographic will serve (explain a process, highlight a trend, support an argument).
- Establishing a hierarchy—main, overriding point to supporting details—for organizing the infographic report.
- Creating a wireframe—a visual outline or layout—for the client's review.
- Advising on the better of two visual approaches to take: the traditional approach (charts and graphs made captivating by the use of color, fonts, and structure) or the metaphorical approach (an artsy rendering that bears little resemblance to charts and graphs).

The number of thriving infographic design firms indicates that many businesses see the need for these kinds of services. A few examples follow:

- Avalaunch Media (avalaunchmedia.com)
- ConceptDrop, matches clients with infographic designers (www.conceptdrop.com)
- Info Graphic World (infographicworld.com)
- Lemonly (lemonly.com)
- SlideGenius (go.slidegenius.com)
- Upwork (www.upwork.com)

We have discussed guides for spacing, fonts, emphasis techniques, and the use of headings in reports, and you have seen those guides applied in different report formats. Some reports—print newsletters, for example—require even more specific attention to page layout.

Producing Print Newsletters and Similar Reports

A newsletter, according to Dictionary.com, is a written report, issued periodically, typically by a business, institution, or other organization.[21] Newsletters are a conventional form of content marketing—a way of distributing information to attract and retain customers, promote brand awareness, and boost sales and profits. Today, print newsletters are used for marketing in both business-to-business (B2B) and business-to-consumer (B2C) settings.

In addition, newsletters are used extensively by not-for-profit organizations to proclaim their stated missions. And many associations, churches, clubs, and interest groups use newsletters to encourage and expand interest and maintain group cohesion.

E-mail newsletters and online newsletters are indeed common; and newsletters printed on paper have notable advantages, whether hand delivered, placed in high-traffic areas, or sent via U.S. Postal Service. The same might be said for newsletter-like documents: booklets, brochures, fact sheets, flyers, handbills, leaflets, pamphlets, and prospectuses. Advantages of printed newsletters for business promotion are indicated by these facts.[22]

- The marked decrease in postal mail makes a print newsletter stand out to the recipients, while e-mail newsletters often get lost in overly full inboxes. Print newsletters allow people to disconnect from unrelenting online chatter.
- Consumers prefer print newsletters to e-mail—even the 18 to 34-year-old demographic. Consumers in general, and older ones in particular, perceive print mail as more legitimate than e-mail and admit to giving print mail more attention.
- E-mail is ephemeral while print newsletters last longer and allow for repeated use.

- Distribution costs are relatively low because your organization owns the mailing list.
- Print materials involve the tactile sense, leaving a more lasting impression on the brain than digital materials.

Naturally, print newsletters also have disadvantages:[23]

- The budget and timeline for newsletter production can strain marketing resources.
- Keeping an up-to-date mailing list is challenging, given the level of population mobility.
- Newsletters are too costly for most companies to print in more than one language.

Once you decide to generate a newsletter, your next decision involves the method you will use.

Newsletter Creation Methods

The methods include selecting a newsletter template, hiring a newsletter design and printing service, and designing your own newsletter. All three methods require time and skill to create the first and successive editions.

In general, adopting a template is the least time-consuming and least expensive way to initiate a newsletter. Designing your own newsletter takes considerably more time and effort on the designer's part, resulting in higher initial costs for your organization.

Selecting a Newsletter Template

Your word processing software likely offers an assortment of newsletter templates, including business templates. Templates and samples for printed newsletters also abound on the web. Most of the following websites offer free templates along with a selection of newsletter templates for sale:

- Constant Contact (www.constantcontact.com)
- Fresh Templates (www.freshtemplates.com/newsletter_templates/n014.htm)

60 PRODUCING WRITTEN AND ORAL BUSINESS REPORTS

- Graphic River (graphicriver.net/category/print-templates/newsletters)
- iNewsletter Templates (www.inewslettertemplates.com)
- Lucid Press (www.lucidpress.com/pages/templates/newsletters)
- Office-Xerox (www.office.xerox.com)
- Page Prodigy (www.pageprodigy.com/free-Newsletter-templates)
- Powered Template (www.nl.poweredtemplate.com/brochure-templates/newsletters/index.html)
- Smilebox (www.smilebox.com)
- StockLayouts (www.stocklayouts.com/Templates/Newsletter/Newsletter-Templates-Designs.aspx)

Four-page templates are the most popular. Many organizations create two-page newsletters; and, of course, some companies use 6- 8-, 12-, and 16-page layouts. Choose the number of pages you need for vital information; that is, without resorting to space-wasting filler items unrelated to your newsletter's purpose.[24] Figure 2.10 shows a four-page layout to be printed front and back on 17-inch × 11-inch paper that will be folded in the center, creating an 8.5-inch × 11-inch newsletter.

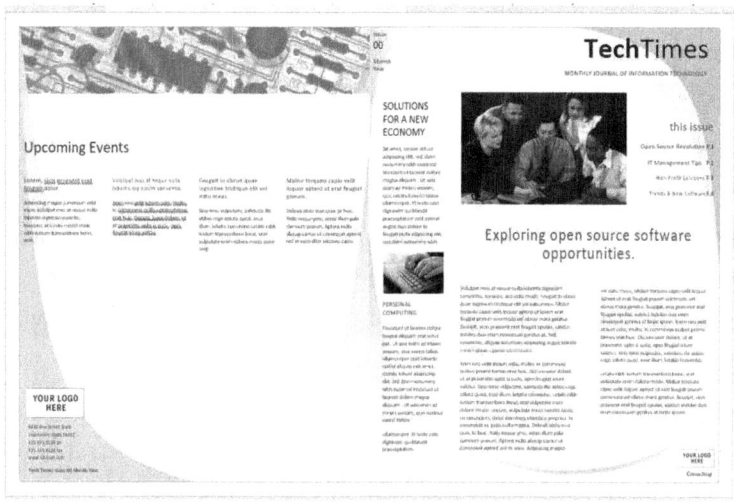

Figure 2.10(a) Newsletter template (pages 4 and 1)

Figure 2.10(b) Newsletter template (pages 2 and 3)

Hiring a Newsletter Designer-Printer

Using a design and print service involves sharing your vision. Either in person or on the web, you provide information and make choices that will eventually determine the appearance of your newsletters. Naturally, you provide all the content for each newsletter edition. Follow the guidelines in Chapter 1 for revising and editing reports to ensure accuracy of your newsletter text and illustrations before making it available.

A list of design and print services includes these names:

- Company Newsletters (companynewsletters.com)
- Dazzle Printing (www.dazzleprinting.com)
- Headline Design & Print (www.helloheadline.com)
- LKCS (www.lk-cs.com/design/graphic-design?gclid=CLfgw-fze-c4CFdgUgQodZ3MB1Q)
- Sun Solutions (www.sunsolutionsusa.com/index.html)
- Talk Design & Print (www.talkdesignandprint.com)

In some of these services, you may be asked to choose a design template at the company's website and then indicate your desired color, font,

62 PRODUCING WRITTEN AND ORAL BUSINESS REPORTS

and other changes as well as the type of paper to be used for printing. In other cases, you may converse with a representative of the design service and share your vision by answering the rep's questions. In this setting, you can ask for designer and printer recommendations.

In either situation, be sure you approve page proofs (near-final sample of pages for your inspection and correction) before your newsletter is printed. If you request a change in content or design, ask to see page proofs again.

Designing Your Newsletter

Begin designing with a pencil sketch of how you want the finished newsletter to appear. A useful technique is to sketch the contents on paper by blocking areas for headlines, main text, and visuals. This sketch will help you plan page layout for effective visual impact. The sketch in Figure 2.11 shows a four-page newsletter to be printed on 11 × 17 paper and folded into a standard-sized document.

The sketch in Figure 2.11 demonstrates the criteria of effective newsletter design: balance, consistency, contrast, focus, and proportion.

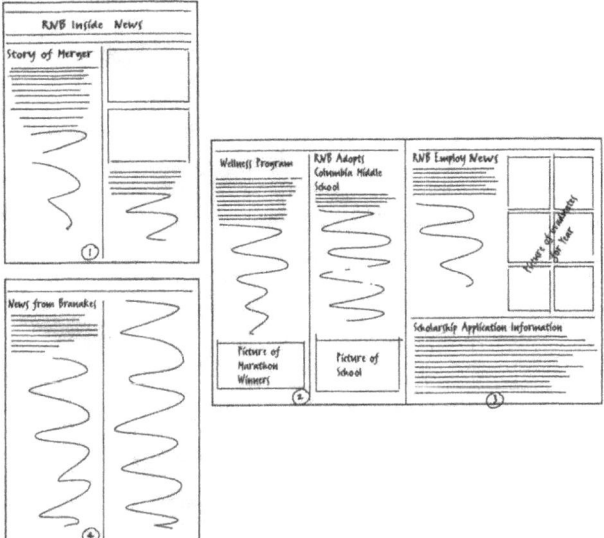

Figure 2.11 Sketch of newsletter page design

- *Balance*: the visual harmony of top, bottom, and side margins as well as placement of text and graphics on a page. To achieve visual balance and compensate for optical illusion, the bottom margin should be slightly larger than the top margin.
- *Consistency*: harmony of fonts, font styles, font sizes, heading structure, and visuals. You can mix these elements sparingly and still achieve consistency in appearance.
- *Contrast*: use of blank space, shaded areas, and visuals in documents. Use contrast techniques to relieve visual tedium.
- *Focus*: methods used to attract reader attention. Focusing techniques include placement of visuals; emphasis techniques, such as bold, italics, underline, ALL CAPS, and bullets or numbering; and use of color.
- *Proportion*: the relationship of font size in headings and text, the relationship of the size of a visual to the surrounding text, and the relationship of text and blank space. The most important information should have more space assigned to it than the least important information.

Each page appears clean, open, and uncluttered—an invitation to start reading!

An original sketch may need tweaking once content is in place. However, the basic design should be kept intact. Instead of changing the design to accommodate the text in your draft, consider effective ways to make the text more concise to fit your design.

Additional Guidelines for Newsletter Production

Effective newsletters—like all good reports—begin with careful planning, starting with defining your purpose and what you want your newsletter to accomplish and continuing with analyzing your audience (intended readers and possible others) and the overall context, or circumstances, including the season of the year when your newsletter will be distributed.

However, newsletters differ considerably in content and format from the business and research reports discussed previously. Therefore, use the following guides to deal with those differences.

Design Guides

Appearance is critical for getting potential readers' attention. The layout largely determines what recipients do upon opening your newsletter: read it or toss it. The legibility of text and ease of reading affects whether the readers continue. Keep the following layout and text guides in mind when designing newsletters or evaluating newsletter templates:

- Use big headlines and other large elements, such as drop caps (first letter of paragraph that is much bigger than the characters that follow) and pull quotes (short, thought-provoking quotations from the body of an article and used as a subheading or shaded text box).[25]

  However, not all headlines should be the same size. Variation looks more interesting and enables readers to read articles in the order of importance.[26]
- If your newsletter budget cannot cover full-color printing, instead of black-and-white, settle on a two-color, or two-ink, design. Thus, you choose an accent color to be used for certain elements in addition to the black ink used for paragraphs. Then both the black and accent could be used for shading sidebars, pull quotes, and so on in varying degrees, such as 60%, 40%, and 20%.[27]
- Use color consistently. For example, select one color for all headlines and another color or shade for all borders around graphic elements. Use only black for the main text and print every newsletter on white paper.[28]
- Help readers navigate your newsletter by using jump lines (directional text, such as continued on page 3, column 2) marking the end of the first part of a divided article. Also use end signs (a graphic element or tiny icon marking the end of an article).[29]
- Use one font size from 12 to as low as 9 for the main text. Even smaller font sizes (8 to 6) are acceptable for footnotes and explanatory comments. Use no more than six different font sizes on a page.

- Use multiple columns on each page. Many designers favor a three-column format. The design in Figure 2.10(a), page 60, involves a two-column layout, while the sketch in Figure 2.11 (page 62) shows three columns on page 1 but four columns on pages 2–4. In any case, for added visual interest, vary the number of columns the articles span.[30]

Content Guides

Once your design draws readers' attention, your newsletter content is what keeps it—or not. Use these guides to keep your audience reading your first edition and all that follow:

- Include a nameplate, table of contents, call box, and running head to guide your readers through the newsletter and build their confidence in your organization.[31]
  - *Nameplate.* The nameplate contains the newsletter title, date, and volume number, along with the organization's logo or tagline or both. The nameplate is a branding opportunity; make it the biggest element on your newsletter. Note the nameplate in Figure 2.10(a), page 60.
    Grab readers' attention with a captivating name for your newsletter, instead of a generic one. Use a name that is likely to have wide appeal now and into the future. In Figure 2.10, the name TechTimes is more engaging than, say, Journal of Information Technology or Ipsum Software News.[32]
  - *Table of contents.* On the front page list topics of three or four articles on successive pages. Include a relevant picture for each article listed if you have room. In Figure 2.10(a), notice the table of contents under the heading "This Issue."
  - *Call box.* Reserve a small area on page 2 or 4 to list contact information for the newsletter staff and publisher and perhaps one or two other company representatives.

- ○ *Running head.* Include the newsletter name, date, volume number, and page number at the top of each page, except the front page.
- Provide descriptive, catchy article headlines in abbreviated sentences. Incorporate an article's most engaging news in its headline.[33]
- Establish several newsletter sections that you will feature regularly. For example, Eagle Legacy Credit Union's newsletter might include headquarters news and branch news sections in each edition, along with employee benefits news and sales tips for credit union employees. Another regular section might include information about the newest service being offered to customers.[34]
- Include only articles that will generate the results you want. You planned the newsletter with your overall purpose in mind. Take planning a step further by identifying the objective for every article.[35]

  Earlier we discussed the importance of writing reports objectively and confidently. Your newsletter is no exception. Provide useful information for your readers, not sales hype.[36]

  Place your most helpful, interesting, timely article on page 1. Regular features, such as President's Letter or Salesperson of the Month, do not have to appear on the front page every time.[37]
- Use a direct structure for all articles; that is, begin with the information most important to readers.[38]

Guides for Visuals

In formal written reports, writers often use the introduce-display-discuss technique for incorporating visuals into reports (described in Chapter 4). Newsletters, however, will benefit from a different technique. Basically, place a visual where it is most likely to attract readers' attention.

All visuals should fit with your overall purpose and complement the newsletter content. Here are additional guides for the effective use of visuals in newsletters and similar documents.

- Keep the number of visuals small enough that each stands out. A good guide is to use no more than two visuals on an 8.5-inch × 11-inch page.
- In addition to photographs, use sidebars (short articles of explanatory or supplementary information in a text box beside main articles), graphs, tables, and maps.[39]
- Take newsletter photos using a digital camera, rather than your phone or tablet. In addition, set the camera for the largest picture size and highest resolution. Thus, you practically ensure crisp, clear images.[40]
- Most newsletter photographs should involve a person or several people—mainly customers and staff. Instead of portraits, use action shots for added interest. In addition, stand close to the photo subject(s) so that they fill the frame.[41] As a general rule, include a photo caption.
- When a photo is too large for the space, cut (crop) unnecessary parts from the visual. For example, a picture of a person standing may be cropped to show only the person's head and shoulders. If the photo cannot be cropped, resize, or scale, it in both height and width (the aspect ratio). Scaling an image in one direction only will distort the appearance and sometimes the meaning conveyed.
- Touch-up your photos with image-editing software before inserting them into your layout. Adjust the brightness, color, contrast, and so on to prevent a murky appearance.[42]
- Consider eye movement when placing photos on a page. For instance, a profile photograph of a person should be placed so that the person is looking into the page rather than off the side of the page.

Newsletter Do's and Don'ts

In addition to the design, content, and illustration guides, keep these ideas in mind to heighten the effectiveness of your newsletters.

- Do print your newsletter on recycled paper and state this fact in a note somewhere on the newsletter. Recycled paper costs the same as new paper, and your organization's eco-friendliness will make a favorable impression on some readers.[43]
- Don't promise newsletters more often than you can deliver them. If the nameplate indicates it is a monthly newsletter, then strive to send each issue about the same time every month.[44]
- Do allow 7 hours of editorial time for each 8.5 by 11 page, or 28 hours for a four-page newsletter. Add hours for designing, checking page proofs, and so forth.[45]
- Do take multiple shots for each photograph you plan, using slightly different angles and poses. Thus, you can choose the best photo in each instance.[46]
- Don't reprint articles from print publications or the web in your newsletter without written permission from the copyright holder (publication or website sponsor where the article appeared). Doing so is copyright infringement,[47] a dispute usually resolved through litigation in civil court. Likewise, before using an image found on the web, determine whether it is copyrighted. If so, obtain permission before including it.
- Do indicate the source of any information from a print publication or website that you summarize for inclusion in your newsletter.[48]

An attractive, reader-friendly format enhances a report's contents. However presented—e-mail, memo, letter, manuscript, web page, report deck, infographic, or newsletter—the format must entice readers, lead them effortlessly through the report, and maintain their interest.

Summary

An effective format is both attractive and functional. Ideally, the format motivates readers to respond to the report as you, the writer, had hoped.

A company may adopt standards for its documents and presentations and expect all writers in the organization to meet those standards. In the absence of such standards, follow these basic guides when formatting a paper document (memo, letter, or manuscript).

Document Formatting Checklist

- ☐ *Spacing.* Use single spacing, or some slight variation of it, for paragraphs.
  - o Omit paragraph indentations.
  - o Leave blank lines below each paragraph.
- ☐ *Fonts.* For paragraphs, choose a regular, proportionally spaced, serif font, such as Times New Roman. For headings in manuscript format, choose a sans serif font, such as Arial (bold is optional).
  - o The font size for paragraphs may be 10-point to 14-point, though 10-point may be too small for some readers.
  - o For headings in manuscript reports, use display sizes— 16-point, 18-point, and 20-point.
- ☐ *Emphasis techniques.* Strictly limit the use of ALL CAPS, bold style, italics style, and underlining. Add emphasis with bullet points, numbered items, and shaded text.
  - o Remember, a long LINE OF ALL CAPS IS HARD TO READ—and denotes shouting.
  - o Use bold to draw readers' attention to a few words, a phrase, or a short sentence.
  - o Use italics sparingly. Since it is hard to read, italics *forces slower, more careful reading.*
  - o Use bullet points when the order of listed items is irrelevant. (When sequence or ranking matters, use numbers instead of bullets.)
    - – Introduce bulleted or numbered lists with a unifying phrase or sentence.

- Include two or three points, never just one.
- Write all bulleted or numbered items in the same grammatical form; starting each item with an imperative (commanding) verb is a common practice.
- Choose one traditional bullet style for a report, such as ones used in this chapter. Unconventional bullet styles may be used in a newsletter.
- Align bullets or numbers at the paragraph point; use hanging indentation; and generally use the same spacing between bulleted or numbered items as between your other paragraphs.
- Call attention to an example, a long quotation, or other critical information using light shading on the text.

☐ *Headings*. Headings represent the outline, or organization, of your report; and they guide readers through it. The style of headings should show the relationship of report sections:
  - Make all Level 1 headings look alike; all Level 2 headings should look alike—but different from Level 1 or Level 3 headings. Put the same amount of space below a heading that you use between paragraphs.
  - Do not place a heading at the end of a page.
  - Insert text below every heading; do not place a Level 2 heading immediately below a Level 1 heading.

The chapter introduces seven report formats—three paper formats (memo, letter, and manuscript) and four electronic formats (e-mail, web page, slide deck, and infographics). Two principles apply equally to all of them.

- Choose a simple, practical design—one that makes needed information easy to find.
- Know what formatting options you have within your organization. Companies often set formatting standards for everyone in the organization to use.

Checklist for Report Formatting

- ☐ *E-mail format* (for short external or internal reports).
  - o Use standard e-mail headings, including Cc (courtesy copy) and Bcc (blind courtesy copy) headings.
  - o Include a strong subject line.
  - o Fill in the subject field, using caps and lower case, before typing your report—so you do not forget to identify its subject.
  - o Use six to eight descriptive words, with the key words first.
  - o When replying to a reply, change the subject line to match your new message.
  - o Use an informal salutation (greeting), depending upon how well you know the recipient. Drop the salutation if that person omits it in reply.
  - o Use headings and spacing to show organization of your e-mail content.
  - o Use one medium or large (about 12-point or 14-point) sans serif font throughout your e-mail report.
  - o Omit paragraph indentations; insert a blank line below each paragraph; and emphasize key points with a bulleted list. Allow lines of text to wrap naturally.
- ☐ *Memo format* (for relatively brief internal reports only). A standard memo heading includes guidewords: To, From, Date, and Subject and sometimes Cc (courtesy copy).
  - o Omit courtesy and professional titles on the To and From lines unless otherwise indicated.
  - o Use position titles on the From and To lines if you are new to the job.
- ☐ *Letter format* **(for external reports of up to three pages).** At minimum, a letter includes the following parts—always in this order and left-aligned on the page.

You will need to know how to apply specifications and guidelines for each report format. You may find the following checklist helpful:

- ☐ *Include sender's identification.* In the absence of a company letterhead, type the organization's complete mailing address an inch or so down the page. Use a letterhead for the first page only; after that, use plain paper with this heading: receiver's name, page number, and date.
- ☐ *Include date written or mailed.* Put the date a few blank lines below a letterhead or immediately below a return address. Spell out the month; type the day as a cardinal number (10, not 10th), and the four-digit year: June 8, 2016.
- ☐ *Include receiver's address.*
  - o Place the complete letter address several lines below the date.
  - o Use a courtesy or professional title with the person's name; but omit these titles if you do not know the person's gender or a woman's title preference.
  - o Include the receiver's position title; put it beside the name (comma between) or on the next line.
  - o Remove the excess space between lines of the address.
  - o The delivery address on the envelope should be identical to this one.
- ☐ *Include a salutation.*
  - o Start the greeting with Dear.
  - o If the letter address contains a courtesy or professional title, use it with the person's last name only.
  - o Use a first-name-only greeting only if you know the person well.
  - o Consider omitting the salutation and the complimentary close, when the address lacks a person's name.
- ☐ *Include a complimentary close.*
  - o Leave a blank line below the letter body, or message.
  - o Use a traditional close: Sincerely is a good choice as it fits in both formal and informal situations.
- ☐ *Include your signature block.*
  - o Leave a couple blank lines below the complimentary close, above your name.

- Type your name and position title or department affiliation beside your name (comma between) or immediately under it.
- Sign the letter in the space above your typed name.

☐ *Provide an envelope.*
- Use a window envelope or prepare an envelope by typing the letter address near the horizontal and vertical center.
- If using a plain envelope, include your name and address in the upper-left corner.

☐ ***Manuscript format*** (for internal or external reports exceeding three pages). Include at least a title page and a cover letter. Add other parts (table of contents, list of visuals, glossary, and so on) as needed. Observe these formatting conventions.
- Use single-spaced or multiple-spaced, blocked paragraphs unless otherwise indicated. Put a blank line above and below headings and between paragraphs.
- Use one serif font only or a serif font for paragraphs and a sans serif font for the title and Level 1 and 2 headings.
- Use a one-inch top margin on each page after the first and a one-inch bottom margin on all pages—usual default setting of word processing applications. On page 1, place the report title roughly two inches from the top and leave several blank lines below it.
- Use a left margin of 1.5 inches when binding on the left. Otherwise, make it one inch—same as the right margin.
- Include a title page that contains the report title, for and by whom it is written, and the report's completion date. Page borders and company logos may be added.

☐ *Manuscript format on the Internet*
- Create the report in Adobe Acrobat or convert your file to PDF.
- Use the site's content management system (CMS) to upload your prepared file.

- Use a file transfer protocol (FTP) to add your file to a website that does not have a CMS.
- Use a size 12 or 14 font.
- Limit report length to 60 pages or about 35 kilobytes.
- On the website, warn website users when a link will open a PDF.
- Use an image optimizer program to compress any photos in your report.
- Include convenient links in the report to aid navigation.

☐ *Web page format.* Ensure that web reports contain accurate HTML code and are quick to download and easy to navigate. Include your main point in the first lines. Aid readability by following these guides.
- Use short pages with ample blank space, short paragraphs, and interesting headings.
- Use consistent heading styles and give every report page the same appearance.
- Separate visuals from text with surrounding blank space.
- Omit links within paragraphs; instead, put them at the end of the paragraph or in a menu.
- Choose a light color for the background. Then select two or three font colors that contrast with the background.
- Use bold and full capitalization sparingly; avoid italics; and limit underlining to hyperlinks.
- Pick one serif and one sans serif font, and use the latter for paragraphs to be read from a computer screen or mobile device. And use standard letter spacing and line spacing.
- Keep the lines fairly short—around 55 characters.
- Use bullet points to get readers' attention.

WAI (the Web Accessibility Initiative) aims to make the web available to people with a range of disabilities. Employ these measures to make web pages accessible to hearing-impaired or vision-impaired individuals.

- ☐ Insert alt text (a text alternative) for all visuals (for example, charts and graphs, video clips, and photographs). And provide a transcript for podcasts, audio clips, and the like.
- ☐ When including a video in your report, provide closed captions or a sign language version for users who are deaf or hard-of-hearing.
- ☐ Omit any design elements—such as animation—that are incompatible with text-only browsers and large-print and voice software. Omit all references to colors used on the page in deference to people with colorblindness.

To ensure satisfactory viewing of your online report, test your web page over a low-speed modem connection, on a low-resolution computer monitor, and in different browsers.

- ☐ *Report deck format.* Although created with presentation software, report decks are meant to be clear to users without a presenter. Thus, a report deck is usually sent as an e-mail attachment and viewed by the recipient on his or her computer screen or mobile device. Generally, reports in this format contain more visuals than text. Follow these guidelines for good results from your report decks.
  - o Prepare a title slide (page) containing the report title, company name, your name, and the date.
  - o Include a contents slide, listing the name of each report section. For long reports, add page numbers and insert links for navigating the report deck.
  - o Establish your design on a master slide, using a solid background.
    - At the upper-left or upper-right on each slide, place a tracker (header) showing which report section the slide represents.
    - Place a footer on each slide: slide number, project name, and brand or copyright information.

- ☐ Write a title (headline) statement or question on each slide (page), using sentence case. Resize the headline text box if necessary to fit two lines of 24-point text. Below the headline add content to support the statement or answer the question.
- ☐ Use mostly visuals to convey your message, with some explanatory text.
  - o Use abbreviated or concise sentences, not paragraphs.
  - o Use bullets on some pages, but not all.
  - o Avoid using any text smaller than 18-point, especially if you will project the report deck during a presentation.
- ☐ *Infographics format.* This format shows data visually rather than describing it textually. The infographics format takes advantage of our brains' ability to process images faster than words, an important benefit as our information overload keeps growing.

Reports in infographics format may be used as standalone reports, as enhanced report illustrations, as executive summaries, or as online reports. Most creators of this format use an infographics maker, such as Venngage, Piktochart, or Easel.ly; or they engage the services of an infographics designer, such as Avalaunch, Info Graphic World, or Upwork. When using an infographics maker, follow these guides:

- ☐ Become thoroughly familiar with your data and the story it tells.
- ☐ Identify what you want readers to take away from your visual report.
- ☐ Sketch a storyboard, laying out the data-story left to right and top to bottom.
- ☐ For the small amount of text involved, use unusual fonts that are also very readable.
- ☐ Choose calm, harmonious colors, avoiding a white background and dark and neon colors. The rule of three is reliable for color selection: three complementary colors with

> the lightest in the background. If you need more colors, use shades of the original three.
> ☐ As a test, ask someone unfamiliar with your data to interpret your infographic report.

Newsletters and similar documents—brochures and fact sheets, for example—remain popular for promoting businesses and not-for-profit organizations. In our digital world, print materials stand out. And many consumers, including those 18 to 34, view a paper document as more credible than e-mailed information. In addition, the impact of print materials lasts longer than that of digital materials.

For generating a newsletter, choose the method that will best fit your budget and time available:

☐ Select a business newsletter template from your word processing software or the web.
☐ Hire a designer-printer service, such as Company Newsletters or Sun Solutions.
☐ Design your own newsletter.

Whichever creation method you choose, use this checklist to ensure that the design meets these effectiveness criteria before you insert your content.

> ☐ Each page shows a *balance* of blank space and printed area.
> ☐ Fonts and colors are used *consistently* throughout the newsletter.
> ☐ Pages involve pleasing *contrast* of blank space, shading, and visuals.
> ☐ Emphasis techniques, including placement, *focus* readers' attention.
> ☐ The sizes of fonts and visuals are in *proportion* to their importance.

Ensure a newsletter layout that will pique readers' interest the moment they open it and help them navigate its pages. Use this checklist to evaluate the design.

- ☐ The layout involves two, three, or four columns, with some articles spanning two or more columns.
- ☐ Headlines vary in size with key articles headlined in a display font and the newsletter title the largest font of all.
- ☐ All headlines are the same color or shade; likewise, the drop caps, the pull quotes, and the sidebars.
- ☐ Paragraphs are typed in a serif font, size 9 to 12.
- ☐ Jump lines direct readers to the next part of divided articles, and end signs follow the last word of each article.

Use the newsletter content so that your audience will continue reading. The following checklist is useful for evaluating newsletter content:

- ☐ The title suggests the presence of practical news-you-can-use for readers.
- ☐ Headlines consist of catchy, descriptive sentences that include the main point of the article.
- ☐ Most articles represent one of several regular-feature sections, but a few articles are special features.
- ☐ All articles fit your purpose and are likely to achieve the results you want.
- ☐ Page 1 includes a table of contents; each following page is numbered. The publication date and volume number are included.

Visuals are placed in newsletters to draw attention and garner interest in the accompanying articles. Use this checklist to assess the visuals in your newsletters.

- ☐ The newsletter contains an average of two or three visuals per page.
- ☐ Besides photos, other graphics (charts, maps, tables) are used now and then; and textual graphics such as shaded drop caps, pull quotes, and sidebars add visual interest to the pages.
- ☐ Photos—mostly action shots—were taken with a digital camera at the highest resolution and size. Thus, every photo is clear and crisp and fills the frame.
- ☐ Photos have been cropped or scaled to an appropriate size, and scaled photos are free of distortion.

The following checklist contains additional points to keep in mind before releasing your newsletter:

- ☐ If printed on recycled paper, a note indicates the percentage of recycled paper involved.
- ☐ No articles or photos have been reprinted from the web or other source without permission from the owner. Proper credit is given for material summarized from a published source.
- ☐ This newsletter will reach readers on time, according to your announced publication schedule.

In every case, choose a format and features that will (1) best meet the needs of your readers and (2) most likely accomplish your purpose for planning and producing the report.

CHAPTER 3

Illustrating Reports

If you have tried to follow complex written instructions—such as those for assembling a bicycle—or listened to a detailed explanation including many numbers—such as an insurance agent's description of the rate structure—you can appreciate the complementary value of visuals (photos, diagrams, graphs, and tables) to words, either written or oral.

Data visualization—our endless attempt to compress data into images—is society's way of dealing with the information overload of our age. Data visualization (data viz) runs a wide gamut. Have you noticed that some manufacturers supply only visuals as directions for use or assembly of their products? The infographics format discussed in Chapter 2 is also part of what data viz means, and there are additional meanings.

While it includes using the most effective traditional graphics to tell a story and make a point, data visualization also involves finding new ways to encode and plot data into pictures that people everywhere can apprehend quickly and retain permanently.

In effect, data visualization upends business research. Traditionally, business people used prescribed graphics in research reports to help readers understand what the writers already knew from their thorough collection, preparation, and (statistical or nonstatistical) analysis of the data.

Increasingly, however, business people and others chart data as they collect it, and the graphics *are* the analysis. They collect massive blocks of big data—the billions of nonrelational or unstructured raw data generated by the Internet, smartphones, cars with onboard computers, social networks such as Facebook, and even the digital storage of medical records—and use large-scale data processing engines, such as Apache Spark (spark.apache.org) to put these data in graphic form. When studied, these charts often reveal patterns and relationships in the data.[1] Once identified, the data connections can be used "to predict human behaviors, solve problems, identify shopping habits, thwart terrorists…"[2] *Note*: To be precise, the initial analysis involves looking at plotted data to see what they seem to say. If this exploratory analysis uncovers meaningful information, then confirmatory analysis using more traditional methods will likely follow.

For a data viz demonstration, see David McCandless' TED talk on You Tube: "The Beauty of Data Visualization" (www.youtube.com/watch?v=pLqjQ55tz-U&feature=youtu.be). McCandless turns complex data sets (such as worldwide military spending, media buzz, and Facebook status updates) into diagrams that reveal previously unseen patterns and connections.[3] This presenter makes a strong case that data visualization is the best way to deal with information overload.

Purposes of Visuals

While many writers readily think of using visuals in long reports, such aids can also increase the effectiveness of short reports. You should use visuals to emphasize, clarify, simplify, reinforce, and summarize information in both simple and complex oral or written reports. Further, visuals may be used to add interest, improve credibility, and increase the coherence of written messages.

Emphasize

Newspaper reporters and advertising copywriters are well aware of the value of photographs, diagrams, and charts to emphasize important facts. For example, a photo of people milling about and waving placards in front of a government building emphasizes the number of people involved in a protest far more effectively than a verbal report that "1,500 people demonstrated in front of the State House." Similarly, a line chart showing steadily increasing sales emphasizes the increase more effectively than does a written narrative alone.

Reports often cover many points, but not all are of equal importance. Visuals can be used effectively within reports to emphasize specific information. In addition, a visual on the report cover can draw the reader's attention to the main point of that report. Assume, for example, that you must prepare a report to employees to show that health insurance claims have increased dramatically while employee contributions to the health insurance plan have increased minimally during the past 10 years. For emphasis, you could prepare line charts showing claims and contributions as percentages of total wages for 10 years. Those charts could be placed strategically within the report. As an alternative, however, you could place a multiple-line chart on the report cover showing the relationships of employee claims and contributions, thereby emphasizing a significant fact to readers as soon as they pick up the report.

Clarify

A second purpose of visuals is to clarify something that may be difficult to express clearly in words alone. Assume that you wish to explain to your employees how payments for insurance benefits have been distributed among various benefit categories. Although you could provide that information in narrative form, the same data could be conveyed more clearly in a bar chart.

Simplify

Another purpose for visuals is to simplify data. Simplification involves breaking a complex whole into its component parts while preserving the essential nature of the whole. A pie chart may be used to simplify information. It presents the essential components (amount in each benefit category) while retaining the whole (total benefit payments).

Another visual often used to simplify a complex process is a diagram. A diagram shows relationships and abstract information without displaying numerical data. An example appears in Chapter 1 in Figure 1.2, which shows the steps and stages for drafting a report. The Venn diagram in Figure 3.1 compares and contrasts the attributes of three coffee shops.

Reinforce

To reinforce is to make stronger or more pronounced. Repetition is one form of reinforcement that helps people remember something important, but reinforcement is usually most effective when information is presented in more than one way, rather than through mere repetition.

84 PRODUCING WRITTEN AND ORAL BUSINESS REPORTS

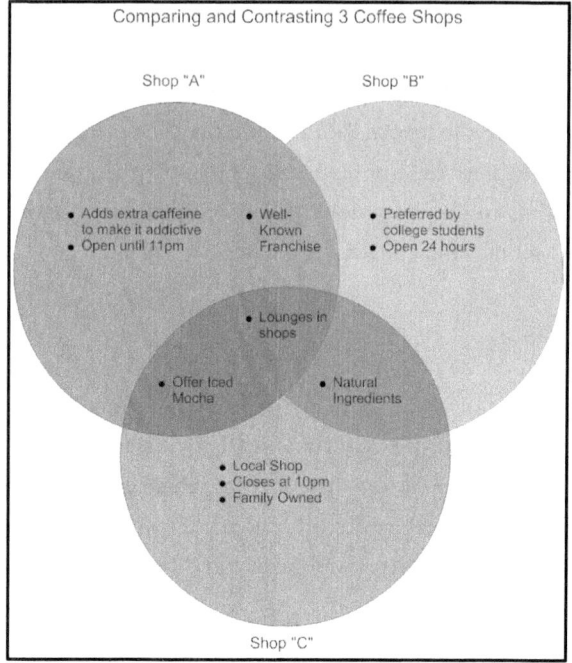

Figure 3.1 **Example of Venn diagram**

Source: SmartDraw Templates.

You can increase reader retention and recall of important facts by using visuals to reinforce your report narrative. For example, if you were asked to present a case for your company's participation in a major project, your visuals would probably include information about the company's past performances with projects similar to the one being considered. You would show charts reflecting the creative methods used by the company to keep costs down, performance statistics to indicate your high-quality standards, and your best idea-to-production times to show the audience how adept your company is at meeting target dates.

To be most effective as reinforcers, visuals should be used selectively. If minor as well as major verbal information is supplemented by a visual, the visuals become common, and their reinforcing value is reduced.

Summarize

Visuals can effectively summarize detailed information. A summary covers main points succinctly without providing all details. A good summary presents a reader with essential information and minimizes the amount of reading required to obtain that information.

If constructed accurately, a single visual, such as a chart, infographic, map, or table, can summarize several pages of narrative. Therefore, business reports today often replace a classic executive summary with a visual depicting the report's major findings.

In the report body, a visual cannot fully replace the narrative as a summary. While visual provides major points, the narrative may describe fine points that cannot be included in the visual summary.

Add Interest

When you go to the next page of a website, newspaper, or magazine, do you immediately begin to read the narrative or do you first look at pictures or charts? Most people look at the visuals first.

Visuals are effective tools to create interest and to relieve the tedium of a lengthy narrative. They make a report more attractive. Even in short reports, visual devices such as bullets (•), squares (□), or pointers (▶) can add interest. In addition, the text graphics called SmartArt in Microsoft Word are useful for adding interest. These visuals also indicate the relationship between pieces of information, as shown in Figure 3.2.

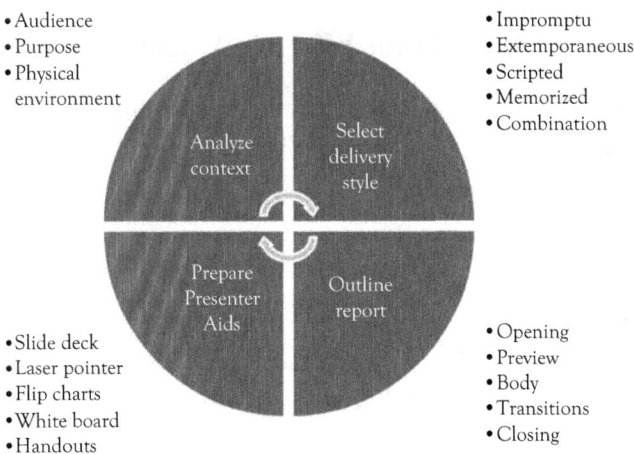

Figure 3.2 Example of SmartArt used to show relationships

Source: Clippinger (2016).

Improve Credibility

Visuals tend to add a sense of credibility that words alone cannot convey. The statement that profits have "increased dramatically" during the past five years may be interpreted as self-serving puffery. But that same statement may seem credible if it is accompanied by a line chart that shows sharply rising profits.

Graphics and pictures create a sense of precision. Many readers tend to believe that a writer who uses well-designed, accurate visuals is a confident, credible information source.

Increase Coherence

Effective reports are coherent—that is, all parts come together in logical relationships. The report writer may understand the relationships because of extensive exposure to the data, but the report will not be effective unless those relationships are also made clear to the reader(s). Visuals such as line charts, tables, or diagrams can show the relationships among different parts of a report.

As you study the visual examples in this chapter, consider which of the purposes—to emphasize, clarify, simplify, reinforce, summarize, add interest, improve credibility, and increase coherence—each visual would serve if it appeared in a report.

Criteria for Effective Visuals

To use visuals effectively in reports, become familiar with basic principles that apply to all visuals. In addition, follow guides for identification and placement of visuals in reports and strive for ethical representation of information.

Basic Standards

Well-constructed visuals meet four standards for effective graphics: simplicity, contrast, unity, and balance.

Simplicity

The most effective graphics are simple. Regardless of how complex the subject, the visual itself should include only information that is absolutely necessary to support the writer's message. Each visual should focus on one main point. A complex, cluttered visual presents too many stimuli to the viewer, thereby diverting the reader's attention rather than focusing it on the main point to be conveyed. Besides, as the number of stimuli increases, the possible interpretations of the visual also increase, adding to the likelihood of misunderstanding.

Edward Tufte, considered by many to be the preeminent authority on data visualization, refers to confusing, distracting visual features as chartjunk. He cites five forms of chartjunk:[4]

- *Decorative form:* Graphs designed to look like an object without regard for clarity of data representation.
- *The grid:* Graphs printed against dark grid lines that compete with the data. The grid should be muted or suppressed.
- *Moiré vibration:* Optical (op) art—an abstract art that gives the illusion of movement by the precise use of pattern and color, or in which differing patterns overlap.
- *Three-dimensional (3-D) display:* Giving false perspective to a printed chart so that it will resemble a three-dimensional object.

Consider the simplicity and effectiveness of international traffic symbols. Even when people cannot read or understand the local language, they can interpret those traffic signs. In effect, the simplicity of the signs helps to overcome a language barrier, as shown in Figure 3.3.

Figure 3.3 Simplicity of international traffic symbols

Contrast

The second principle to demonstrate in your visuals is contrast. To be effective, a visual must be noticed. Therefore, it must first stand out from

88   PRODUCING WRITTEN AND ORAL BUSINESS REPORTS

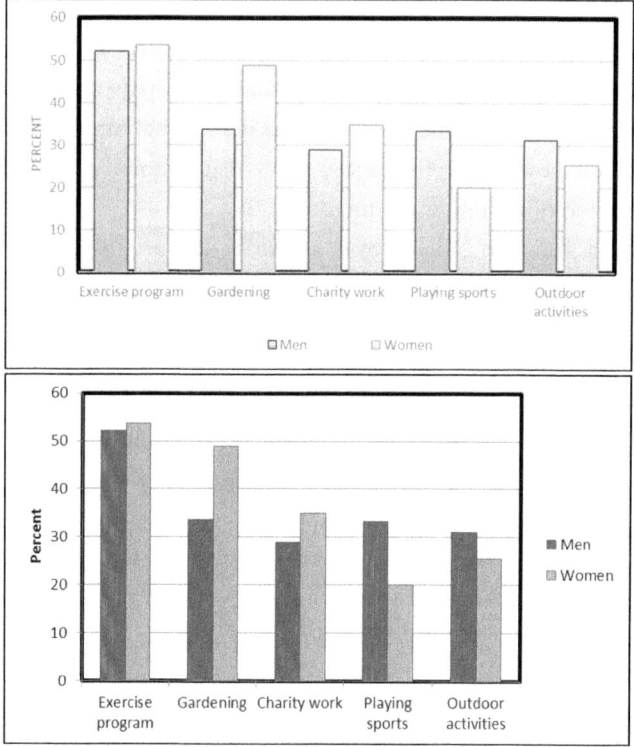

Figure 3.4 Comparison of low (top) and high contrast

its field. In written reports, that field is the page of the report. Contrast is achieved by visually separating the graphic from the narrative. This separation can be accomplished by using additional blank space or horizontal lines between the text and visual or by emphasizing borders of the visual.

Second, contrast must be achieved within a visual itself to clarify the comparisons or relationships that are presented. Contrast within a visual is achieved by differing colors or shades, solid and dotted lines, and different shapes to represent distinct items. Most graphing software offers a range of styles for the visuals created, as shown in Figure 3.4.

Unity

The third principle to observe is unity. An effective visual gives the impression that all parts belong and fit together. A unified chart or table shows the logical relationship of the parts to one another.

Within a visual, a sense of unity can be achieved by proximity, grouping, connecting lines, common shape, or common base. In a report, overall unity can be achieved by displaying all visuals in color or all in grayscale; using the same border style, font, palette, and title placement for all graphics.

Balance

The fourth principle for graphics construction is balance. Balance refers to a sense of equal weight among the components of the visual. When two or more equal things are being described, balance is relatively easy to achieve. Each item can be presented in exactly the same size, shape, or plane of the visual.

In the following examples, balance is contrasted with unbalanced presentations. While the balanced presentations are more attractive, an unbalanced arrangement may be justified under some conditions. For example, the unbalanced bar chart in Figure 3.5 would be justified if the bars were arranged chronologically. But since the bars represent discrete data, such as sales by region, the balanced presentation in descending order is preferable.

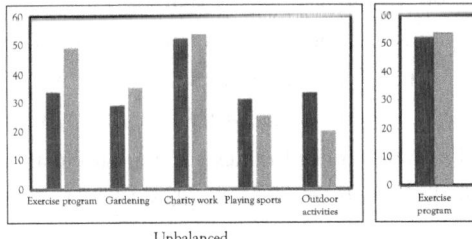
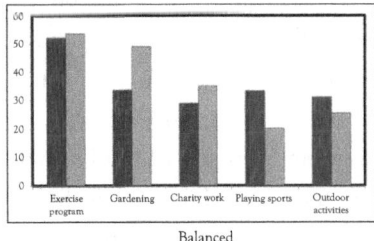

Unbalanced   Balanced

Figure 3.5 Unbalanced and balanced bar graph arrangement

In pie charts, balance can be achieved by beginning the largest segment at the top of the circle. The other segments should follow in a circular direction, by size, ending with the smallest. Again, rationale may exist for an unbalanced presentation. If two pies, for example, show contributions of parts to the whole for two different years, logical arrangement would be to place the segments of the first pie according to the principles of balance and the segments of the second pie in that same sequence to facilitate comparison of the related parts. Unbalanced and balanced arrangement are contrasted in Figure 3.6.

90 PRODUCING WRITTEN AND ORAL BUSINESS REPORTS

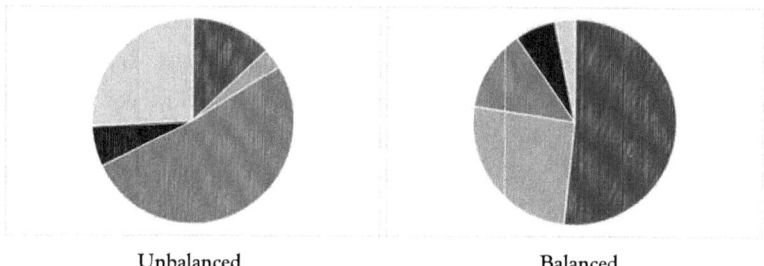

Unbalanced   Balanced

Figure 3.6 Unbalanced and balanced pie chart arrangement

Identification and Placement

When your report contains several visuals, identify each by a label, number, and title. For efficiency, some writers label all visuals as illustrations (for example, Illustration 1, Illustration 2, and so on). An alternative practice is to differentiate tables from other visuals, usually referring to charts, diagrams, maps, and so on as figures or illustrations (for example, Table 1, Table 2, Figure 1, Figure 2, and so forth). Current practice is to use Arabic, not Roman, numerals to number the visuals.

A title must be descriptive but concise. A well-written title for a visual answers the what and when questions about the data, and in many cases the title should also answer who and where. For example, Microcom Sales by District, 2016 and 2017, is a more meaningful title for a chart than Microcom Sales or Sales by District. Titles of tables are normally placed above the table, while titles of charts or figures may be placed at either the top or the bottom. Since most readers in the Western world read a page from top to bottom, it is reader-friendly to place the number and title at the top of all visuals so the reader sees such identifying information before studying the visual. Remember to be consistent with your placement of titles.

Besides identifying the visual by label, number, and title, you should identify the data source. If you used secondary data, the source may be identified in a shortened form, assuming that full identification is provided in the report's list of sources. An example of noting a secondary source is "Source: Statistical Abstract of the United States, 2015." If the data are from a primary source, such as observation, experimentation, interviews, questionnaire surveys, and searches through company records, the simple notation "Source: Primary" is adequate.

The most effective placement of visuals is in the report body, not in an appendix, unless you know that your main reader prefers that visuals be grouped in an appendix. Visuals should be placed where they are needed for emphasis, clarity, simplification, reinforcement, summary, interest, credibility, or coherence. And a visual should be placed as near as possible to the accompanying narrative. An effective three-step procedure for incorporating a visual into a report is to introduce the graphic, display it, and then discuss it.

Introduce the Visual

In the introductory statement, mention a key fact that the visual illustrates. Focus on the information contained in that visual, not on the visual itself. Following the introduction, identify the visual by number or title to help the reader locate it in the report. If the visual is on another page, also include the page number in the identification. The following examples contrast less effective and more effective introductions.

Less Effective: Illustration 1 shows sales for oat bran, rice bran, and wheat bran in 2017.
More Effective: Oat bran substantially outsold both rice bran and wheat bran in 2017. (See Illustration 1.)
Less Effective: As Figure 1 shows, a research plan contains 12 parts.
More Effective: Planning research is a 12-part process, as demonstrated in Figure 1, page 4.

Display the Visual

Following the introduction, display the visual as soon as possible. Separate the visual from the narrative with additional blank space or horizontal lines to achieve contrast. Some report writers include a two- to three-inch column on the left of each page and place small, simple graphics in it, beside the introduction on the right; but, integrate larger illustrations with the text as just described.

If space permits, place the visual on the same page as the introduction. If the visual does not fit on the same page, do not leave a large patch of blank space at the bottom of the page; just continue with your discussion and place the visual at the top of the next page.

Visuals must fit within the margins of the report narrative and should not be so large that they distract from the narrative. If necessary, reduce the visual so that it will fit attractively within the report margins while retaining legibility.

When large visuals must be used, they may occupy a full page and may be placed vertically or horizontally. Whenever possible, display full-page visuals on the page immediately following the one on which the visual is introduced.

Discuss the Visual

While a visual can add interest to a report or summarize essential information, it is your responsibility as the report writer to interpret the data in that visual. After introducing and displaying the visual, discuss it in an interpretative manner. Interpretation requires more than merely repeating the data presented in the visual. Your discussion must clarify data or add details that cannot be captured visually.

When your discussion requires only one paragraph, you may combine the introduction and discussion. In that situation, display the visual after the discussion. If the discussion is lengthy, however, the introduce–display–discuss sequence is more effective. An acceptable pattern for introducing, displaying, and discussing visuals is demonstrated in Figure 3.7.

> 6
>
> Especially disconcerting is the low volume of tourist spending for accommodations, food service, and recreation/arts/entertainment. Although rich in history and recreational opportunities the Hatfield-McCoy region received fewer tourist dollars from those categories than did any other region.
>
> The number of jobs created by tourism is also a significant measure of economic impact. (See Table 2.) In terms of jobs created, the regions ranked in the same order as on the measure of tourist spending, with the exception of the Eastern Panhandle and New River-Greenbrier Valley regions, which switched positions. Again, the Hatfield-McCoy region scored lower than all other regions on this measure, garnering fewer than 3% of tourism-related jobs.
>
> **Table 2. Direct Employment Generated by Tourism in West Virginia, 2014**
>
> | Region | Number of Employees |
> |---|---|
> | Eastern Panhandle | 9,000 |
> | Northern Panhandle | 8,700 |
> | Metro Valley | 6,600 |
> | New River-Greenbrier Valley | 6,900 |
> | Mountaineer Country | 5,500 |
> | Potomac Highlands | 3,800 |
> | Mountain Lakes | 2,200 |
> | Mid-Ohio Valleys | 2,100 |
> | Hatfield-McCoy Mountains | 1,300 |
> | Total Direct Employment | 46,100 |
>
> Source: Dean Runyan Associates, pp. 26 and 27.
>
> The Dean Runyan study revealed interesting facts about the total impact of tourism on the state. Another study focusing on day travelers (Lawson International, 2014) provides insights into a market setment that could prove to be especially profitable for the Hatfield-McCoy Mountains region. Day travelers are West Virginia residents and nonresidents who travel at least 50 miles to a tourist destination but do not include an overnight stay.
>
> The Lawson study estimated that 39.9 million day trips were taken to and in West Virginia in 2013, 62% of which were marketable trips (that is, not for business or to visit friends and relatives). Those marketable pleasure trips brought in $2.1 billion, or $84.89 per person, in West Virginia that year (Lawson, pp. 7-17). The Runyan report (p. 10) listed total direct spending by tourists in 2013 at $4.5 billion. So day travelers who came strictly for pleasure accounted for almost 47% of that year's tourism spending in the state.

Figure 3.7 Placement of visuals in a report

Ethical Representation

A final criterion for effective visual aids is that all visuals must be ethical representations of data. A report narrative may present comprehensive and accurate data, but readers tend to gain first impressions of information from visuals.

Visuals can sometimes have more impact than their accompanying text for three reasons.[5]

- Visuals have an emotional impact that words lack.
- Skimmers of items will see visuals even when they do not read the text.
- Readers remember visuals longer than the descriptive text.

A report narrative may present comprehensive and accurate data, but readers tend to gain first impressions of information from the visuals. Those first images and the impressions they leave often influence the reader more strongly than does the verbal narrative.

Distorted graphs are sometimes deliberately deceptive—to mislead or, perhaps, shock readers. More often the writer does not fully understand the data behind the graph. Most misleading graphs include one of these problems:[6]

- Data are omitted.
- The vertical scale of a bar or line chart skips numbers.
- The vertical scale does not start at zero.
- The vertical scale is too big or too small.
- Graph labels are incomplete or inappropriate.

The article "Misleading Graphs: Real Life Examples" (www.statistic-showto.com/misleading-graphs) includes recent examples of distorted visuals in news media.

Choosing and Constructing Visuals

Although visuals serve many purposes in reports, those purposes are achieved only if the appropriate graphic is chosen. Knowing the characteristics of various graphics will help you choose visuals to achieve your purposes.

Data Visualization Studies

Our eyes and mind evaluate graphical cues with different degrees of accuracy.[7] Studies show that the colors used in a graphic display can affect the time required to read it.[8]

Graphic Cues and Perceptual Accuracy

In a classic study, William Cleveland asked participants to make judgments involving different visual cues. Using results of these experiments, along with other information, the researcher ranked the cues from most accurate to least accurate for perceiving data, as shown in Figure 3.8.[9]

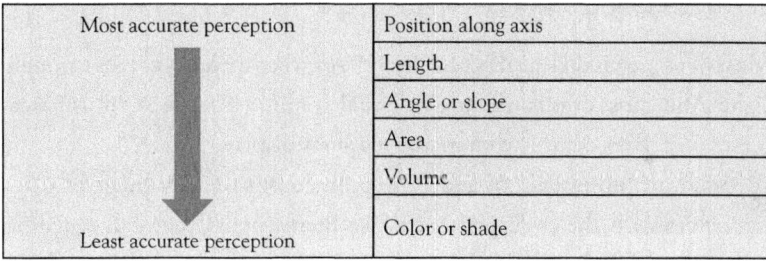

Figure 3.8 Rank order of visual cues
Source: Valiela (2001), p. 188.

Recently, Jeffrey Heer, a data visualization expert, led a similar study and drew similar conclusions. Specifically, Heer's team ranked eight data encodings from most accurate to least accurate:[10]

- Position on a common scale
- Position on a nonaligned scale
- Length
- Slope
- Angle
- Area
- Volume
- Color or shade

The information in Figure 3.8 as well as Heer's findings indicate that readers will decode your graphs most accurately when you use bar graphs and line graphs, which involve data points on an axis or two, bars of varying lengths on a common baseline, or lines that form angles or slopes as they rise and fall.

Area charts, including stacked line graphs and pie charts, are inherently harder to read. In his book *Show Me the Numbers*, Stephen Few noted that "our visual perception is not designed to accurately assign quantitative values to 2-D areas."[11] Few then pointed out that adding a third dimension, a popular graphics enhancement, only makes charts more difficult to read accurately. Additionally, visuals that convey meaning solely by color are frequently difficult to read accurately, given the fact that approximately 8% of the U.S. population is colorblind.

Color Associations and Perceptual Speed

Most of us are visual learners; that is, 90% of what we learn comes through sight. And most of our reaction to visual stimuli (62% to 90%) is based on color.[12] Thus color is vital to any graphics display.

Stanford professors Lin and Heer pointed out the advantage of pairing colors with the concepts that evoke them—what they call semantically resonant color choices.[13] At the risk of overgeneralizing, semantic resonance means you use blue for blueberries, orange for oranges, and yellow hues for bananas and lemons when charting produce items in a grocery department.

In their study published in *Harvard Business Review*, Lin and Heer asked people to complete identical comparison tasks, one using semantically resonant colors and the other using nonresonant colors. Each comparison involving semantically resonant colors took 10% less time to complete than the nonresonant comparison. Although the actual amount of time was small (one second), "these seconds add up, especially for data analysts who make untold numbers of comparisons during their workday."

Likewise, semantically resonant colors give readers the advantage of familiar color relationships, reducing their need to look at the legend accompanying the graph or chart.

Not only tangible objects but also many concepts have colors associated with them. And these associations vary from one culture to another. For example, in the U.S. culture red is associated with danger, debt, and stop. In China, red is the color of luck. Black represents mourning in the United States; in China, white does.

The list of color meanings[14] in Figure 3.9 is not meant to be comprehensive. Also, the following meanings are traditional but may not be current in these cultures because old associations fade with time and multicultural awareness. The Internet, by allowing people to learn about other cultures and adopt what they like from them, has contributed greatly to the cross-cultural adoption of colors and ideas.

Color	Western Cultures	Eastern Cultures
Blue	Trust, authority, conservative, corporate, peace, calm, masculinity	Immortality, femininity
Green	Luck (four-leaf clovers), spring, new birth, regeneration, nature, environmental awareness	New life, regeneration, hope, fertility
Orange	Affordable or inexpensive	Happiness, spirituality
Purple	Royalty, spirituality, wealth, fame	Wealth, sorrow, comforting, death
Yellow	Happiness, joy, hope, cowardice, caution, warning of hazards and hazardous substances	Sacred, imperial, honor, masculinity

Figure 3.9 Comparative meanings of various colors

In his book *Visualize This*, Nathan Yau noted that though people have been graphing data for centuries, researchers began studying the relative effectiveness of various graphs only a few decades ago. "In that respect," Yau wrote, "visualization is a relatively new field."[15] The popularity of infographics may lead some business people to abandon traditional graphics. A better choice is to use the findings of visualization studies to maximize the efficacy of every visual.

Graphing Software

You are likely familiar with the charting tools in Microsoft Excel. While author Stephen Few is not a proponent of Excel, he used that program to create most of the graphs and tables in *Show Me the Numbers*.[16] He did so "in part to demonstrate that good design can be achieved even if you have no software but Excel."[17]

In addition, many charting applications are available online for generating graphs. In most cases, these applications allow you to build in animation and interactivity. Additionally, the online software can link the graphics you create directly into your website, eliminating the need for you to be proficient in scripting language and application program interfaces (APIs).

The following list includes a few examples of online graphics software:

- amCharts (www.amcharts.com)
- ChartGo (www.chartgo.com)
- Flot (www.flotcharts.org)
- Highcharts (www.highcharts.com)
- JPowered (www.jpowered.com)
- SmartDraw (www.smartdraw.com)

> Author Nathan Yau recommended the following graphics software and commented on each program.
>
> - *Adobe Illustrator* (www.adobeillustrator.com). This application is the industry standard for all types of illustration (except photo editing), not just graphs. If graphs and tables are the only illustration you do, you may want to consider some of the other options, given Illustrator's price. Adobe provides many tutorials for Illustrator.[18]
> - *Corel Draw* (www.coreldraw.com/us). This Windows-only package, generally less costly than Illustrator, is comparable to it in the illustration tools it offers.[19]
> - *Google Spreadsheets* (www.google.com/sheets/about). This application has been called "the cloud version of Microsoft Excel" because of the familiar spreadsheet interface. It offers the standard chart types; in addition, it includes specialized

tools called gadgets. Using time series data, one gadget makes a motion (animated) chart and another creates an interactive chart.[20]
- *Inkscape* (inkscape.org). This free, open-source application is comparable to Adobe Illustrator and nearly as popular. Numerous tutorials are available at inkscapetutorials.wordpress.com.[21]
- *Tableau* (www.tableau.com). For Windows only, this program is designed to explore and analyze data visually, not just graph it. You can import data from a variety of sources, including Excel, database servers, and text files. The makers of this high-powered, high-priced package also offer a fully functioning free trial.[22]

Animation and Interactivity

Animation and interactivity separate web page graphics from printed ones.

Any graphic mentioned in this chapter can be animated in a web page report. Animation is mostly used for getting web viewers' attention and includes bouncing, flashing, pulsing, shaking, stretching, swinging, and wobbling. Subtler animation involves the use of transitions by which a graphic appears mobile upon entry or exit or both. Clicking a link might cause a bar graph or pie chart or map to bounce, fade, flip, rotate, slide, or zoom onto or off the screen.

Business graphics often involve interactivity to enhance web users' experience at a website. Experts in the field recognize three levels of interactivity: low, medium, and high.[23]

- Low-level interactivity. Users see certain stored data when they point to or hover over a visual (pop-up windows on a static image).
- Medium-level interactivity. Users can click a visual to view more detailed data or link to related data.
- High-level interactivity. Users can influence or modify content of the visual; for example, they might be able to zoom in

on the data or filter the data that is shown (display data on a line chart for certain years only or expose data on a statistical map for certain areas only). And at this level, users can choose their own navigation path in the data and the website.

While animation and interactivity are common website features, little formal research is available to inform business people for using them.

The following principles are derived from comments of a few business bloggers.[24]

- Focus first on conveying clear, easy-to-follow data, not on achieving a particular level of interactivity.
- Know your audience, how they think, and their reasons for visiting your website. Then provide only the level of data that will help solve a problem of theirs.
- Omit higher levels of information beyond the audiences' current interest, as it may create confusion and detract from their user experience.
- Try to get a sense of your audience's need or preference for guidance through data versus finding their own path.
- Make every graphic visually appealing and highly relevant. Always aim for high-quality graphics.
- And make your graphics mobile-friendly, too, as more and more people navigate the web using a tablet, smartphone, or another handheld device.
- Ensure that every click by a user provides access to new data.
- Encourage social sharing by including the most appropriate social media links for each report graphic.
- Include calls to action, such as sign up for e-mail or request a quote. Provide a maximum of one such link per page.
- Consistently check for problems, such as a graphic that does not load or a failed hyperlink.
- Survey web page users from time to time on their satisfaction with their user experience at your site.

Guides for Specific Visuals

Following are guides for constructing various bar graphs, line graphs, area charts, and relationship charts. (The words chart and graph are used interchangeably throughout the chapter.) Then construction guides are provided for tables, followed by discussions of statistical maps and photographs.

Bar Graphs

A bar graph uses two or more rectangles along with vertical and horizontal axes to represent information. When the rectangles are placed vertically, the chart may be called a column chart; when the rectangles are placed horizontally, the name horizontal bar graph applies.

Uses

Bar graphs are used to compare discrete (noncontinuous, distinct, unconnected) quantitative data, such as the numbers of females and males in a training program, the sales volumes of two or more products in a stated time period, or the distribution of time among several activities. A bar graph provides a quick visual impression of the relationships between or among the compared components (called variables). A variable is a factor that may change (vary) in value. A simple bar chart compares two or more variables on one dimension, as shown in Figure 3.10. The graph compares five variables, or categories, by percent of respondents in each category.

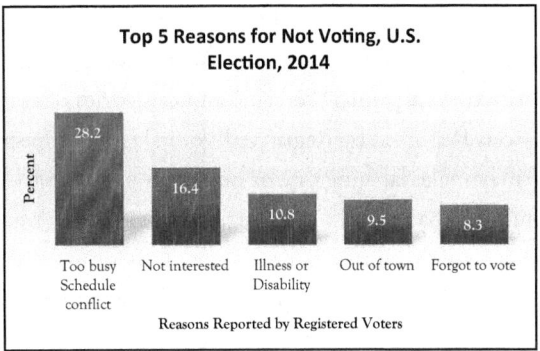

Figure 3.10 Simple bar graph

Source: Current Population Survey (2014), U.S. Census Bureau.

Construction Guidelines

Following these guideliness will help you construct effective bar graphs:

- Plan size and page location carefully, using the introduce-display-discuss pattern. Allow sufficient space so that the graph, including its title and source note, will not be crowded. Resize the graph as needed while maintaining legibility. Resizing is easier when you copy a graph from your graphics software and paste it as a picture into your report. However, if you wish to keep the report graph linked to the original data table, paste the graph as text. Then change dimensions, keeping the aspect ratio.
- Achieve balance in the length and width of bars. All bars must be the same width, and the space between bars should be no less than half the width of the bar itself. If the output of your charting software does not follow this rule, try a different style. For readability, vertical bars should be no longer than seven inches, and horizontal bars should not exceed five inches. Unless it is logical to do otherwise, arrange your data table so that bars will be in ascending or descending order by length.
- Arrange data so that the unit of measurement shows on the horizontal (x) axis for graphs having horizontal bars and on the vertical (y) axis for graphs having vertical bars. Always check to ensure that your charting software drew the axes and scale units accurately, with all steps of a scale representing the same unit size and placed at equal distances from one another.
- Label the graph. For each axis, as shown in Figure 3.10, identify the scale units (Percent) and categories of comparison (Reasons Reported by Registered Voters). A very specific chart title may make labeling one or both axes unnecessary.
- In multiple-bar graphs, use sharply contrasting colors to differentiate categories. When you will distribute a report from a monochrome (all-black) printer or a photocopier, ensure contrast by using a grayscale palette (black, white, and shades of gray). Provide a key or legend within the graph to interpret the colors or shades.

Variations

The construction guides are also applied in the following variations of the simple bar graph.

A multiple bar chart compares two or more variables on two or more dimensions, as shown in Figure 3.11. This chart compares two variables (ages 18 to 24 and ages 25 to 44) on five dimensions (reasons for not voting).

A segmented bar chart adds another dimension to a comparison, as shown in Figure 3.12. The parallel, segmented bars clearly show the ethnic backgrounds of voters in each of the six national elections.

Another variation of the bar graph is the bilateral bar graph, which permits display of positive and negative values. Figure 3.13 displays the data table in the graph for those readers who want precise data.

A pictograph, or pictogram, is a bar chart or line chart that uses images or symbols to depict its data. A staple of journalists and forerunner of infographics, a pictograph's simple images add interest and emphasis and, according to studies, make data easier to read and remember. Notice how the goal of Women for Women International—to help women around the world, particularly in war-torn countries, improve their economic well-being—is emphasized in Figure 3.14, page 105.

Bar graphs are an effective way to compare items between different groups. They are a very useful visual to use in business reports, both written and oral (presentation slides). These graphs allow report readers to see patterns or trends more easily than looking at the same numerical data arranged in a table.

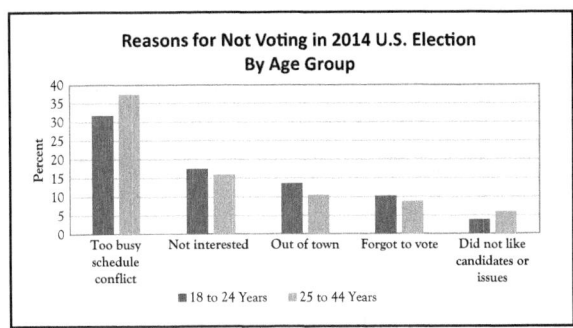

Figure 3.11 Multiple-bar graph

Source: Current Population Survey (2014), U.S. Census Bureau.

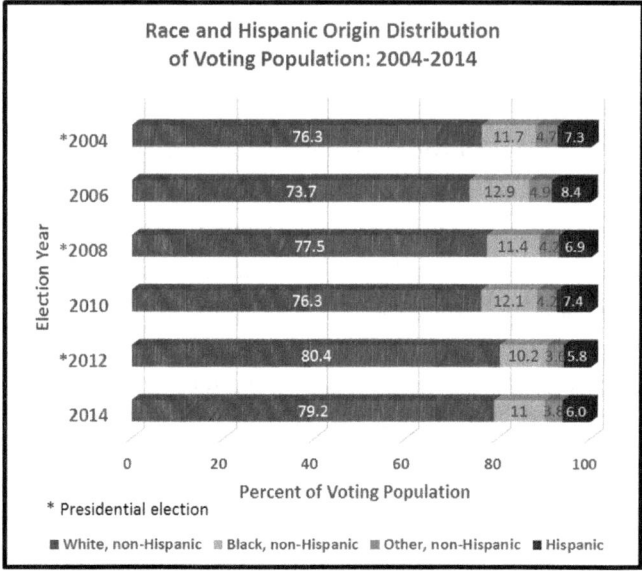

Figure 3.12 Segmented bar chart

Source: Current Population Survey (2014), U.S. Census Bureau.

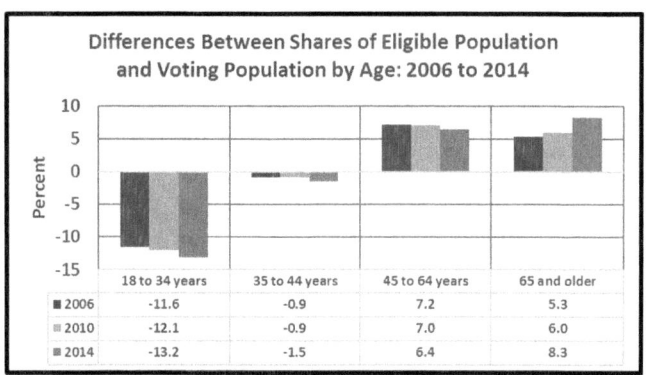

Figure 3.13 Bilateral bar graph

Source: Current Population Survey (2004–2014), U.S. Census Bureau.

Line Graphs

Line graphs are used to compare continuous (connected, unending) data. A line graph consists of a vertical axis, a horizontal axis, and one or more plotted lines. Each axis contains a measurement scale that identifies the factors of comparison: income, age groups, time periods, percentages,

ILLUSTRATING REPORTS   105

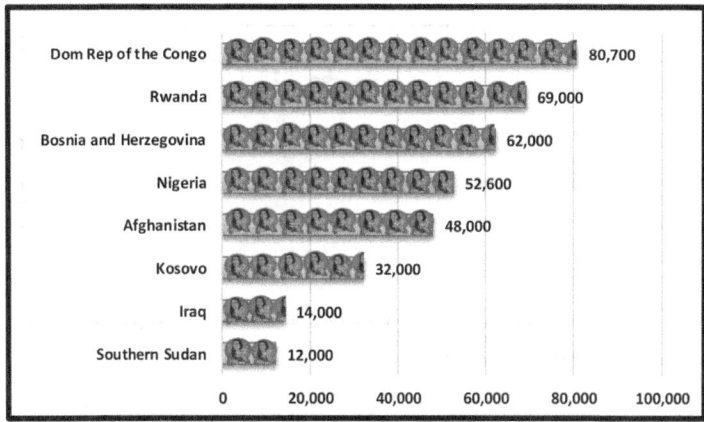

Figure 3.14 Pictograph (variation of a bar graph)
Source: What We Do. (2016). Women for Women International.

ratings, amounts, and so on. Traditionally, the horizontal dimension represents time and the vertical dimension represents values. There are underlying assumptions of continuity and equal intervals in the measurement scales. For example, a time scale is based on the assumption that time is continuous and that all scale points represent equal time intervals.

Uses

Line graphs show the relationship between the variables on the vertical and horizontal axes. A basic line graph contains one line showing changes in the dependent variable (shown on the vertical axis) for each classification of the independent variable (shown on the horizontal axis). In business reports, one of the most commonly used line graphs shows trends or changes in a variable over time—as shown in Figure 3.15.

Another often-used line graph is a frequency distribution (frequency polygon), which shows the relationship between two factors (excluding time), such as anticipated sales at various unit prices or unit costs at various production levels.

Line charts should not be used to compare obviously independent items, such as sales in each of several districts. A bar graph appropriately compares that kind of (discrete) data.

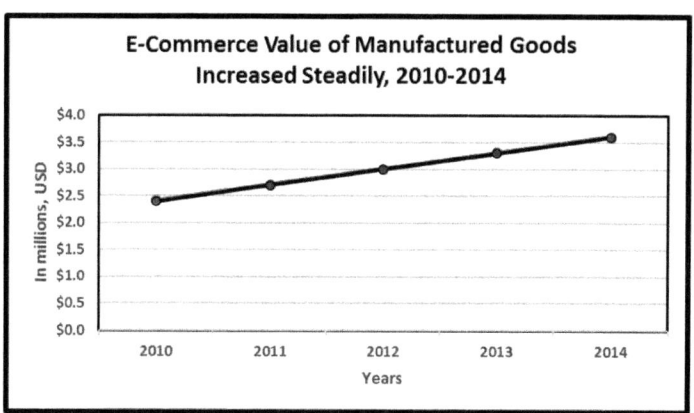

Figure 3.15 Line (time) graph

Source: Annual Survey of Manufactures and the Economic Census, U.S. Census Bureau.

Construction Guides

Following guides will help you construct effective line charts:

- Plan the chart size for readability. The maximum size should occupy less than a full page of the report so that there will be enough space for the title and other identifying information. If you are tempted to use a chart that is larger than a full page, reconsider. You are probably trying to present too much data in a single chart. The minimum width and height should be two to three inches so that the title, scales, and labels are legible.
- Follow standard plotting rules. Use the horizontal axis to designate the independent variable; that is, the method of classification, such as time, scores, or age groups. Use the vertical axis to show the dependent variable; that is, classification range, such as dollar amounts, frequencies, or units.
- Use accurate, nondistorting scales. Observing the products of your charting software, you will likely see the three-quarter rule applied. That rule states that the height of the vertical axis should be about three-quarters the length of the horizontal axis. Check distances on the axes of your graphs: Are distances between markers identical on each axis? And are distances between markers on the *x* and *y* axes about the same?

Both attributes are necessary to prevent distortion. In addition, notice that the vertical scale begins at zero. *Note*: If the entire plotted line lies considerably above zero—as it does in Figure 3.15—you may break the vertical scale to show omission of unnecessary data.
- Label the graph. Identify scale units on the *x*-axis and *y*-axis. In multiple-line graphs, use sharply contrasting colors to differentiate the variables and provide a legend within the graph to interpret those lines. As with all graphs, full labeling includes an appropriate title and source notation.

Variations

A multiple-line chart permits comparison of both trends and relationships. For example, a multiple-line chart can compare total growth in the value of manufactured goods with growth in the value of e-commerce manufactured goods as shown in Figure 3.16.

A bilateral line chart permits plotting of both positive and negative values. To accommodate negative values, the vertical scale must continue below the zero point, as is shown in Figure 3.17.

An interesting variation of the line chart: the high-low, or stock, chart. A high-low chart permits you to show variations in values for a factor during a time period—such as daily, monthly, or annual rainfall—as well as the average value of the factor. A bar marks the high and low values,

Figure 3.16 Multiple-line chart

Source: Annual Survey of Manufactures and the Economic Census, U.S. Census Bureau.

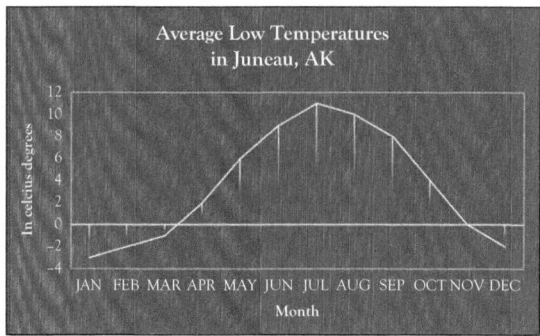

Figure 3.17 Bilateral line chart

Source: Climate Juneau—Alaska (2016), U.S. Climate Data (2016).

and a line is plotted through the bars to show the average values. Quarterly stock prices for a hypothetical company are shown in Figure 3.18.

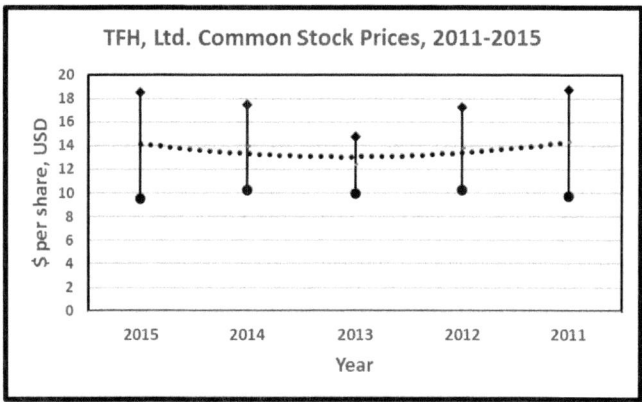

Figure 3.18 High–low (stock) chart

Source: Primary.

Area Graphs

A stacked variation of the line chart is called an area chart or band chart. In this graph, the factors that contribute to a total are identified, and a line is plotted for each factor. The areas between the plotted lines—supposedly—represent the respective contributions of the factors to the total. The data plotted in Figure 3.16 could also be plotted as an area chart, as is done in Figure 3.19.

Area charts are problematic for a couple of reasons. As already noted, we generally do not perceive areas very accurately. So we tend to read area

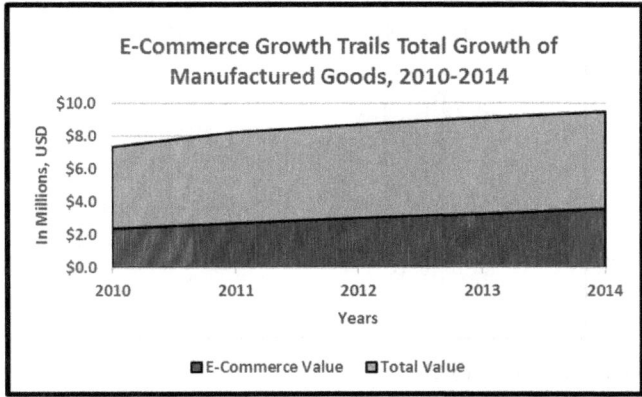

Figure 3.19 Area (stacked line) chart

Source: Annual Survey of Manufactures and the Economic Census, U.S. Census Bureau.

charts as line graphs, looking at the top edge of each area. Doing so works when you have only two areas. The line at the top of the chart reveals the total units for the time period. And the line formed by the baseline area reveals the units contributed by that part. But when you have three or more areas, the lines between the first and last areas reveal nothing meaningful. The slopes of lines at the top of those areas is influenced by the slopes of the areas below them—and the areas themselves are practically impossible to discern.[25]

Therefore, use stacked-line graphs when readers need only a rough idea of how the parts compare to each other in their contributions to the total. To present such data precisely, use two line charts, one showing the total and one showing the parts.[26]

Pie (Circle) Chart

You are likely familiar with the area graph called a pie chart. This graph is a circle divided into segments. The circle represents the whole amount (100%), and each segment represents a proportion of the whole.

Uses

A pie (circle) chart is effective when you want to emphasize relative proportions. Pie charts permit rough comparisons of parts that make up a whole. A circle graph, is shown in Figure 3.20.

110 PRODUCING WRITTEN AND ORAL BUSINESS REPORTS

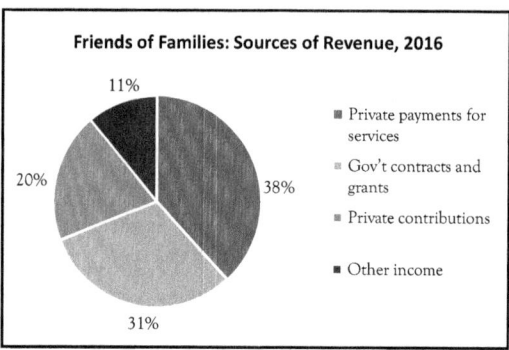

Figure 3.20 Pie (circle) chart

Source: Primary.

Two or more pies can also be placed side by side to compare factors at different times, such as expenditures in two different years, or to compare two related factors, such as sources and uses of funds.

Author Stephen Few does not use pie charts and recommends that we all follow his lead. He states that pie charts are even harder to read accurately than other area charts. "If they're fairly close in size, it's difficult if not impossible to tell which is bigger, and when they're not close in size, the best you can do is determine that one is bigger than the other, but you can't judge by how much." To emphasize the point, Few provides the following example in Figure 3.21 of a pie chart and bar chart portraying the same data. The pie chart segments seem to be very close in size, but the same data on a bar chart tells a different story.[27]

Of course, the pie segments could include data labels; but, remember, visuals generally influence readers more than the associated text. If precision is your goal, then present the data in a table, the most numerically precise graphic.

Pie charts are often shown as objects in three dimensions, but the addition of 3-D generally makes the charts even harder to read than the 2-D areas. Notice in the following examples in Figure 3.22 (page 112) that the 20% segment appears larger than the 25% segment in the 3-D pie. The segment at the six o'clock position in a 3-D chart usually will appear larger than it does in 2-D. In his YouTube video "Data Viz: You're Doin' It Wrong," an expert graphics designer Noah Iliinsky cites this foreshortening as distortion that can be prevented by spurning 3-D displays.[28]

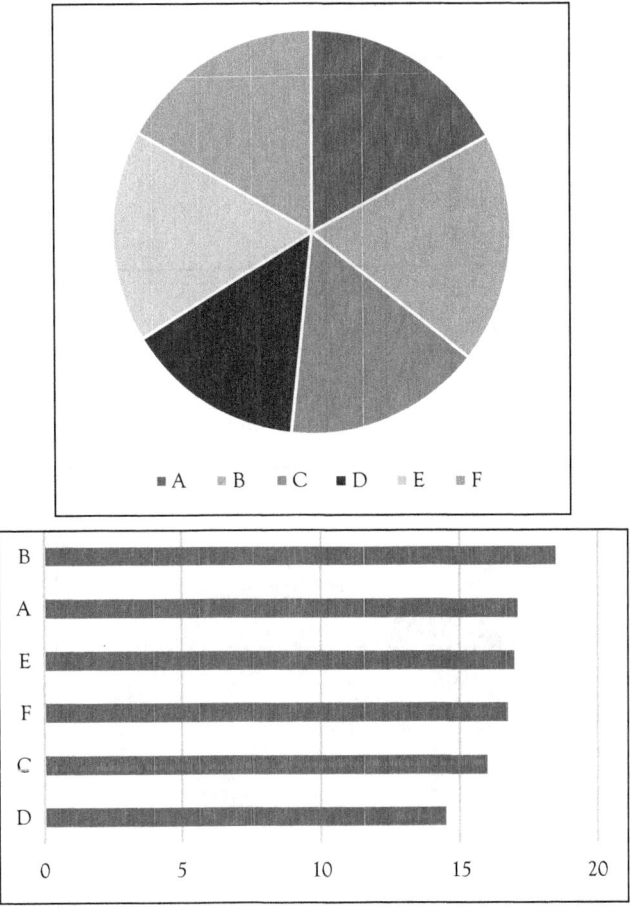

Figure 3.21 Comparison of precision difference between a pie and bar chart

Source: Few (2012), pp. 94–95.

The following guides are designed to help if you choose to use pie charts in spite of prior comments.

Construction Guides

To construct pie charts, follow these guides:

- Keep the number of segments to a minimum. While the recommended maximum was seven or eight segments, recent

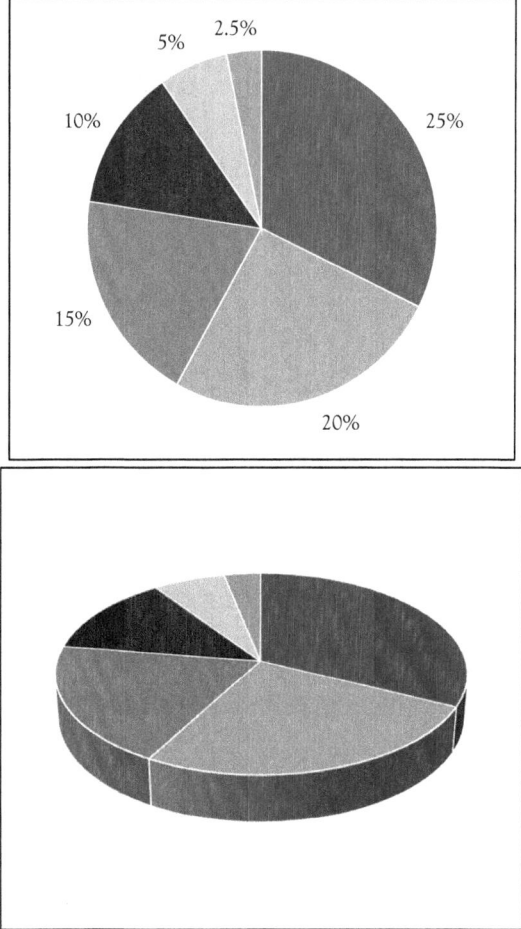

Figure 3.22 Comparison of a 2-D and 3-D pie chart

studies suggest drawing the line at about five segments. Too many slices in the pie increases the difficulty of comparing them.
- Balance the segments. Since people in the Western world tend to read pie charts in a clockwise (top to bottom toward the right) direction, illustrators recommend placing the largest segment first, beginning at the top. Place other segments around the circle in descending order of size unless logic requires some other arrangement. For example, the 2016 revenue data

presented in Figure 3.20 (page 110) could be presented for 2019 in a side-by-side pie chart. If that were done, pie slices would be sequenced the same in both charts, even though the 2019 chart may not be arranged largest to smallest.
- Label the chart. Appropriate labeling includes a title, a source-of-data notation, and identification of the segments. The title must include the factor being analyzed and the time represented by the chart. Give each segment a meaningful name and identify its proportion of the whole. If space permits, place that identifying information on the face of the pie within the appropriate segments. If space is limited, place the identifying labels around the perimeter of the pie.
- Show segment values accurately. When segment values are stated in percentages, the segments must always total 100%. Although pie chart units are most often in percentages, units may also be in absolute numbers. If you state units in absolute numbers, be sure that each segment size still represents its accurate proportion of the pie.

Variations

Pie charts may employ various techniques to emphasize certain segments or to increase interest. One such technique is to separate one segment or all segments; another, is to explode one segment. Only the segment that is being referred to should be exploded. Another technique is to add a bar or brackets to explain one of the segments. These techniques are demonstrated in Figure 3.23.

Bar and pie charts permit comparison of discrete, independent items. When you wish to show relationships between or among continuous, dependent variables, a line chart is an appropriate tool.

Graphics to Avoid

Regardless of the graphics software you use, keep in mind that while you strive for balanced, consistent, simple, and unified visuals, the software vendors strive to sell software. And doing so sometimes means offering

114 PRODUCING WRITTEN AND ORAL BUSINESS REPORTS

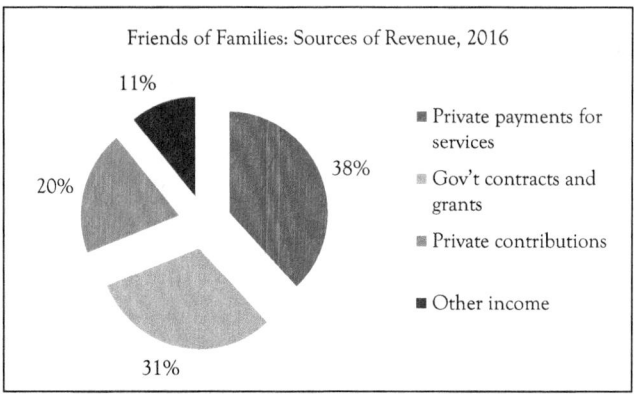

Exploded pie

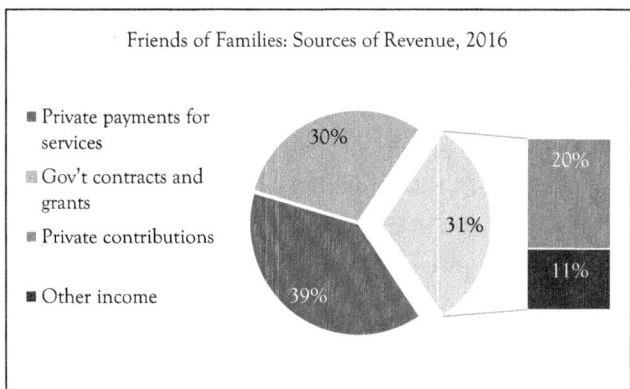

Pie with segment extracted and combined into stacked bar

Figure 3.23 **Enhanced pie charts**

gewgaws along with sound graphing tools. Few's chapter titled "Silly Graphs that are Best Forsaken" cites four graphics that are included in Microsoft Excel 2016 and shown and explained at the FusionCharts website: www.fusioncharts.com/ chart-primers.

Avoid the following four visuals if you can:

- *Donut chart.* The donut is a pie chart with a hole in the middle, and some people attempt to display parts of a whole with it. Pie charts with more than five slices are hard to read because of our native inability to perceive areas accurately. Donut charts compound this perception problem.[29]

- *Funnel chart.* This cone-shaped graph is used to show the progressive reduction of data—usually sales data—as it passes from one phase to another. Data in each phase is represented as a different portion of the whole (100%). In a sales funnel, all potential customers make up the 100%. The funnel narrows as some of those individuals become leads, and it continues to narrow until a small percentage of the prospects place an order, accept delivery, and pay for the product. But this graph forces a funnel shape that may not match the numerical values, or it turns out barely resembling a funnel.[30]
- *Spider web chart.* This graph—laid out in a circular, rather than linear, manner—is also called a radar chart. A spider web chart attempts to display data as a flat surface of three or more numerical variables shown on axes starting from the same point (center of the spider web). While a spider web chart looks more interesting than conventional graphics, it conveys less detail and takes notably longer to comprehend.[31]
- *Waterfall chart (misused).* A waterfall chart, a special vertical bar chart, is meant to show how a value (such as an account balance) increases and decreases over time to come to a final value. Whole columns represent the beginning and ending values, while floating columns denote in-between values. Columns are usually color-coded to differentiate positive and negative values. Too many times, though, people try using the waterfall to show part-to-whole relationships. A simple bar chart conveys that relationship more effectively.[32]

While bar, line, and circle charts show quantitative relationships, the next section presents charts showing nonquantitative information.

Relationship Charts

A relationship chart shows how several nonnumeric factors act together. Two relationship charts that you may find useful in reports are the flowchart and the factor relationship chart.

Flowchart

A flowchart shows how a series of activities, operations, events, or other factors fit together to accomplish a full cycle. Complex flowcharts are often used as engineering or systems analysis tools. Flowcharts also can be used effectively in business reports to condense, clarify, or simplify a procedure.

A flowchart consists of a title, shapes (circles, rectangles, squares, triangles, and so on) to represent various elements in the process, labels to identify each element, and lines or arrows to connect the shapes and show the direction of flow. Although flowcharts may use a rectangle or a square for each element, many flowchart designers use the standard flowchart symbols shown in Figure 3.24.

A flowchart describing the procedure for processing an electronic payment is shown in Figure 3.25.

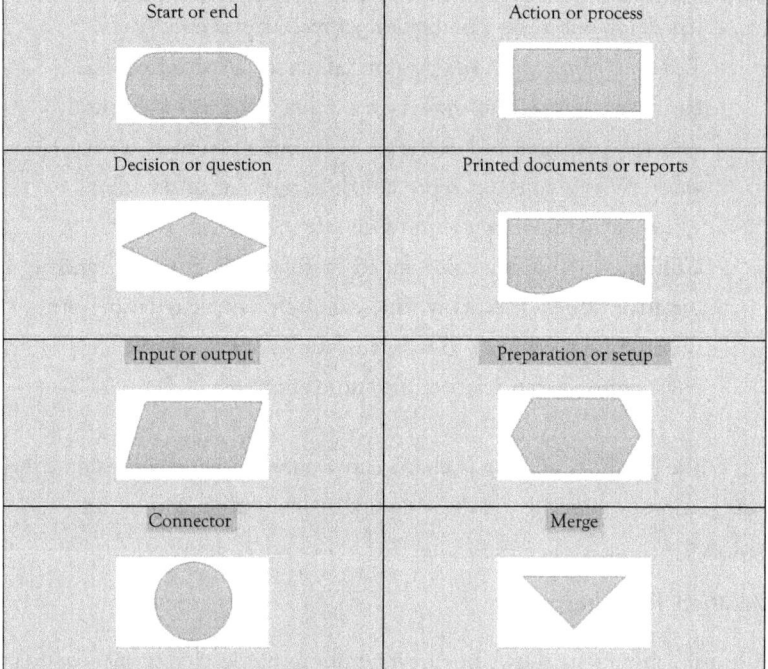

Figure 3.24 Flowchart symbols

Source: SmartDraw Software. "Flow Chart Symbols."

ILLUSTRATING REPORTS 117

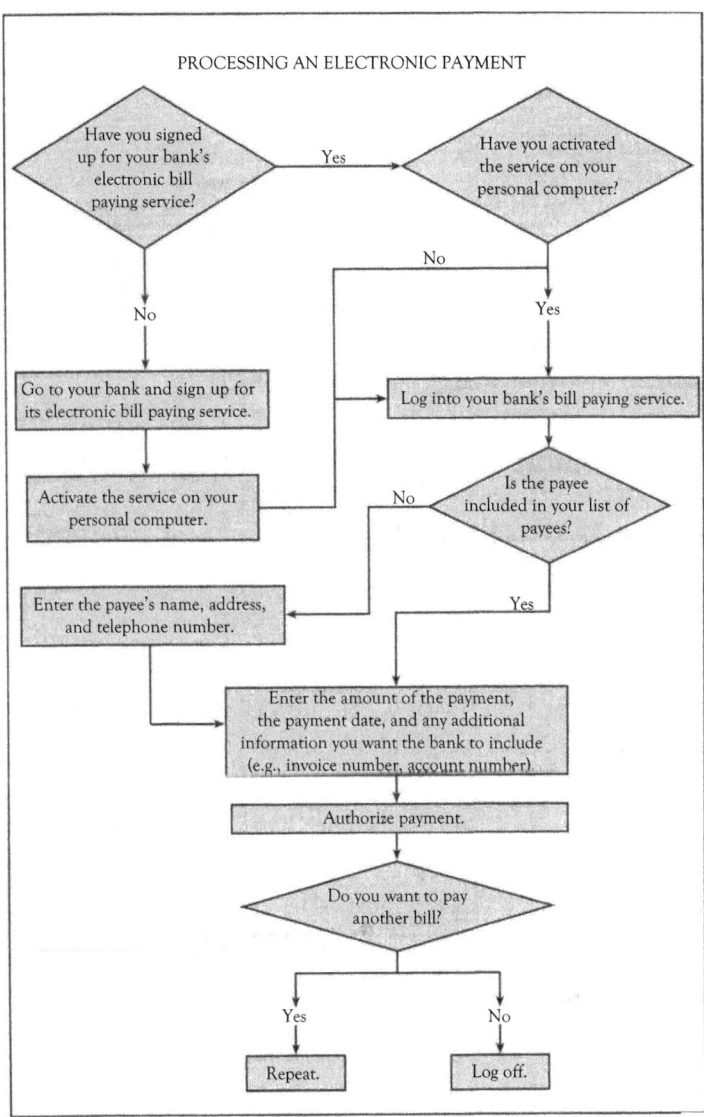

Figure 3.25 Flowchart

Source: Kuiper and Clippinger (2013), p. 132.

Factor Relationship Chart

A factor relationship chart is useful to describe nonlinear relationships. Such a chart shows how primary factors and secondary factors interact with one another. The chart illustrated in Figure 3.26 consists of a title,

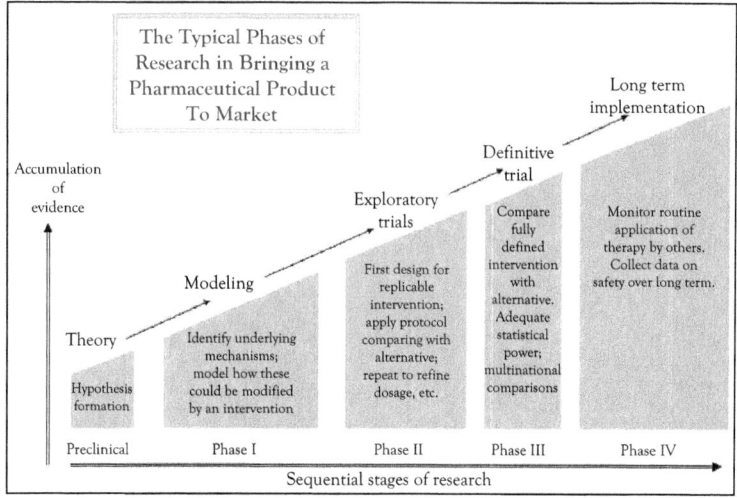

Figure 3.26 Factorial relationship chart
Source: Society, the Individual, and Medicine (2015).

shapes to represent various factors that interact with one another, labels to identify those factors, and multiple arrows to show how the factors interact.

Although bar charts, pie charts, line charts, and relationship charts summarize and simplify information, the amount of information that can be shown in such charts is limited. When numeric detail is desired, a table is the best visual.

Tables

Both formal and informal tables are used in reports. A table consists of columns and rows of quantitative data, along with labels to identify the data. A formal table also has a title and generally has more identifying information than does an informal table.

A table surpasses all charts in ability to present detailed information. Consequently, you should use a table when you want the reader to compare exact figures. As the number of dimensions to be compared increases, the need for identifying labels also increases. Therefore, formal tables are required for the presentation of complex data.

Formal Table

As with charts, a formal table is separated from the report narrative and is identified by title. And a formal table is numbered and shows a source notation, just like graphs (see Figure 3.27). In addition to columns and rows of numbers, other features of a formal table include column heads, stubs to identify rows, and stub heads. Features of a formal table are identified in Figure 3.27.

Formal tables may contain a spanner head, which unifies the column heads. For clarity, you may use horizontal and vertical lines to separate heads. In long tables, you can improve readability by leaving a blank row about every five rows. Another option is to alternate five plain rows and five lightly shaded rows.

Informal Table

An informal table is a brief tabulation run in with the text. This type of table has no title, and column and stub heads may also be omitted if the text clearly identifies the table's contents. An informal table in a report is shown in Figure 3.28.

Construction Guides and Variations

Follow these guides to construct effective tables:

- Use the tabs in your word processing application to create an informal table.

Table 1. U.S. School Enrollment by Ethnicity ← Title

Stub head		Spanner head →		Ethnicity					
Stub	Column heads →	White		Black		Hispanic		Other*	
Year	Total	No. (000)	Percent	No. (000)	Percent	No. (000)	Percent	No. (000)	Percent
→ 2012	49,771	25,386	51.0%	7,803	15.7%	12,104	24.3%	4,479	9.0%
→ 2014	50,132	25,007	49.9%	7,828	15.6%	12,740	25.4%	4,557	9.2%
→ 2016	50,385	24,566	48.8%	7,806	15.5%	13,306	26.4%	4,706	9.5%

Figure 3.27 Formal table

Source: Digest of Education Statistics, Table 203.50.

* Includes Asian/Pacific Islander, Native American, Alaska Native, and children identifying as two or more races.

Resources Needed

All research will be conducted by the staff of the Government Affairs Division as part of our normal duties. We will use approximately 100 employee hours to prepare the data collection instruments, enter and analyze the data, and prepare the final report. We anticipate spending approximately 24 employee hours conducting the town-hall meetings. Standard cost allocations for respective grades will be applied. In addition, the project will incur direct costs for printing, supplies, postage, and town-hall meetings. The total project budget is $5,750:

Staff labor	$3,750
Printing and supplies	750
Postage	750
Meeting expenses	500
Total	$5,750

Presentation of Results

I will present our findings, conclusions, and recommendations to the management committee in a formal written report prior to our September 20 management meeting and will be prepared to discuss the report at that meeting.

Request for Approval

Approval of this proposal by January 20 will permit the Government Affairs division to work this project into our schedule and adhere to the proposed schedule given in this proposal. Please call me at extension 497 with any questions.

Figure 3.28 Informal table in a report

- To create a formal table, use either a worksheet in your spreadsheet software or the table feature in your word processing application. Using a worksheet allows you to keep your table linked to the worksheet. Thus, when you change

data in the worksheet, the table is updated, too. A worksheet also allows you to insert trend lines (tiny line graphs) in the table.
- For a report in e-mail format, do not insert a formal or informal table on the e-mail screen. Send it as an attachment instead.
- Title each formal table as you would title a graph, including the five W's (who, what, when, where, and why) or at least the most relevant of the five.
- Supply column headings with the same care used for axis titles and data labels.
- Avoid rounding numbers too much. Generally, run numbers from one to four decimal places, depending on the level of precision needed.
- In general, left-align words and right-align numbers. Except for the far-left column, words may be centered if you prefer. Always left-align the far-left column and align decimal numbers at the point.
- Size your table to fit the contents, adjusting column width and row height as needed. Allow text to wrap in columns and make all number columns about the same width.
- Make a formal table more attractive and open by omitting most shading and most horizontal borders. Then, if you need to emphasize selected data, highlight those cells, columns, or rows with borders or light shading, as shown in Figure 3.29.

Although charts and tables are the most common visuals in reports, other graphics are also used to add interest.

Statistical Maps

A statistical map—also called a thematic map—presents numerical data (a theme) superimposed on a map of the geographical or spatial units to which the data are related. A few examples of business themes include

Table 1. U.S. School Enrollment by Ethnicity

Year	Total	Ethnicity							
		White		Black		Hispanic		Other*	
		No. (000)	Percent	No. (000)	Percent	No. (000)	Percent	No. (000)	Percent
2012	49,771	25,386	51.0%	7,803	15.7%	12,104	24.3%	4,479	9.0%
2014	50,132	25,007	49.9%	7,828	15.6%	12,740	25.4%	4,557	9.2%
2016	50,385	24,566	48.8%	7,806	15.5%	13,306	26.4%	4,706	9.5%

Figure 3.29 Formal table with visual enhancements

Source: Digest of Education Statistics, Table 203.50.

* Includes Asian/Pacific Islander, Native American, Alaska Native, and children identifying as two or more races.

building locations, demographics (such as age, birthrate, employment base, gender, households, housing units, language spoken, and literacy rates), landmarks, transportation (airports, highways, railroads, rivers, and so on), municipalities, and population centers. Although the same data could be presented in a table or a bar chart, the map image helps readers associate the data more directly with specific spaces or geographic areas and to identify geographical trends. One statistical map technique is illustrated in Figure 3.30.

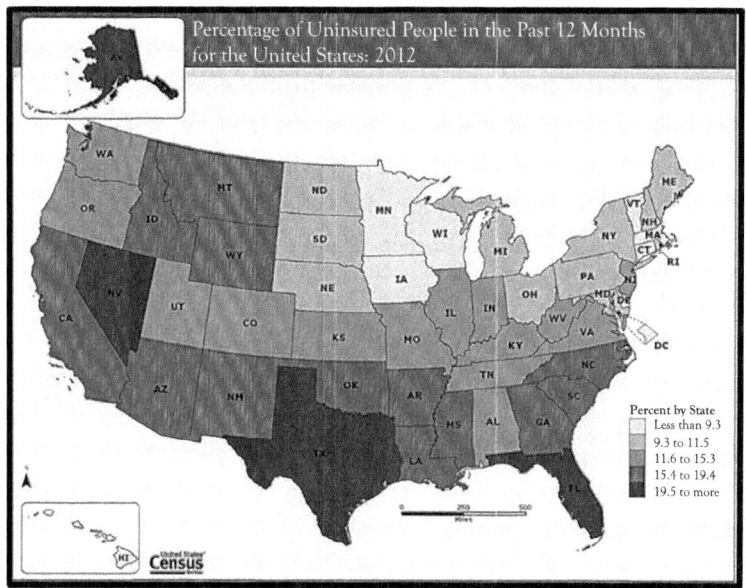

Figure 3.30 Statistical map

Source: 2012 American Community Survey, U.S. Census Bureau.

Uses

Maps are outstanding for showing geographic patterns for analyzing markets, conducting direct marketing, planning and routing calls on customers, and planning and planting a new business. Maps, however, cannot provide precise values with which users can do their own calculations. Thus, maps are for display rather than as a source of reference material.[33]

The simplest statistical map has data values posted on a static (as opposed to animated or interactive) map at the related location.

To create an interactive map, you might obtain a diagram from one of the following map sources and overlay it with your numerical data:

- Bing static map (msdn.microsoft.com/en-us/library/ff701724.aspx)
- CartoDB static map (carto.com)
- Google static map (developers.google.com/maps/documentation/static-maps)
- HERE static map (developer.here.com/develop/rest-apis)
- Mapbox static map (www.mapbox.com/help/create-a-static-map)
- MapQuest static map (developer.mapquest.com/products/maps)
- Yandex static map (staticmapmaker.com/yandex)

The Static Map Maker site (staticmapmaker.com) provides one location for accessing all seven mapmakers and tailoring them to your needs.

A choropleth, or color-shaded, map, the most common type, is particularly suitable for showing standardized data, such as rates, densities, or percentages. As shown in Figure 3.30, a different color or shade is used for each data category. Experts recommend at least three and a maximum of seven categories. Thus readers can identify which areas have high, low, or medium values. Use a choropleth map when data are standardized, discrete, and rather evenly distributed within map areas.[34]

A proportional, or graduated, symbol map uses symbols (usually circles) that are scaled in size to the values they represent, so that the largest symbol will fall in the area with the highest value. Use a graduated symbol map when there is a lot of variation and range in the data. A graduated symbol map must not be used for standardized data such as rates or percentages. It is a good choice for count data.[35]

On a dot map, individual events or groups of events are marked with a dot, allowing users to see geographic patterns in the dot clusters. One map can show multiple data sets by using dots of different shapes or colors. A dot map is best used for count data. Creating and designing this kind of map is more complicated than a proportional symbol map, which is also used for count data.

To create a choropleth, graduated symbol, or dot map, you will need a geographical information system (GIS); that is, business mapping software, such as Maptitude (www.Caliper.com).

Other online mapmakers for business users include:

- ArcGIS (www.esri.com)
- Map Business Online (www.mapbusinessonline.com)
- Mapline, an easy-to-use program that can upload your spreadsheet data from Microsoft Excel for inclusion in the map (mapline.com)
- PostGIS (postgis.refractions.net)
- Qgis, an open-source program (www.qgis.org)

Construction Guides

> After becoming familiar with the GIS of your choice, use this list of best practices for mapping.[36]
>
> - Provide a clear, descriptive title, indicating the geographic areas used. Consider the five W's as you would for any other graphic.
> - Indicate the time period(s) of the data. For example: Date from years 2001 to 2016. Also indicate currency of the geographic boundaries.
> - Include a key to explain what the colors, shades, or symbol sizes mean.
> - Include a source note, indicating where you obtained the data applied to the map or the source of the map-data

combination when you use a ready-made map. *Note*: Data and maps provided by the U.S. Census Bureau and many other U.S. government agencies are not copyrighted. For any other map, determine if it is copyrighted. If so, request permission from the copyright holder to use the map in your report.
- Adjust map size to ensure clarity of all parts and data. Generally, you will need a larger map when showing small areas, such as counties or districts, than when showing large areas, such as regions of a country or the world.
- Provide labels for the main map areas, but avoid cluttering the map or obscuring the statistics. Consider providing a separate reference map that contains only the area names and boundaries.
- Choose up to six classes for your data and decide the best way to divide them. The GIS you use will offer various ways to classify the data and ask you to choose one:
    - *Equal ranges.* Example: 0–14, 15–29, 30–44, and so on.
    - *Natural breaks in the data.* If data values tend to cluster into distinct groups, you may wish to adjust the ranges so that all areas falling into a particular group are the same color on the map.
    - *Percentiles.* Example (quintiles): 1%–20%, 21%–40%, 41%–60%, and so forth.
    - *Polarized ranges.* If data cluster toward one (or both) ends of the range of values, use this option. Example: If your theme is wealth, you might decide that the least prosperous 75% of areas are one shade, but the wealthiest areas are highlighted by having different shades for the top 25%, 10%, and 5%.
- Do not assume that the default values suggested by your GIS (for choropleth map ranges, for example) are necessarily the best. Always examine the data and its context to see if it could be presented a better way; then adjust the GIS settings.

- Choose colors wisely. GISs allow you to choose from a wide array of colors.
  - Instead of using unrelated colors for each data category in a choropleth map, use a gradation of one color along a range (Figure 3.30, page 122).
  - In general, use light shades (except white) for low values and dark hues for high values. Reserve white to indicate missing or unavailable data.
  - Keep in mind earlier comments about the meanings of colors. Be aware that those meanings are not the same across cultures.

To streamline color selection, use ColorBrewer (colorbrewer2.org). After indicating the nature and context of your data and the type of background you want to use, choose one of the color schemes provided. When you find a scheme you like, note the six-digit hex number for each color. (Hex is short for hexadecimal, a base-16 numbering system.) Later, in your GIS, you can enter those hex numbers and match the ColorBrewer scheme you chose. Incidentally, ColorBrewer allows you to limit color scheme options to ones that are colorblind safe, printer friendly, photocopy safe, or all three.

Variations

Many variations of statistical maps can be designed, including separating and enlarging or exploding part of a static map. In web page format, a map may be animated, interactive, or both, using the mapping applications in the previous list (page 123).

Computer or video animation shows change in a map area over time, either much faster (usually) or slower than real time. For example, you can animate changes to watch growth or decline of a business across a geographic region. Then if the map is also interactive, readers can easily focus on their area to see how things have changed.

Examples of medium and high interactivity levels may be seen at Maptitude (www.Caliper.com/ovuwebpg.htm).

The Mass Stats (Massachusetts statistics) map allows users to select from 10 themes, over a hundred maps, and roughly 370 cities and towns, all by clicking. The SRPEDD (Southeast Regional Planning and Economic Development District) Signalized Intersections map involves a high level of interaction: Users can change the map's scale; navigate the map by dragging to re-center it, zooming in, zooming out, and panning; click the map to display information about an intersection; and query the map to determine the jurisdiction, signal type, year of signal permit, level of service, volume, delay, and accident data; and view photographs of an intersection.

Maps, a subdivision of data visualization, enable readers to explore your data more deeply than graphs allow. And as scaled-down versions of their real world, maps appeal to readers on a personal level.

Photographs

Because of their universal appeal, photographs effectively capture reader attention, a fact that prompts many corporations to use photos extensively in annual reports. You may also find opportunities to use photographs effectively in other business reports, especially those prepared in report deck or web page format.

Photographs tend to add a sense of reality to a report. Viewers know that pictures can be posed and that good photographers stage a picture; nonetheless, many readers perceive photos as truth. Because of that fact, an ethical obligation exists to ensure that photographs represent accurately the conditions they are intended to portray. For example, a photo of employees at work should accurately portray the environment in which the majority of your employees work. Picturing the most favorable working conditions that perhaps only a few enjoy would present a distorted view of reality.

With digital cameras, high-quality photos are easy to take and integrate within reports. As an alternative to doing your own photography, consider the wide range of stock photos available online. You may be familiar with Google Images (images.google.com) and Yahoo (images.search.yahoo.com) as sources of free photos.

Dozens of websites offer millions of images, including these sites.[37]

- FFCU (Free for Commercial Use) (www.freeforcommercial-use.net)
- Gratisography (www.gratisography.com)
- IM Free (www.imcreator.com/free)
- Kaboompics (kaboompics.com)
- Pexels (www.pexels.com)
- Pixabay (pixabay.com)
- SkitterPhoto (skitterphoto.com)
- Unsplash (unsplash.com)

Before downloading a photo and attempting to use it, check the license.[38] If you want only free and royalty-free photos, look for the CC0 or CCZ label, which stands for Creative Commons Zero license. A CCZ photo can be downloaded and used any way you want, for commercial or noncommercial purposes, without charge and without your requesting permission. Some free photos are labeled Creative Commons with attribution. This license is like CC0—but with the condition that you include a photo credit. The credit usually involves the photographer's name and a link, but check for and use the exact wording. *Note*: Whenever in doubt about terms of use for any image, contact the copyright holder directly or try to contact the site where you found the image. Do this to prevent copyright infringement (use of someone else's copyrighted work without permission), a legal matter handled by the courts. Upon obtaining permission to use a copyrighted image, include a photo credit. Credits may be placed under each photo or in an appended list.

Whether a photograph comes from your smartphone, digital camera, or a stock photo website, you may need or want to edit, or modify, it. Most photo editing is done using photo editing software, such as Photoshop, accessible free at Adobe Creative Cloud (www.adobe.com/creativecloud.html). Extended versions of Photoshop and other Adobe apps are available with a paid subscription. Photo editing is done to remove blemishes, using airbrushing or retouching, and to fix errors, such as red-eye effect, hot-spot (excessive light in a small area), and inadequate contrast.

The following list includes a small sampling of available online photo editors:[39]

- Gimp (www.gimp.org)
- Paint.Net (www.techradar.downloads-hub.com/downloads/paint-net)
- Pixlr (pixlr.com)
- PhotoScape (www.photoscape.org/ps/main/index.php) and PhotoScape X for Mac (x.photoscape.org/mac)
- Serif PhotoPlus X8 (www.serif.com/photoplus)
- SumoPaint (www.sumopaint.com/home)

The old saying "A picture is worth a thousand words" captures the essence of data visualization. And all of the highlighted business report visuals—not just photographs—turn data into powerful pictures. *Note*: The following print report includes most of the graphics discussed in this chapter: 2015 Annual Starbase Report (www.dodstarbase.org). Click About Us; then select Annual Reports.

Summary

Business leaders and other professionals constantly look for ways to manage and present voluminous data. A major way of dealing with data glut is to encode data and form images. Data visualization is the umbrella term for efforts to convert data into pictures. Data viz includes infographics, collection and analysis of big data, and effective use of traditional visuals (charts, graphs, maps, photos, and tables).

> When creating a business report, plan its visuals carefully to:
>
> ☐ Emphasize major points and separate them from minor points;
> ☐ Clarify information that words alone can hardly express;
> ☐ Reinforce the report narrative, aiding reader retention and recall of the information;
> ☐ Summarize essential information while omitting nonessential details;
> ☐ Add interest and ease the tedium of large text blocks;
> ☐ Improve believability by lending a sense of exactness; and
> ☐ Increase the report's coherence and show relationship among its parts.

Become familiar with the criteria for effectiveness in report visuals, and use the following checklist to assure effectiveness.

> In each report examine your visuals and note if you have maintained these four basic standards:
>
> - ☐ Simplicity.
>   - o Make each visual focus on just one point; include essential information only.
>   - o Omit chartjunk, such as 3-D display, a dark grid that obscures data, and moiré vibration that makes a printed graphic move on the page.
> - ☐ Contrast.
>   - o Separate each graphic from the text by space and lines or borders.
>   - o Assure that the colors within a visual can be distinguished at a glance.
> - ☐ Unity.
>   - o Assure that each visual looks like its parts naturally belong together.
>   - o Use arrows, commonalities, grouping, and proximity to achieve unity.
> - ☐ Balance. All parts of each visual appear to be equally important, regardless of the value each represents.

Check your techniques for identifying and placing graphics within your text.

> Go through your near-final draft, evaluating your visuals using this checklist.
>
> - ☐ Graphics are integrated with the text (unless you were advised to place them in a report appendix).
> - ☐ Each visual has a label, such as Figure; a number; and a concise, descriptive title.

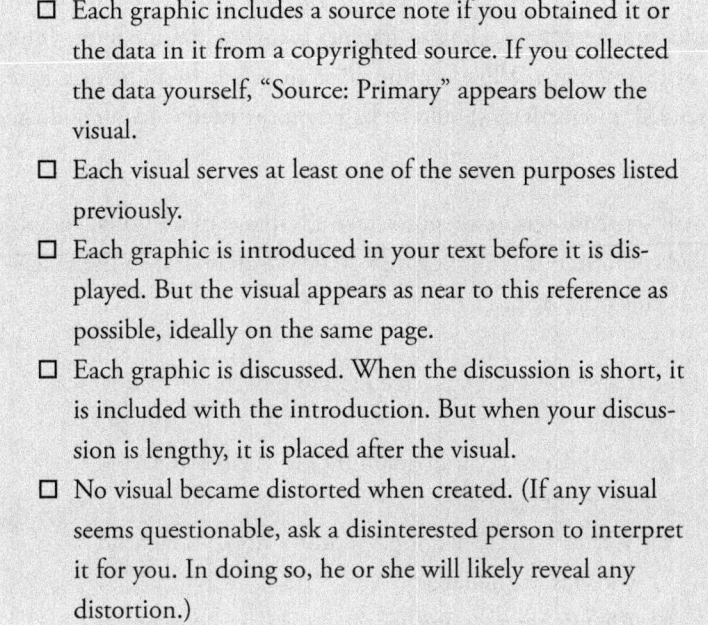

- ☐ Each graphic includes a source note if you obtained it or the data in it from a copyrighted source. If you collected the data yourself, "Source: Primary" appears below the visual.
- ☐ Each visual serves at least one of the seven purposes listed previously.
- ☐ Each graphic is introduced in your text before it is displayed. But the visual appears as near to this reference as possible, ideally on the same page.
- ☐ Each graphic is discussed. When the discussion is short, it is included with the introduction. But when your discussion is lengthy, it is placed after the visual.
- ☐ No visual became distorted when created. (If any visual seems questionable, ask a disinterested person to interpret it for you. In doing so, he or she will likely reveal any distortion.)

Knowing the attributes of different visuals will help you choose graphics wisely in keeping with your purpose. The human brain is better at reading some graphics than others. People are adept at discerning positions on a horizontal or vertical scale or axis (bar and line graphs) and judging length (column and bar charts) and angle or slope (line graphs). However, we are notably less able to read areas (area charts or stacked line graphs and pie charts) and volumes. People also are particularly weak at interpreting visuals strictly on the basis of color.

However, color does affect a visual's success. Of particular importance is the use of semantically resonant colors. That is, every item or idea should be represented graphically by the color that most people associate with it. These familiar associations help readers interpret visuals faster and retain the information longer.

Besides the charting tools in Microsoft Excel, many graphing applications are available to you online, including Chartgo, Highcharts, and SmartDraw. Other charting applications include Adobe Illustrator, Corel Draw, Inkscape (a free, open source program), and Tableau.

The graphics in web page reports may be animated to incite curiosity and add interest. Many web page graphics involve a low, medium, or high level of interactivity. While a minimalist approach to animation is recommended, interactivity should be based on the needs of your audience.

As a writer of business reports, take advantage of traditional graphics and commit to maintaining high standards in their use. The following checklist can help:

☐ Bar and column graphs are used to plot discrete numerical values.
  o Each bar or column graph is only as large as necessary to be legible.
  o When resizing, the original proportion of height to width is maintained.
  o All bars are the same width, and spaces between are at least half as wide as the bars.
  o No vertical bar exceeds seven inches; no horizontal bar exceeds five inches.
  o The bars in each graph are in ascending or descending order, unless logic dictates otherwise.
  o The units in each chart are labeled on both axes, unless the chart title eliminates this need.
  o The variable (unit of measure) appears on the horizontal (x) axis in bar charts; it appears on the vertical (y) axis in column charts.
  o A key or legend explains what factor each high-contrast color represents. Distinctive shades of gray along with black and white replace colors when using a monochrome printer or a photocopier.
  o Variations are used appropriately: multiple bar charts (two or more variables), segmented bar charts (different colors in a bar show parts of the whole), and bilateral bar charts (negative values), as well as pictographs (icons make up the bars).

- ☐ Line graphs are used to compare continuous data, such as change in a variable over time.
  - o The x axis shows the method of classification, while the y axis shows the classification ranges.
  - o The y axis begins at "0."
  - o The height of y is about three-fourths the length of x, and distances between the markers on x and y are approximately the same.
  - o Scale units are identified on both x and y, and each graph has a complete title and a source note.
  - o In multiple-line charts, each line is a clearly different color, and a legend decodes those colors.
  - o Stacked line graphs, or area charts, are used to show generally how factors compared in making up the whole. To show an exact comparison, two area charts are used: one showing the individual factors and another showing the total.
- ☐ Two-dimensional pie charts are used to compare approximate contributions of parts to a whole. For a precise comparison of parts to whole, a bar graph or a table is used.
  - o Each pie is divided into fewer than nine slices. To reduce the number of slices, two or more of the smallest ones are extracted and combined in a stacked bar chart.
  - o Colors are harmonious and easy to distinguish.
  - o A data label is shown for each slice, either inside the circle or around its circumference. When totaled the labels equal 100%.
  - o In each circle, the largest segment begins at the top; and other segments are placed in descending order.
  - o To emphasize one factor, that slice is exploded.
- ☐ Flow charts are used to show the steps in a cycle, and a standard symbol is used along with arrows to convey each step.
- ☐ To simplify and summarize nonnumeric, nonlinear data, a factor relationship chart, including clear labels and title, is used.

- A table was used to provide detailed information and exact numbers. Each formal table is numbered and titled and includes a source note.
- Each formal table includes clear column headings and stubs. For added clarity, it may include stub heads and spanner head(s).
- In informal tables, words are left-aligned; numbers are right-aligned or decimal numbers are aligned at the point.
- Columns and rows in each table are sized and enhanced in ways that make it understandable at a glance.

☐ A statistical map is used when your goal is for readers to associate numerical data with specific locations. Map sources include Bing, Google, or Mapbox or created at GIS websites such as ArcGIS, Mapline, and PostGIS.
- The map type selected is most appropriate for conveying your data: a choropleth, graduated-symbol, or dot map.
- Each choropleth map uses a gradation of one semantically resonant color along a range, with light shades representing low values and dark hues denoting high values.
- Each map involves a suitable number of data classes, divided into equal ranges, polarized ranges, percentiles, or at natural breaks in the data.
- Only the main map areas are labeled, so the map is uncluttered.
- Each map is sized to ensure clarity of every part and all data.
- Each map has a descriptive title indicating the geographic area depicted and time period of the data.
- Each ready-made map includes a source note, and each map you created includes the data source.

☐ Photographs are used for realism, and each photo accurately (ethically) represents its subject.

- Each image is of premium quality, whether from your camera, from Google Images or Yahoo Images, or from another stock-photo source, such as FFCU, IM Free, Pexels, and Unsplash.
- Photos that originally contained blemishes, hot spots, low contrast, red-eye, and so on have been corrected, using Photoshop or an online photo editor, such as Gimp, Pixlr, PhotoScape, or SumoPaint.
- Only stock photos available under a CC0 or CCZ license were used without a photo credit. Otherwise, a photo credit shows who owns the copyright and other information that person or company requires.

CHAPTER 4

Reporting Business Research

Business research reports are often classified as information or analytical reports. An information report provides comprehensive data related to a business problem along with interpretation of the data, but it offers no conclusions or recommendations. An analytical report involves conclusions and may also present recommendations. This chapter includes a comprehensive analytical report prepared in manuscript format.

Report Body

The report body must be a complete document that presents all details of the study, from its introduction to its summary (information report) or to its conclusions and recommendations (analytical report). Since the report body should be a coherent unit, it begins with the report title, placed before the first page.

Your job as the writer is to write the report body so clearly and completely that your reader will understand its contents even if that person merely skimmed previous parts. A research report may be written in inductive structure (begins with detailed data and leads to conclusions) or deductive structure (begins with conclusions and traces backward to the data that justify those conclusions).

The inductive structure is appropriate when the reader requires background details before being able to understand or accept the impact of the report. When the report is written in inductive structure, the report title is followed by a coherent introduction; a complete presentation, discussion, and summary of findings; and—for an analytical report—conclusions and recommendations. For an information report, the summary marks the ending.

Introducing the Research and the Report

The introduction provides all information necessary to understand the remainder of the report and establishes the context for interpreting the findings and conclusions.

Typically, the introductory section of a report written in inductive structure includes the background to the problem, a statement of the research problem and purpose, the scope of analysis, and the research procedures. Delimitations (boundaries you set for the study), limitations (conditions you cannot control, which restrict your conclusions or influence research results), and definitions of terms may also be included. The inductive structure introduction in Figure 4.1 shows all of these items.

CHARLESTON AND THE CRUISE INDUSTRY

For more than 25 years, Charleston's Union Pier has served as a home port and port of call for Carnival Cruises and a port of call for other cruise lines. The cruise industry currently contributes approximately $37 million to the region's economy, but the vehicular and pedestrian traffic associated with the departures and arrivals of cruise ships has been the subject of extensive debate among downtown residents, merchants, and professionals.

The South Carolina Ports Authority has begun plans to relocate the cruise terminal to a point north of its present location and relocate existing cargo operations. These changes will open 35 acres of harbor front that can be redeveloped to provide greater public access to the water's edge. Before implementing that plan, the Ports Authority officers wanted to know how much Charlestonians know about the economic impact of the cruise industry and what their attitudes are toward that industry and the proposed revitalization of the waterfront.

Determining Charlestonians' Perceptions of the Cruise Industry

A survey of downtown residents and merchants was conducted during the summer of 2016.

The Problem

The research problem was to assess Charlestonians' perceptions of the economic and social impact of cruise dockings in the Port of Charleston and the possible relocation of the cruise terminal.

The Purpose

The purpose of the study was to assess the business and social climate in which the South Carolina Ports Authority will operate if it implements plans to relocate the cruise terminal. Knowledge of that climate will help the Authority develop operational and communication strategies relative to the relocation.

Scope of Analysis

Three factors were studied:

1. What business impacts do Charleston's downtown residents and merchants perceive to be related to the arrival and departure of cruise ships?
2. What personal and community impacts do Charleston's downtown residents and merchants perceive to be related to the arrival and departure of cruise ships?
3. What knowledge of and attitudes toward relocation of the cruise terminal are evidenced by Charleston's downtown residents and merchants?

In addition, information related to waterfront development was studied to understand more fully the potential impact of community attitudes when a major urban revitalization project is undertaken. That information was helpful while drawing conclusions about Charlestonians' attitudes and making recommendations to the South Carolina Ports Authority.

Delimitations

Because the area between the Charleston Harbor and King Street receives the greatest impact of the presence of cruise ships in the harbor, the analysis was limited to an area bounded by East Bay St. on the east, Broad St. on the south, King St. on the west, and Calhoun St. on the north. This area includes the downtown retail, hospitality, and professional facilities as well as the Ansonborough residential area.

Limitations

Confining the study to the historic Charleston area may have omitted some citizens and merchants who have strong positive or negative feelings about the cruise industry. However, since the downtown community absorbs the major direct impact of visiting cruise ships, the attitudes of that community can best direct decisions related to relocating the cruise terminal.

Since the data were collected during the summer cruise season, the participants' responses may differ slightly from responses they might have made during an earlier or later cruise season. Nonetheless, the responses obtained during a peak tourist season in Charleston were deemed to reflect the strongest feelings and most recent experiences of the participants.

Definitions

For purposes of this study, the term *residents* identifies respondents who live within the targeted Ansonborough section of downtown Charleston; the term *merchants* identifies respondents from the downtown business and professional community.

How the Study was Conducted

The Government Relations division of the Ports Authority used both secondary and primary data to meet the objective of this study.

Secondary Data

Secondary sources concerning waterfront development were studied. The information was useful in evaluating the South Carolina Ports Authority's Concept Plan for the Union Pier Waterfront and the citizens' views of that plan. A list of sources accessed appears in References (page 11 of this report).

Primary Data

Primary data were obtained through a survey of downtown residents and merchants. All residents within the defined area were invited to participate in the study. A systematic random sample of 100 downtown businesses and professional offices was drawn from the Charleston Merchants Association Directory. A copy of the questionnaire and transmittal messages used for residents and merchants appears in Appendix A.

A summary profile of respondents appears in Appendix B. The median age range for both groups was 26-35. Thirty-eight percent of residents were engaged in professions or occupations that were most likely to put them into direct contact with cruise passengers: food services, hospitality services, and retail marketing. Sixty percent of merchants were engaged in those occupations. When the two groups were combined, those occupations represented nearly 50% of respondents. Thus, the responses can be interpreted as heavily weighted by young adults who may have had direct contact with cruise passengers.

Downtown Residents

On May 15 and August 1, 2017, letters were sent to all addresses in the Ansonborough district of Charleston. One half of the district was covered in each mailing. Recipients of the letters were invited to come to a town-hall type of meeting to discuss the impact of cruise dockings on the Charleston business and residential communities. The first meetings were held on June 15 and 16, the days following the departure of a home-port ship. The second series of meetings was held on August 14 and 15, the days after the arrival of a port-of-call ship. After an open discussion of the economic and social impacts of cruise dockings, the residents in attendance were asked to complete a questionnaire related to the presence of the cruise industry in Charleston and the plans to relocate the cruise terminal. Questionnaires were collected as soon as they were completed.

The meetings produced 127 usable questionnaires, 68 from females and 59 from males. The most frequent selections for profession/occupation were retired (25%), retail marketing (17%), food services (15%), and full-time homemaker (14%).

Downtown Merchants

Email messages and an electronic questionnaire were sent to the sample of downtown businesses and professional offices on May 15 inviting them to complete the questionnaire on either June 1-2 or August 13-14. Cruise ships were docked at the Union Pier on June 1(a home-port ship) and on August 13 (a port-of-call ship). Merchants who completed the questionnaire in June were blocked from completing another in August. On August 1 a reminder message was emailed to any merchants who had not completed a questionnaire during the first round.

Ninety-two usable questionnaires were received, 26 from females and 66 from males. The most frequent selections for profession/occupation were food services (33 %), hospitality services (16%), and retail marketing (11%).

Data Analysis

Questionnaire responses were entered into a spreadsheet and summary statistics were computed. It was immediately noticed that residents and merchants were united in their desire to have the cruise terminal moved from its current location. Since over 90% of each group strongly favored the relocation, there appeared to be no value in cross-tabulating the data on that factor. Consequently, responses from the entire group of resident respondents were compared with responses from the entire group of merchants.

What the Study Revealed

The analysis produced guides for waterfront development and assessments of Charlestonians' knowledge and attitudes about the current economic impact of the cruise industry.

*Figure 4.1 Research report introduction**

*Figures discussing research related to the cruise port in Charleston, South Carolina, are based on actual events, circa 2011. However, all names, data, and dates used in the figures are fictional.

142 PRODUCING WRITTEN AND ORAL BUSINESS REPORTS

The report headings need not include the words introduction or problem. Indeed, descriptive headings, such as those used in Figure 4.1, may increase reader interest.

If you prepared a comprehensive research proposal, you can draw much of the information for the introduction from that document. Do not, however, merely copy the proposal. Besides omitting parts of the proposal that are irrelevant, write in a style appropriate for a final report. Also change the perspective—and verb tense—from future to past. Review the proposal shown in Figure 4.2; then note how its major points are included in the report introduction (Figure 4.1).

A Proposal:

The Feasibility of Relocating the Cruise Port At Union Pier, Charleston, South Carolina

A study conducted by the South Carolina Ports Authority in Summer 2016 revealed mixed attitudes about the economic and social benefits of cruise dockings in the Port of Charleston. A sizable majority of merchants approved of the dockings and reported that their businesses had benefited from the cruise traffic. In contrast, a majority of downtown residents expressed considerable dissatisfaction with the increased pedestrian and motor traffic in the area as well as the abrasive announcements made from the ships and pier directed to cruise passengers during embarkation and debarkation.

The Ports Authority is tentatively considering a relocation of the cruise port to an area slightly north of its current Union Pier location. Tentative plans call for redirecting motor traffic along the waterfront and increasing public space to provide greater waterfront access to Charlestonians and tourists. The Authority hopes that relocating the cruise port may reduce some of the dissatisfaction expressed by downtown residents and ultimately make a large portion of the waterfront a major community asset. In general, downtown merchants were knowledgeable about the potential economic and social impact of relocating the cruise port; however, residents had incorrect or inadequate information about that impact.

Statement of the Problem

The focus of this study will be to determine the feasibility of relocating the cruise port to an area slightly north of its current Union Pier location, including related changes in traffic flows and waterfront usage.

Three factors will be analyzed:

1. Optimal location for a new cruise terminal
2. Infrastructure and traffic needs
3. Public use of Charleston's historic waterfront

Purpose of the Study

The purpose of the study is to generate a concept plan for the Union Pier waterfront that will enable the Ports Authority to serve the contemporary needs of the cruise industry while retaining the traditional ambiance of historic Charleston.

Methodology

Both primary and secondary data will be used in the study. Secondary data will be obtained by a review of current security standards related to cruise embarkations and debarkations, records of current use of port facilities both as a cruise terminal and a shipping terminal, Charleston County tax assessor's data, and current zoning regulations.

Primary data will be obtained by way of a photographic survey of the entire area under study, followed by engineering and economic studies of pedestrian and vehicular traffic, infrastructure needed to service the port area satisfactorily, and alternative uses for the Port of Charleston waterfront.

To conduct this study, NKG Design will assign a team of licensed engineers and economic analysts who will employ standard engineering and economic analysis techniques.

> **Time Required**
>
> This study will be completed within six months of contract signing. An interim report will be provided at the end of three months.
>
> **Final Report**
>
> A comprehensive written and fully illustrated concept plan will be presented to the Ports Authority. This plan will be accompanied by all engineering and financial studies conducted to formulate the plan.
>
> **Qualifications to Conduct Study**
>
> NKG Design has a track record of compiling successful concept plans for major urban waterfront renewal projects in North America and Europe. Examples of those projects are available at our website: www.nkgdesign.com.
>
> **Cost**
>
> NKG Design will conduct this study for a turnkey figure of $200,000, with a penalty of $2,000 per day for failure to deliver the final product within six months of contract signing.

Figure 4.2 Research proposal

Clearly some sections of the proposal (such as the time schedule and budget) would be meaningless in the final report.

Interpreting Research Data

You conduct research by collecting data related to the identified problem you intend to solve. That data may come from various sources—both secondary (information that others have accumulated and made available through books, magazines, journals, and other publications) and primary (data acquired at their sources through observation, experimentation, interviews, questionnaire surveys, and searches through company records). As you collect relevant information, you accumulate a mass of facts—your raw data. But decision makers are rarely interested in raw data. Therefore, your duty as a researcher and report writer is to interpret those data, demonstrating their relationship to the project's problem and purpose and the context in which decisions must be made.

The entire process of converting raw data into meaningful information for decision makers is called data analysis. Analysis is a process of data reduction: The mass of raw data is reduced to classes or sets of information; those sets are reduced to major findings; and ultimately the findings are interpreted to yield conclusions and recommendations.

Assume, for example, that you are asked to conduct research to identify potential sites for a new FreshMart supermarket. Your data collection activities will yield many facts, which might include demographic data, responses to a consumer survey, and data about building sites currently on the market.

Your data analysis will require classification of the data into meaningful groups that will permit you to compare the desirability of different sites. One category could be the demographics of defined sections of the city. The many facts about each area—population growth, average household income, effective buying power, new home construction, and so on—can be reduced to major findings. Those findings would include the area that has shown the fastest growth in population, has the highest average household income, has the greatest effective buying power, and has had the most new-home construction during a defined period of time. Those findings may be reduced further into a summary statement identifying one section of the city that demonstrates the greatest economic vitality. Similar data reduction would be required for the facts gathered in your consumer survey and the information about available building sites.

Conceivably, a data set containing hundreds of facts may finally be reduced to one recommendation. Assume that your findings indicate that a revitalized section of the central city shows the greatest economic vitality, consumers in that area expressed the greatest desire for a conveniently located supermarket, and a building site is available in an appropriate location and at an affordable price. Your single recommendation would likely be that the company purchase the site for a new supermarket.

Data analysis is a multistage process. In each stage you move further from the objectivity of the raw data and interject the subjectivity that inevitably accompanies data interpretation. When reporting the results of your analysis, you should carefully differentiate the levels of analysis: findings, conclusions, and recommendations.

Findings

Findings are what your collected data reveal. As you analyze your raw data by statistical or nonstatistical methods, you find out certain things. Findings emerge as a result of data interpretation. An example of data analysis follows.

Assume that you have asked a sample of FreshMart customers to rate the importance of five new services that you propose to offer. The rating scale used was the following:

1 = Very unimportant
2 = Unimportant
3 = Neutral
4 = Important
5 = Very important

Your data analysis then would involve the following steps.

1. Classify the data by tallying the survey participants' ratings for each service. That process would enable you to report a breakdown of the number or the percentage of participants rating a specific service in a particular way. You could report, for example, that 58% of the respondents considered Thursday afternoon wine-tasting parties to be unimportant. You could also report that respondents tended to value lower overall prices more highly than any other proposed service. That level of analysis, however, would not capture the subtleties of the evaluations. To get a better understanding of customers' attitudes, you would have to reduce the data further.
2. The next step would be to reduce the data to a summary figure by computing an average rating for each service. Assume that you computed the following averages:

Service	Average rating
2% discount on purchases totaling $20 or more	4.50
5% senior discount on Wednesday	4.10
Free delivery of orders within a 10-mile radius of the store	1.75
Free Thursday night wine tasting	1.30
Frequent-shopper discount card	3.97

The three highest-ranked items relate to ways in which customers can save money on grocery purchases; the two lowest-ranked items relate to special services for which most stores charge a nominal fee. An appropriate presentation of findings could include the following paragraph.

> Average ratings indicate strong customer interest in new services that enable them to save money. Discounts on all purchases of $20 or more, a senior discount on Wednesday, and frequent-buyer discount cards all received average ratings above 3.95, indicating that FreshMart customers consider those services to be important or very important. In contrast, removing fees from seldom-used services appears to be of little importance to FreshMart customers. Free wine tastings and delivery service within a 10-mile radius of the store were rated very unimportant and unimportant, respectively.

The presentation of findings and discussion of what they reveal comprise the major portion of any research report. In this section, you must present a complete and clear analysis of all data. For coherence, the final paragraph of the introduction or the first paragraph of the findings section should contain a preview of how this section is organized. In the Charleston example, this preview opens the findings section.

> The analysis produced five outcomes, including guides for waterfront development and assessments of Charlestonians' knowledge and attitudes about the current economic impact of the cruise industry. Additionally, the study projected economic benefits of terminal relocation, personal and business experiences related to cruise dockings, and the potential impact of terminal relocation on quality of life.

Your report need not contain an actual heading called "Findings." Instead, coherence should be achieved through descriptive headings and subheadings that provide clues about the information in each section and lead the reader through the analysis. Use a summarizing (talking) heading rather than a one- or two-word label. Notice that headings concisely summarize the content of each major division in Figure 4.3.

4

Additionally, the study projected economic benefits of terminal relocation, personal and business experiences related to cruise dockings, and the potential impact of terminal relocation on quality of life.

Guides for Waterfront Development

One analyst of urban development has observed that few cities have viewed their waterfronts as distinctive elements that should be included in a systematic plan of urban development (Moss, 2004). Recently, however, some major cities have undertaken comprehensive programs of urban waterfront renewal or development. Notable examples of comprehensive planning exist in Baltimore, Maryland; Boston, Massachusetts; Louisville, Kentucky; and Salem, Oregon. Successful projects incorporate local residents' desires for recreational water space and tourist expectations of interesting target destinations (Craig-Smith, 2010).

The importance of planned, ethical waterfront development was acknowledged in 1999 in Urban Waterfront Manifesto (The Waterfront Center, 1999). Several principles included in the manifesto are especially relevant to the proposed relocation of the cruise terminal and related waterfront enhancements. They include the following:

- Meaningful community involvement is integral to valid waterfront planning and development. It should begin early and be continuous.
- Many conversions take 10, 15, or 25 years. The understandable desire to achieve instant results should be resisted in all except the smallest steps.
- Public access to and along the urban waterfront should be the hallmark of all projects, including residential developments. Visual access to the water likewise should be a pervading objective.
- Where possible, a diversity of uses should be included along waterfronts, from passive parks to vibrant commercial attractions. People of all income levels and cultures should feel welcome.

Another publication, Smart Growth for Coastal and Waterfront Communities (National Oceanic and Atmospheric Administration, 2014), presents 10 elements that should be incorporated in waterfront development plans. Elements especially relevant to the current plans for Charleston Harbor include the following:

- Incorporate mix land uses, including water-dependent uses.
- Create walkable communities with physical and visual access to and along the waterfront for public use.
- Foster distinctive, attractive communities with a strong sense of place that capitalizes on the waterfront's heritage.
- Encourage community and stakeholder collaboration in development decisions, ensuring that public interests in and rights of access to the waterfront and coastal waters are upheld.

The Concept Plan for Union Pier Waterfront (Cooper, Robertson & Partners, 2015) prepared for the South Carolina State Ports Authority incorporates the concepts presented in the Urban Waterfront Manifesto and Smart Growth for Coastal and Waterfront Communities. The Concept Plan cites these goals:

- Create a financially viable plan including a new cruise terminal that is attractive and in keeping with the character of historic Charleston.
- Comply with today's enhanced cruise security requirements.

- Mitigate impacts on existing infrastructure and traffic.
- Identify additional uses for the Union Pier property that bring enjoyment to Charlestonians and enhance the local economy.
- Increase public access to Charleston's historic waterfront.

These principles of urban waterfront development and the goals cited in the Concept Plan are relevant in an assessment of Charlestonians' knowledge and attitudes about the proposed enhancements to the Port of Charleston.

Knowledge of Current Economic Impact

Whereas Charleston merchants appeared to have relatively accurate knowledge of both the current economic impact and the potential impact of the proposed relocation of the cruise terminal, Ansonborough residents tended to underestimate the economic impact of the cruise industry.

News reports about the relocation plans have consistently mentioned that the cruise industry is a vital player in the economic health of the Charleston area and the state. In 2014 the cruise industry generated $64 million in direct spending in South Carolina and supported 1,177 jobs (2014 Economic Impact, 2014). A 2015 study by the College of Charleston found that the annual economic impact of the Charleston cruise industry exceeded $37 million and supported over 400 jobs (Smith, 2015).

However, 51 percent of Charleston residents attributed approximately 200 jobs to the industry, with only 17 percent reporting the accurate estimate of 400. Merchants, on the other hand, had an accurate perception of the number of jobs supported by the cruise industry; 74 percent of merchants indicated that the industry supported approximately 400 jobs and 21 percent placed their estimate at 300 jobs. (See Chart 1, page 6.) Similarly, Charleston residents underestimated the monetary impact of the industry; 54 percent of those respondents said that the impact was approximately $25 million. The majority of merchants (61 percent) accurately assessed that impact to be in the $35 million range. (See Chart 2, page 6.)

Overall, the Charleston citizens who participated in the study held incorrect perceptions of the number of jobs and the economic impact that could be attributed to the cruise industry, whereas Charleston merchants appeared to have accurate knowledge about those factors.

Attitudes about Projected Economic Benefits of Terminal Relocation

Ansonborough residents appear to be extremely skeptical about the potential economic benefits directly associated with relocation of the cruise terminal. The dominant attitude (over 60%) about projections of jobs and monetary contributions to the local economy was that such estimations are guesses, not facts; and only 10-13% of respondents thought that the historic district will share in the economic benefits. Although only 13-18% of merchants anticipate that the historic district will share in the increased jobs and $45 million of expenditures, over 75% looked beyond the downtown area, saying that the Charleston area needs such a boost and the project should proceed. (See Chart 3, page 7.)

Personal and Business Experiences

In February 2015, the Ports Authority implemented a new cruise traffic plan (South Carolina State Ports Authority, 2015). Despite changes to traffic flows, a majority of both residents and merchants reported

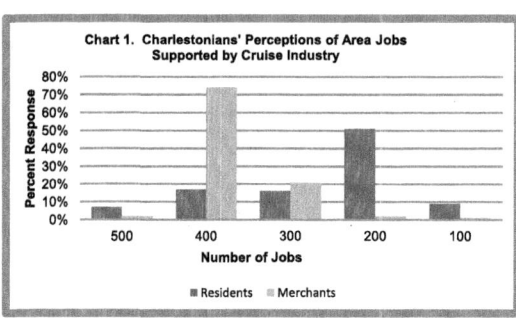

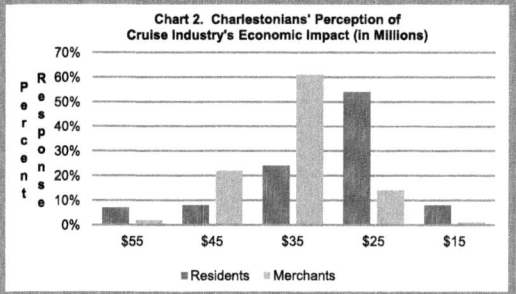

negative experiences related to pedestrian and motor travel; a complement to such reports is the fact that no one in either group reported having experienced decreased pedestrian traffic and a smooth flow of vehicular traffic. In addition, a majority of both groups reported having experienced noise and environmental pollution.

The major difference between the two groups of respondents related to how they interacted with cruise passengers. A larger percentage of residents (73%) than merchants (33%) reported reluctance to leave home.

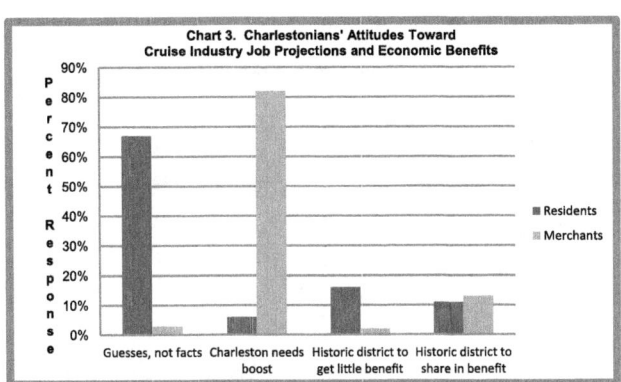

or place of business, suggesting that the residents' contacts may have been more limited. In a related finding, a smaller percentage of residents (20%) than merchants (75%) reported pleasant interactions with the tourists. Fortunately, only five respondents in the residents group and none in the merchants group reported abrasive interactions. Understandably, no residents reported increased or decreased sales related to the presence of cruise ships. A considerably larger percentage of merchants reported increased sales (65%) as opposed to decreased sales (20%). (See Chart 4).

Impact of Terminal Relocation on Quality of Life

As was noted in the methodology section of this report, the strongest agreement between the resident group and the merchant group was in their desire to relocate the cruise terminal. Over 90% of both groups favored the proposed relocation. A majority of both groups also thought that relocating the terminal would result in improved quality of life, as shown in Table 1. Only 5% of each group projected that

Table 1. Charlestonians' Assumptions about
Quality of Life Resulting from Terminal Relocation

Quality of Life	Residents	Merchants
Likely improve	30%	15%
Possibly improve	43%	39%
No change	21%	41%
May decline	3%	3%
Very likely decline	2%	2%

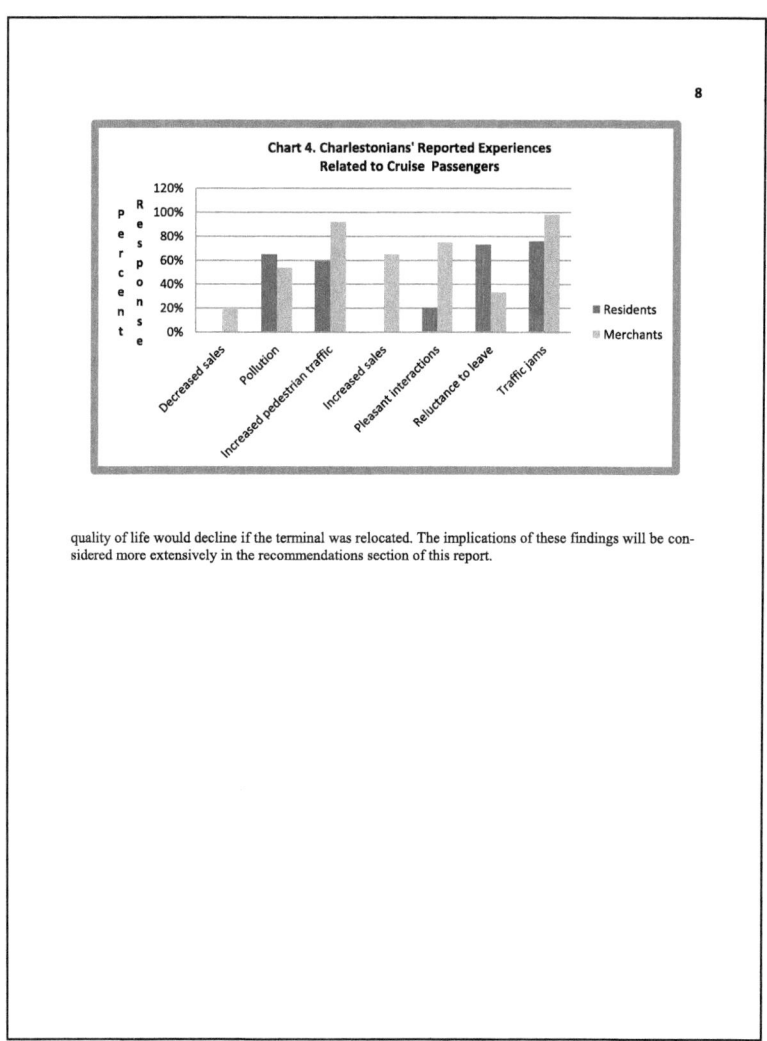

quality of life would decline if the terminal was relocated. The implications of these findings will be considered more extensively in the recommendations section of this report.

Figure 4.3 Research report, the findings section

Follow these guides as you present your research findings:

- Classify or summarize data; present such classifications or summaries in tables, charts, or graphs whenever appropriate.
- Interpret the data; do not merely repeat the raw data or the summary figures shown in your visuals.
- Show similarities and differences among groups of data. If differences exist supply possible explanations for those differences.

The findings you present should permit you to draw conclusions.

Report Summary

Information and analytical reports should always contain an overall summary of the findings. When the analysis is lengthy and complex, you should also summarize your discussion of the findings at the end of each major section. For an information report written in inductive structure, the summary marks the conclusion of the report. In an analytical report, the summary may occupy a separate section, as is shown in Figure 4.4, or may be included in a section with the conclusions.

Summary

The Ports Authority's plans for the cruise terminal and other waterfront enhancements generally adhere to contemporary guides for waterfront development. Ansonborough residents and members of the downtown business and professional community share some attitudes about the cruise industry, but the business community views it a bit more favorably than does the residential community. Overall, Ansonborough residents are less well informed about the economic benefits that the cruise industry has brought to Charleston and are less inclined to believe that the historic downtown community will benefit from a relocation of the cruise port. Both groups shared negative experiences related to pedestrian and vehicular traffic. Compared to the merchants, Ansonborough residents appeared to have had less direct contact and fewer positive interactions with cruise passengers.

Conclusions

The Port Authority has attempted to apply sound waterfront development principles in its Concept Plan for Union Pier Waterfront, including public input. This study has been one attempt to obtain public input.

Communication about the plans seems to have been understood and received favorably by downtown merchants. That communication, however, has done little to change the downtown residents' opinion about the value of the cruise industry.

Downtown Charleston's residents and merchants both perceive that the presence of cruise ships in the Port of Charleston has negatively impacted pedestrian and vehicular traffic. Although residents and merchants have differing degrees of knowledge about the economic impact of the cruise industry, both groups strongly support relocation of the cruise terminal.

Recommendations

These findings suggest that Charlestonians recognize that the cruise business will continue to be a part of the Port of Charleston and their lives. However, they want the negative aspects of that impact to be ameliorated. To enhance citizens' support for the proposed cruise terminal relocation and waterfront enhancements the South Carolina Ports Authority should do the following:

- Publicize the keys aspects of the Concept Plan that include:
  - Improved vehicular traffic flows and parking in the cruise terminal area and downtown Charleston.
  - Improved visual and human access to the waterfront.
  - Ecological reclamation and protection of the waterfront.
  - Reclamation and protection of historical structures in the Charleston Harbor.

- Proceed with port relocation and waterfront improvement plans presented in the Concept Plan in a sequence that will most readily show the greatest benefits to Charleston merchants and residents. Specifically:

  10

- Complete street construction/traffic alteration projects first. Improved traffic flow would immediately be felt by residents and businesses and may improve attitudes toward the presence of cruise ships in the Port of Charleston.
- Upon completion of the street improvements, begin making improvements to the waterfront at the same time that construction begins on the new terminal site. This simultaneous activity will demonstrate to residents and merchants that the Ports Authority is as serious about enabling greater recreational use of the waterfront is it is about improving cruise facilities.
- Issue regular press releases to mark the progress of the project and to inform residents and merchants about construction activities that may temporarily inconvenience them. Constant communication should reassure the citizens of Charleston that the project is moving forward as planned and will soon show major benefits to residents and merchants as well as cruise passengers.

Figure 4.4 Summary of findings

Conclusions

As you can see, the Charleston report (Figures 4.3 and 4.4) is presented in inductive structure. The conclusions and recommendations constitute the final sections of the report. However, the deductive structure is appropriate when readers prefer it or when they have extensive knowledge of the research problem and will easily understand and accept the conclusions and recommendations. In that case, the recommendations, followed by conclusions, may be presented at the beginning of the report body. The opening pages of a report presented in that manner are shown in Figure 4.5.

Charleston and the Cruise Industry

Recommendations

Charlestonians recognize that the cruise business will continue to be a part of the Port of Charleston and their lives. However, they want the negative aspects of that impact to be ameliorated. To enhance citizens' support for the proposed cruise terminal relocation and waterfront enhancements the South Carolina Ports Authority should do the following:

1. Publicize the keys aspects of the Concept Plan that include:
   - Improved vehicular traffic flows and parking in the cruise terminal area and downtown Charleston.
   - Improved visual and human access to the waterfront.
   - Ecological reclamation and protection of the waterfront.
   - Reclamation and protection of historical structures in the Charleston Harbor.

2. Proceed with port relocation and waterfront improvement plans presented in the Concept Plan in a sequence that will most readily show the greatest benefits to Charleston merchants and residents. Specifically:

- Complete street construction/traffic alteration projects first. Improved traffic flow would immediately be felt by residents and businesses and may improve attitudes toward the presence of cruise ships in the Port of Charleston.
- Upon completion of the street improvements, begin making improvements to the waterfront at the same time that construction begins on the new terminal site. This simultaneous activity will demonstrate to residents and merchants that the Ports Authority is as serious about enabling greater recreational use of the waterfront is it is about improving cruise facilities.
- Issue regular press releases to mark the progress of the project and to inform residents and merchants about construction activities that may temporarily inconvenience them. Constant communication should reassure the citizens of Charleston that the project is moving forward as planned and will soon show major benefits to residents and merchants as well as cruise passengers.

These recommendations are based on the conclusions that the South Carolina State Ports Authority has attempted to apply sound waterfront development principles in its Concept Plan for Union Pier Waterfront, including public input. Communication about those plans seems to have been understood and received favorably by downtown merchants. That communication, however, has done little to change the downtown residents' opinion about the value of the cruise industry.

Downtown Charleston's residents and merchants both perceive that the presence of cruise ships in the Port of Charleston has negatively impacted pedestrian and vehicular traffic. Although residents and merchants have differing degrees of knowledge about the economic impact of the cruise industry, both groups strongly support relocation of the cruise terminal.

Charlestonians' Perceptions of the Cruise Industry and Proposed Port Enhancements

For more than 25 years, Charleston's Union Pier has served as a home port and port of call for Carnival Cruises and a port of call for other cruise lines. The cruise industry currently contributes approximately $37 million to the region's economy, but the vehicular and pedestrian traffic associated with the departures and arrivals of cruise ships has been the subject of extensive debate among downtown residents, merchants, and professionals.

The South Carolina Ports Authority has begun plans to relocate the cruise terminal to a point north of its present location and relocate existing cargo operations. These changes will open 35 acres of harbor front that can be redeveloped to provide greater public access to the water's edge. Before implementing that plan, the Ports Authority officers wanted to know how much Charlestonians know about the economic impact of the cruise industry and what their attitudes are toward that industry and the proposed revitalization of the waterfront.

Research Plan

A survey of downtown residents and merchants was conducted during the summer of 2016.

The Problem

The research problem was to assess Charlestonians' perceptions of the economic and social impact of cruise dockings in the Port of Charleston and the possible relocation of the cruise terminal.

The Purpose

The purpose of the study was to assess the business and social climate in which the South Carolina Ports Authority will operate if it implements plans to relocate the cruise terminal. Knowledge of that climate will help the Authority develop operational and communication strategies relative to the relocation.

> **Scope of Analysis**
>
> Three factors were studied:
>
> 1. What business impacts do Charleston's downtown residents and merchants perceive to be related to the arrival and departure of cruise ships?
> 2. What personal and community impacts do Charleston's downtown residents and merchants perceive to be related to the arrival and departure of cruise ships?
> 3. What knowledge of and attitudes toward relocation of the cruise terminal are evidenced by Charleston's downtown residents and merchants?

Figure 4.5 Beginning of a report in deductive structure

Conclusions must be logical inferences supported by findings. As you draw conclusions, you are moving further from the objectivity of the data and relying on your perceptions of what the data mean. To avoid unwarranted subjectivity in conclusions and to state them effectively, follow these guides:

> - Conclusions must not be a mere restatement of the findings.
> - Conclusions must be objective and flow logically from the analysis. If the data contradict anticipated outcomes, you must put aside your expectations and base conclusions on the available data.
> - Conclusions must be relevant to the stated problem and purpose of the report.
> - Conclusions must not introduce new material. All relevant data and analysis must be presented before a conclusion can be drawn.
> - Several findings may be used to support a single conclusion. You need not draw a conclusion from each major finding.

> On the other hand, one major finding may lead to more than one conclusion.
> - You should always review your conclusions to ensure that your data analysis, or findings, support them.

The following examples contrast inappropriate and appropriate conclusions related to the survey of FreshMart customer preferences.

Inappropriate Conclusions

> *Restatement of findings:* FreshMart customers rated services providing discounts on purchases higher than eliminating fees for seldom-used services.
>
> *Not justified by findings:* FreshMart customers will not respond to reduced fees for seldom-used services. Customers want lower grocery prices, not parties or cheaper delivery service.
>
> *Not related to problem of report:* FreshMart can gain a competitive edge by offering a variety of price-reduction strategies. (This conclusion is not justified if the stated problem is to determine customer preferences for new services and no data were gathered to determine their inclinations to choose a supermarket on the basis of the availability of those services.)

Appropriate Conclusion

> *Justified by findings, not merely a restatement of findings, related to research problem:* FreshMart customers are more interested in ways to save money on their grocery purchases than in saving money on peripheral services. FreshMart can satisfy some of the desires of current customers by offering discounts on purchases.

In Figure 4.4, pages 154 and 155, note the relationship of the findings summary and the conclusions.

Since research is problem oriented, you are usually expected to carry your analysis one step further—to make recommendations.

Recommendations

Recommendations are confident statements of proposed actions based on the conclusions. Recommendations must be context relevant; that is, they must respond to the purpose of the study and be appropriate for the specific audience. As you write recommendations, observe the following guidelines:

- Verify that specific conclusions and findings justify each recommendation. Some report writers number the summary statements of findings and conclusions so that they can refer easily to such supporting information when they write recommendations.
- State recommendations in imperative sentence structure. Begin each with an action verb.
- State recommendations specifically, including a recommended plan for implementation, if appropriate.
- Suggest additional research to investigate unanswered questions that became evident during your study.

Returning to the FreshMart study, assume that the purpose of FreshMart's survey was to increase customer satisfaction and loyalty by providing desired services. The following example shows an appropriate way to state your recommendations.

Recommendations

To increase customer satisfaction and loyalty, FreshMart should initiate two new services as soon as possible and determine the feasibility of a third. Specifically, FreshMart should:

1. Give a 2% discount on orders totaling $20 or more. This recommendation can be implemented by:
   - Programming point-of-sale registers to compute a 2% discount on total orders of $20 or more.
   - Training checkout associates to highlight the savings on each receipt and point it out to the customer.
2. Give an additional 3% discount to all seniors on Wednesday. This recommendation can be implemented by:
   - Designing and publishing an attractive newspaper advertisement announcing the new policy.
   - Training checkout associates on how to recognize customers who appear to be 60 years of age or older and how to enter the discount for such customers.
3. Investigate the feasibility of issuing a frequent-shopper discount card. Specific facts needed include:
   - How to identify frequent shoppers.
   - Type of discount that should be offered.
   - Cost of providing the card, maintaining records, and fulfilling the discount program.

Again, recommendations are most meaningful when they are related to the stated purpose of the study. Notice the relationship of the purpose, conclusion, and recommendation in the following example.

Purpose: To assess the business and social climate in which the South Carolina Ports Authority will operate if it implements plans to relocate the cruise terminal. Knowledge of that climate will help the Authority develop operational and communication strategies relative to the relocation.

Conclusion: Communication about the plans seems to have been understood and received favorably by downtown merchants. That communication, however, has done little to change the downtown residents' opinion about the value of the cruise industry.

> *Recommendation:*
>
> Publicize the key aspects of the Concept Plan. Specifically:
>
> - Improved vehicular traffic flows and parking in the cruise terminal area and downtown Charleston.
> - Improved visual and human access to the waterfront.
> - Ecological reclamation and protection of the waterfront.
> - Reclamation and protection of historical structures in the Charleston Harbor.

Review your recommendations to ensure that your conclusions support them. Some writers, perhaps in a mistaken attempt to compose a dramatic ending to the report, introduce new data with the conclusions or recommendations. That practice, however, tends to confuse the reader and destroys report coherence.

For example, a writer might be tempted to withhold the quality-of-life information from the report findings (Figure 4.4, pages 154 and 155). Such a writer might think that this information would give final, solid justification for the recommendation to carry out the proposed port enhancements in parallel projects. However, since the data about quality of life is closely related to respondents' perceptions of the cruise industry, it should be—and was—included as part of that analysis.

The recommendations indicate completion of the analysis and propose actions that are justified by that analysis. Recommendations may also suggest other research that should be undertaken.

Report Supplements

Report supplements may be added to provide additional information that will be of interest to some readers. The supplements include any information that may be useful—but not essential—for understanding the analysis, conclusions, and recommendations. Supplements may include endnotes, a list of secondary sources, a glossary, an appendix, and an index.

Reference List

A reference list must be included when secondary sources are cited, whether you use in-text citations or endnotes. Include in the list all secondary sources that contributed data for the study. Figure 4.3 demonstrates how to use in-text citations when you want to acknowledge specific sources within the text. (On page 4 of Figure 4.3 note the five in-text citations.) Figure 4.6 shows a reference list that readers might use to consult any or all cited sources.

References

2014 Economic impact of the cruise industry in America by state. (2014). Retrieved from: http://www.cruiseindustryfacts.com/newsroom/data-and-reports/2014

Cooper, Robertson & Partners. (2015, July 18). Concept plan for Union Pier waterfront. Retrieved from http://www.scspa.com/UnionPierPlan /pdf/Union

Craig-Smith, S. J. (Ed.). (2000). *Recreation and tourism as a catalyst for urban waterfront redevelopment.* Westport, CT: Praeger Publishers.

Johnson, T. & Howard. E. (2012). South waterfront urban renewal feasibility study. City of Salem Retrieved http://www.cityofsalem/Departments/Urbandevelopment/UrbanRenewal/Documents/SWF

Moss, M. (2004). The urban waterfront: Opportunities for renewal. Retrieved from http://www.mitchellmoss.com/articles/urbanwaterfront.html

National Oceanic and Atmospheric Administration. (2014, September 9). Smart growth for coastal and waterfront communities. Retrieved from http://coastalsmartgrowth.noaa.gov

Ryckbost, P. (2010, April 14). Redeveloping urban waterfront property. Retrieved from http://www.umich.edu/~econdev/waterfronts

Smith, B. (2015, February 2). "Growing cruise industry means big money for Charleston, SC." *USA today.* Retrieved from http://www.usatoday.com/travel/cruises/2010-02-02-south-carolina-cruise-industry_N.htm

South Carolina State Ports Authority. (2015, February 11). SCSPA implements new cruise traffic measures. Retrieved from http://www.scspa.com/about/news/pressroom/pressroom.asp?PressRelease=264

The Waterfront Center. (1999, July 10). Urban Waterfront Manifesto. Retrieved from http://www.waterfrontcenter.org/about/manifesto.html

11

Figure 4.6 References list*

* References are shown in APA (American Psychological Association) style.[1] APA style is often used by professionals in the social and behavioral sciences, of which business is one.

Glossary

A glossary—a list of selected words with their meanings—is required only when the report contains terms that may be unfamiliar to some readers. Including a glossary is advisable when the readership consists of some persons who know the technical terminology and others who do not. That practice provides definitions for readers who need them without cluttering the report with information that is unnecessary for many readers. If the report contains few technical or unfamiliar terms or words are given a specific meaning in the report, those terms may be included in the introductory section of the report, as is done in Figure 4.1, page 140 (Definitions).

Appendix

An appendix includes items referred to but not displayed in the report body. Similarly, all items displayed in an appendix must be identified at some point in the report. Plan and organize an appendix, or series of appendices, as carefully as other report parts. Do not use an appendix to share interesting, superfluous information. When adding more than one category of information, use more than one appendix, labeling them Appendix A, Appendix B, and so on. Materials often displayed in appendices include:

- Copies of transmittal letters;
- Questionnaires or interview guides;
- Data tabulations;
- Statistical formulas; and
- Supporting graphs, charts, and diagrams.

Remember, however, that visuals intended to clarify, emphasize, or summarize parts of the report should be incorporated into the report narrative unless you are specifically requested to group them in an appendix. In Figure 4.3, report pages 6, 7, and 8 show effective ways to incorporate figures and tables into the report narrative. Figure 4.7, report pages 12 through 16 shows the Charleston report's Appendix A and Appendix B.

Appendix A. Data Collection Instruments

Text of E-mail Transmittal Message to Merchants

To: Carriage Properties

Subject: Charleston and the Cruise Industry

As a person who conducts business in Historic Downtown Charleston, you are aware that the presence of cruise ships in Charleston Harbor has generated controversy in this community. Although the cruise business has made positive contributions to the Charleston economy, some citizens fear that cruise ships will change the gracious ambiance of this area.

You have an opportunity to enter the debate on this controversial issue. The SC Ports Authority is conducting a study to evaluate attitudes of downtown merchants and citizens toward the cruise industry and the proposed relocation of the cruise terminal. We value your input. Please log onto www.SCPorts.com/survey and complete the questionnaire that you will find there.

Your response before June 14 will ensure that your voice is heard as the SC Ports Authority makes decisions about how to accommodate the wishes of our citizens while also making the Port of Charleston an attractive entry into our beautiful city.

Transmittal Letter to Residents

S. C. Ports Authority

P O Box 22288 Charleston, SC 29413 864.111.1111

May 15, 2016

Dear Ansonborough Resident:

As a resident of the Ansonborough District of Historic Charleston, you take pride in your home and the gracious ambiance of downtown Charleston.

In recent months, the *Charleston News and Courier has* published comments about the presence of cruise ships in Charleston Harbor and cruise passengers in the historic district. Although many citizens realize that the cruise industry has a positive impact on the Charleston economy, some fear that its presence may distract from our traditional way of life.

The South Carolina Ports Authority wants to hear from you on this issue. On June 12 and 13 we will conduct town-hall meetings at St. Phillips's Episcopal Church, 142 Church Street. At those meetings members of the Ports Authority will explain our tentative plans to relocate the cruise terminal and improve the Charleston Harbor waterfront. The entire project is intended to give Charlestonians and tourists better access to that wonderful resource.

Please plan to attend one of those meetings. You will be given an opportunity to discuss your views of the cruise industry and the proposed relocation of the terminal. The enclosed questionnaire should help you prepare for the meeting.

You may complete the questionnaire before the town-hall meeting, or you may wait to fill it in until after you have heard the discussion. We will collect completed questionnaires at the end of the meeting.

We look forward to seeing you at a meeting on June 12 or 13 at 7:30 p.m. to discuss what we can do to improve everyone's enjoyment of our downtown waterfront.

Sincerely,

Bryant T. Joseph, VP
Terminal Development

Enclosure: Questionnaire

14

Questionnaire for Merchants and Residents

Questionnaire: Charleston and the Cruise Industry

Please share something about your knowledge, attitudes, and experiences related to the impact of the cruise industry in Charleston. There are no correct or incorrect answers. We are looking for your honest assessments.

1. Approximately how many jobs in the Charleston area are supported by the cruise industry?

    500____   400____   300____   200____   100____

2. Approximately how much economic output (in millions) is generated by the cruise industry in Charleston?

    $55____ $45____ $35____ $25____ $15____

3. Which of the following conditions do you associate with the presence of a cruise ship in port? (Check all that apply.)

    ____ Abrasive interactions with cruise passengers.
    ____ Decreased pedestrian traffic in neighborhood.
    ____ Decreased sales of food, lodging, and/or merchandise and services.
    ____ Environmental/noise pollution.
    ____ Increased pedestrian traffic in neighborhood.
    ____ Increased sales of food, lodging, and/or merchandise and services.
    ____ Pleasant interactions with cruise passengers.
    ____ Reluctance to leave home or place of business.
    ____ Smooth flow of vehicular traffic.
    ____ Traffic jams.
    ____ Other (Please describe.)

One option the Ports Authority is considering is to relocate the cruise terminal to a point somewhat north of Union Pier.

4. At this time, do you favor or oppose relocation of the cruise terminal? (Check one.)

    Favor ____

    Oppose ____

5. Relocating the cruise terminal is projected to bring approximately 350 jobs to the Charleston region and contribute $45 million to the local economy during the 12 months of construction. Which of the following statements **best** reflects your attitude about those projections?

    ____ Projections are guesses, not facts.
    ____ The Charleston area needs that kind of economic boost; let's do it.
    ____ The Charleston historic district will receive little of that benefit.
    ____ The Charleston historic district will share in that benefit.

6. If the cruise terminal is relocated (check one):

   ____ My quality of life will very likely improve.
   ____ My quality of life may possibly improve.
   ____ I anticipate no change in my quality of life.
   ____ My quality of life may decline.
   ____ My quality of life will very likely decline.

7. Please provide some information about yourself to help us process the answers to this survey.

   - Your age range is:
     Under 25____   26-35____   36-45____   46-55____   56-65____   Over 65____

   - You are:
     Female____   Male____

   - Your profession or occupation is best categorized as:

___ Advertising, media, marketing, and public relations	___ Hospitality and leisure services
___ Artistic endeavors	___ Legal services
___ Banking, economics, and financial services	___ Manufacturing
___ Business, management, and human resources	___ Public sector, politics, and policy
___ Consulting	___ Real estate services
___ Development and non-governmental not-for-profit	___ Retail
___ Education and religious services	___ Technology
___ Energy and environment	___ Transportation
___ Engineering and construction services	___ Wholesale distribution
___ Healthcare services	___ Retired
___ Homemaker (Full-Time)	___ Other: _____

Please return your completed questionnaire to:

South Carolina State Ports Authority
P O Box 22288
Charleston, SC 29413

Appendix B. Profiles of Respondents

Gender	Residents	Merchants
Female	68	26
Male	59	66
Total	127	92

Ages of Respondents	Residents	Merchants
	No.	No.
46-55	3	8
56-65	21	10
36-45	24	22
26-35	31	27
Under 25	22	23
Over 65	26	2
Total	127	92

Profession/occupation	Residents	Merchants
Artistic endeavors	5%	8%
Education services	9%	4%
Food services	15%	33%
Full-time homemaker	14%	0%
Hospitality services	6%	16%
Legal services	2%	10%
Medical/dental services	5%	3%
Other	2%	4%
Real estate services	4%	7%
Retail marketing	17%	11%
Retired	25%	0%
Wholesale distribution	2%	3%

16

Figure 4.7 Report appendices

Index

An index is a list of key words or topics found in some, typically longer reports. Generally, an index is included only if the reader would not be able to locate specific information without that aid. In most situations, a comprehensive table of contents along with clear, concise division headings should be sufficient to direct the reader to specific topics.

The parts for a formal business report should be adapted to meet your specific reporting requirements. Be mindful of your audience and include all parts that will assist your readers. Remember your objectives: to establish rapport with report readers, stimulate interest in the report, and facilitate use of the report. Include the parts that will help you achieve those goals.

Report Preliminaries

The preliminary parts of a formal report, setting the stage for the report and enabling readers to access the information easily, help to make the report user-friendly. Those preliminaries provide a convenient way to physically transmit the report, establish a context for understanding it, and enable the reader to locate specific information quickly. Some preliminary parts may be omitted in informal situations or when the report is quite short and the topic is straightforward.

Although the report preliminaries are the first pages the report user sees, many of those parts can be compiled only after you have written the full report. The preliminary parts must accurately reflect the report's content and structure. If you revise your report in any way after you have written the preliminaries, be sure to check the accuracy of all preliminary parts and, if necessary, revise them before finalizing the report for delivery. For example, be sure that your table of contents accurately shows the final content and page numbering of your report.

Cover or Binder

A reader must be able to handle the report document conveniently. Although some readers may prefer that you present unbound pages, perhaps enclosed in an envelope or a file folder, many prefer that you bind the report securely, as well as providing an electronic version. A cover or binder protects the pages of a printed report and prevents them from loosening while the current readers—and future ones—use the report. Your report cover should show at least the title of the report; if the title is long, a shortened form may appear on the cover. You may also include a design or illustration to suggest the content of the report and stimulate interest.

Flyleaves

A blank sheet may be placed at both the front and the back of the report to protect other pages and provide a space for readers' comments. Those sheets, called flyleaves, are optional. Since they tend to connote a higher level of formality, include flyleaves only when you think the situation justifies such formality. Note, for example, that most hardcover books contain flyleaves, but many softcover books do not.

Title Page

The title page usually contains four facts: the full title of the report and the identity of the person or agency for whom the report was prepared, including contact information. Include the author's identity and contact information (unless advised to omit it). Such information will help readers provide feedback, such as questions, commendations, or requests for new projects. You will also include the report's completion or submission date on the title page.

The title of the report should provide a concise statement of the report's content. Follow these guides for writing an effective report title:

- Include as much 5W information—who, what, why, when, and where—as is possible without creating a cumbersome title.
- To achieve conciseness, avoid using unnecessary words and phrases such as "an analysis of" or "the determination of."
- Use a talking title to stimulate interest more readily than a purely descriptive title.

The following examples contrast a cumbersome, verbose title with a descriptive title and a talking title.

Cumbersome, verbose: A Comprehensive Analysis of Charlestonians' Knowledge of and Attitudes toward the Cruise Industry in Charleston

Descriptive: Assessing Charlestonians' Knowledge and Attitudes about the Cruise Industry

Talking: What Should the Ports Authority Do to Improve Charlostonians' Attitudes about the Cruise Industry?

For the title page you may use a traditional format or any creative format that effectively conveys the required information. A nontraditional format is demonstrated in Figure 4.8.

174 PRODUCING WRITTEN AND ORAL BUSINESS REPORTS

Charleston and the Cruise Industry

Charlestonians' Knowledge and Attitudes about the Cruise Industry

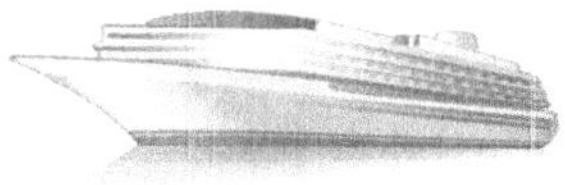

Prepared for—

Bryant T. Joseph, Vice President, Terminal Operations

SC State Ports Authority

P.O. Box 22287

Charleston, SC 29413

Prepared by—

Government Relations Division

South Carolina Ports Authority

September 2017

Figure 4.8 Nontraditional title page

Notice that no page number appears on the title page. A traditional title page format is demonstrated in Figure 4.9.

Charleston and the Cruise Industry

Charlestonians' Knowledge and Attitudes about the Cruise Industry

Prepared for—
Bryant T. Joseph, Vice President
Terminal Operations
SC State Ports Authority
P.O. Box 22287
Charleston, SC 29413

Prepared by—
Government Relations Division
South Carolina Ports Authority

September 2017

Figure 4.9 Traditional title page

Transmittal Message

The transmittal message, in letter or memo format, presents the report to your primary reader(s). A letter is used for external reports and a memo for internal reports.

If you have written the report in an impersonal style, the transmittal message gives you an opportunity to speak more personally to your primary contact person and to reinforce goodwill. The message may include any comments that will stimulate interest in the report, confirm confidence in you as the researcher and writer, and perhaps lead to further interesting, responsible assignments. Appropriate content for the transmittal message includes some, but not necessarily all, of the following: a review of the research problem, purpose, and methodology; highlights of major findings; significant recommendations; comments about the research experience; an offer to discuss the report or assist with future projects.

The transmittal message is often bound within the report, either before or after the title page, but some writers prefer to present it as a separate message accompanying the report. If presented separately, e-mail format would be appropriate for an informal report. See Figure 4.10 for an example of a separate transmittal message accompanying the report.

Memo

To: Bryant T. Joseph, VP, Terminal Development
From: Melvin L. Barbara, VP, Government Relations
Date: September 27, 2017
Subject: Citizens' Attitudes toward Cruise Industry and Port Enhancements

On January 15, 2017, you authorized me to proceed with a study of Charlestonians' attitudes toward the cruise industry and the proposed port enhancements. The accompanying report presents the results of that study. Although the study was initially intended for internal use only, subsequent events have suggested that the Ports Authority may want to share the report with other constituencies. Consequently, I have presented the report in a somewhat more formal style than we normally use for internal reports.

In addition to the survey proposed in January, my research team studied documents related to waterfront development and enhancement.

> We used that information to evaluate the 2016 Concept Plan for Union Pier Waterfront and to evaluate how the Ports Authority can best communicate with the public as it launches this major waterfront revitalization project.
>
> My staff and I appreciate the opportunity to conduct this research. We are prepared to discuss the report at the September 30 management committee meeting.

Figure 4.10 Transmittal message

In this example, as the transmittal message indicates, the report will likely be circulated outside the organization for which it was prepared. Therefore, the separate transmittal memo is appropriate.

Authorization and Acceptance Messages

The authorization message provides evidence of permission to undertake the project, and the acceptance message gives evidence of agreement to do the task. Those messages are often exchanged before the project is undertaken, sometimes orally and sometimes in writing. If written, they may be included in the report as formal notice to secondary readers that the project was appropriately authorized and accepted. However, if the transmittal message includes reference to the authorization, as is done in Figure 4.10, those messages may be omitted from the report.

If authorization and acceptance messages had been included in the illustrated report, they would be similar to the following examples.

Authorization Message (Letter or Memo Format as Appropriate)

> Please proceed with the study of citizens' attitudes toward the cruise industry and enhancements to the Port of Charleston.
>
> As we discussed this morning, the State Ports Authority must be fully aware of current perceptions of the cruise industry and proposed port enhancements. The research proposal you presented convinced me that your department is the right one to undertake this study. You have my full support.

You agreed to submit a written report of your findings, conclusions, and recommendations no later than September 30. I would appreciate a progress report on July 30 about the first phase of the study.

Acceptance Message (Letter or Memo Format as Appropriate)

Thank you for authorizing the Government Relations Division to analyze citizens' perceptions of the cruise industry and proposed port enhancements. My research team has already begun to prepare data collection instruments.

You will have a report of the research no later than September 25. As you requested, I will submit a progress report on July 30.

You may also occasionally submit unsolicited reports. In such an instance, authorization and acceptance messages do not exist, and the transmittal message must indicate clearly why you are submitting the report.

Contents

In a lengthy report, a table of contents and list of tables and figures help the reader get an overview of the report and easily refer to specific parts of the report (see Figure 4.11).

Table of Contents

List of Illustrations iii

Executive Summary iv

Determining Charlestonians' Perceptions of the Cruise Industry 1
    The Problem 1
    The Purpose 1
    Scope of Analysis 1
    Delimitations 2
    Limitations 2
    Definitions 2

How the Study was Conducted 2
    Secondary Data 2
    Primary Data 2
        Downtown Residents 3
        Downtown Merchants 3
    Data Analysis 3

What the Study Revealed 3
    Guides for Waterfront Development 4
    Knowledge of Current Economic Impact 5
    Attitudes about Projected Economic Benefits of Terminal Relocation 5
    Personal and Business Experiences 5
    Impact of Terminal Relocation on Quality of Life 7

Summary 9

Conclusions 9

Recommendations 9

References 11

Appendix A. Data Collection Instruments 12
    Text of E-Mail Transmittal Message to Merchants 12
    Transmittal Letter to Residents 13
    Questionnaire for Merchants and Residents 14

Appendix B. Profiles of Respondents 16

List of Illustrations

Chart 1. Charlestonians' Perceptions of Area Jobs Supported by Cruise Industry 6
Chart 2. Charlestonians' Perceptions of Cruise Industry's Economic Impact (in Millions) 6
Chart 3. Charlestonians' Attitudes toward Cruise Industry Jobs Projections and Economic Benefits 7
Table 1. Perceived Quality of Life Resulting from Terminal Relocation 7
Chart 4. Charlestonians' Reported Experiences Related to Cruise Passengers 8

Figure 4.11 Table of contents

The table of contents must list all items that appear after that page: any preliminary pages that follow and all chapter or section headings and subheadings used in the report. Do not list preliminary pages that appear before the table of contents. The number of the page on which each first-level division begins must be included. Notice that preliminaries, except the title page, are numbered with lower-case Roman numerals. Most writers include page numbers to mark the beginning of each subdivision as well. The use of dot leaders (shown) guide readers' eyes from topics on the left to page numbers on the right. Some writers use an outline numbering system, such as the decimal system demonstrated in Figure 4.12, to identify entries in the table of contents.

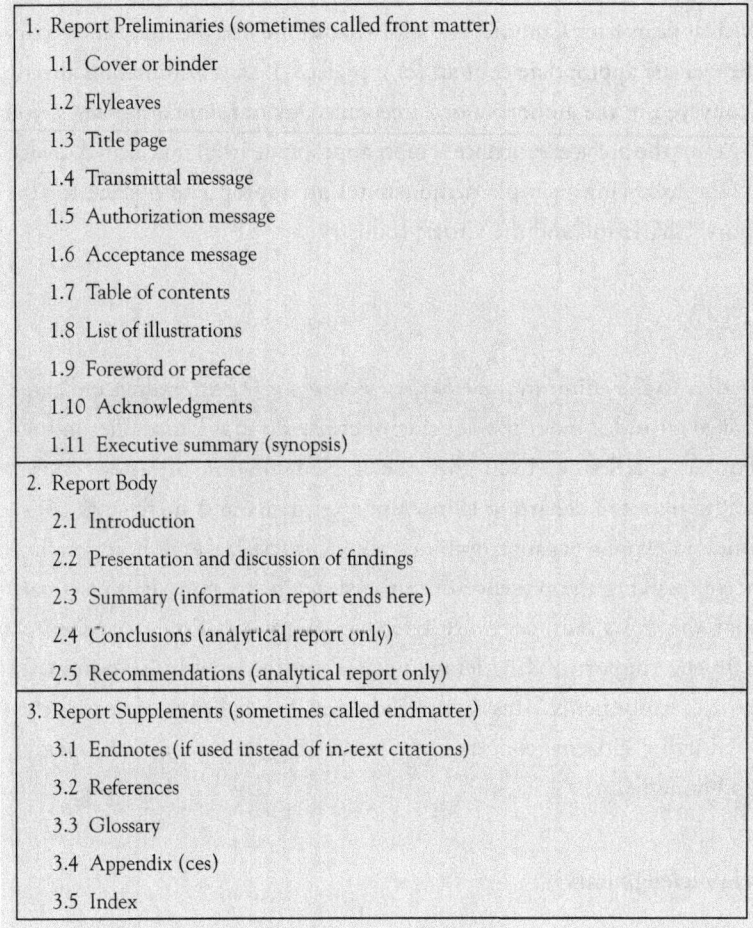

Figure 4.12 Decimal numbering system

When the report includes visuals, list those tables and figures by number and title, after the table of contents, as shown in Figure 4.11.

When only one or two visuals are used, some writers list them in the table of contents. However, the reader can locate the visuals more easily if they appear in a separate list. If the list is short and space permits, the list may be included on the same page as the table of contents. The list of tables usually precedes the list of figures; but if few visuals are used, tables and figures may be grouped in a single list of illustrations.

Preface

A preface should present some special details about the report and create interest. The preface is not as comprehensive as the executive summary, which appears later. Comments about what stimulated the study and its significance are appropriate content for a preface. If that information already is conveyed in the authorization, acceptance, or transmittal messages, you may omit the preface. A preface is most appropriate in an unsolicited report.

The following example demonstrates an appropriate preface for the report, Charleston and the Cruise Industry.

> Preface
>
> Letters to the editor in the *Charleston News and Courier* often indicate mixed attitudes about the docking of cruise ships at Union Pier in the Port of Charleston. Even after the implementation of a new cruise traffic plan for departing ships, some residents and merchants continue to express negative opinions about pedestrian and motor traffic accompanying the presence of cruise ships in the port. It is essential that the Ports Authority use effective communication strategies to gain the support of Charletonians as it proceeds with the proposed port enhancements. This report addresses the challenge of accurately identifying citizens' concerns and addressing those concerns openly and honestly.

Acknowledgments

Include an acknowledgments page when you want to give credit to people who have assisted with the project. When such recognition is included in the transmittal message, the acknowledgments page is omitted. Acknowledgments are often written in the first person (report writer refers to self and team using I, we, me, us, my, mine, and our), even if the report itself is written in the third person (report writer refers to self and team as the writer, the research team, and so on). The following example demonstrates appropriate acknowledgments for the Charleston report.

Acknowledgments

Many people contributed to the success of this study, and I am grateful to all of them. A special thank you goes to several who contributed in unique ways.

Mary Ann Conrad of the Charleston Merchants Association generously shared the association's directory, from which a sample of merchants was drawn. Harry Hatfield of the Ports Authority's information technology division helped set up the electronic survey that was sent to the merchants. The vestry of St. Stephens Episcopal Church permitted use of its parish hall for the town-hall meetings held in the Ansonbourgh district. Individuals attending the town-hall meetings and merchants who completed the on-line survey willingly provided information about their perceptions of the impact of the cruise industry in Charleston. Their candid comments provided the data necessary to gain a needed perspective. Without their assistance, we would not have been able to produce this report.

To all, a hearty "Thank you."

Marvin L. Barbara
VP, Government Relations
S. C. Ports Authority

Executive Summary

The executive summary, sometimes called a synopsis, immediately precedes the body of the report. Traditionally, an executive summary included the research problem, purpose, research methods, major findings, conclusions, and recommendations. A growing trend is to present the executive summary in the form of an infographic. Whether presented in graphic form or text form, the summary must contain enough information to help each reader decide how much of the full report he or she should read (see Figure 4.13).

Executive Summary

The findings suggest that Charlestonians recognize the cruise business as an ongoing presence in the Port of Charleston and their lives. However, they want the negative aspects of that presence to be ameliorated.

To increase citizens' support for the proposed cruise terminal relocation and waterfront enhancements, the South Carolina Ports Authority must launch an extensive communication campaign. The campaign should publicize specific aspects of the concept plan, emphasizing the benefits to Charlestonians, such as improved vehicular traffic flows and parking, improved visual and human access to the waterfront, ecological reclamation and protection of the waterfront, and reclamation and protection of historical structures in the harbor. As the work progresses, the Authority should issue regular press releases to mark the progress of the project and to inform residents and merchants about construction activities that may temporarily inconvenience them. Constant communication should reassure the citizens of Charleston that the project is moving forward as planned and will soon show major benefits to residents and merchants as well as cruise passengers.

Further, as the Ports Authority proceeds with port relocation, it would be wise to simultaneously begin the proposed waterfront improvements. Such a dual approach will most readily help downtown residents and merchants experience some of the benefits of the project. The following sequence is recommended:

- Complete street construction/traffic alteration projects first.
- Upon completion of the street improvements, begin making improvements to the waterfront at the same time that construction begins on the new terminal site.

The objective of this study was to assess the business and social climate in which the South Carolina Ports Authority will operate if it implements plans to relocate the cruise terminal. Knowledge of that climate will help the Authority develop operational and communication strategies relative to the relocation. Three factors were studied:

1. What business impacts do Charleston's downtown residents and merchants perceive to be related to the arrival and departure of cruise ships?
2. What personal and community impacts do Charleston's downtown residents and merchants perceive to be related to the arrival and departure of cruise ships?
3. What knowledge of and attitudes toward relocation of the cruise terminal are evidenced by Charleston's downtown residents and merchants?

The analysis revealed that the Port Authority's plan to relocate the cruise pier and enhance the Port of Charleston incorporates many principles generally considered essential in contemporary waterfront development. Yet there is no consensus among Charleston residents and merchants about the value of the cruise industry and the proposed waterfront development.

Figure 4.13 Executive summary

Although an analytical report may be written in inductive structure, many readers prefer that the executive summary be written in deductive structure, beginning with the recommendations. One technique for drafting an executive summary is to reduce each major section of the report to one paragraph. After condensing the report in that way, you can revise the draft by arranging the paragraphs into the desired structure and adding transitions to link the paragraphs into a coherent summary.

Some executives prefer that the summary be no longer than one page. The length and complexity of the report, however, most often govern the length of the summary. Unless instructed to do so, do not feel that you must limit the summary to one page.

Working Jointly and Separately on Team Research Reports

In reality, collaborative research and writing are not strictly team efforts. As noted in Chapter 1, collaboration actually involves a combination of collective and independent work, depending on the stage of the project. While project planning needs to be done jointly, the actual collection and analysis of research data may be done independently for greater efficiency.

Working together, the team should plan the research project by:

- Identifying the audience, purpose, and scope of the research project;
- Reviewing the overall project together to ensure a common understanding of the expected outcomes;
- Developing a tentative outline for the final report so that all necessary topics are covered and to guide their data collection and analysis;
- Agreeing on the writing style (formal or informal);
- Making format decisions or choosing a report template that all members will use for their report drafts;
- Assigning specific data-collection responsibilities to individuals on the team; and
- Identifying possible data sources.

When a study involves the use of primary data—as in the FreshMart study and the Charleston study—one or two members of a team might be responsible for designing the survey instruments—the questionnaires or interview guides. However, all members should critically review these instruments before they are used.

During data collection, it may be efficient for team members to function independently, each designated person collecting and interpreting data for the segment of the study assigned to him or her. The team should come together, though, to discuss the data, evaluate its adequacy, and agree on its interpretation. Naturally, if the data are inadequate to fulfill the purpose of the research, team members must return to data-gathering.

Once the team has adequate research data, the members should review the report outline they developed together and adjust it as necessary. Then one or more members is ready to begin drafting the report document, as described in Chapter 1. The final draft should be read carefully by the entire team for any needed changes before the report is finalized.

Summary

Business research reports provide comprehensive data related to a business problem along with interpretation of that data. Some of them are strictly informative (offer no conclusions or recommendations) while others are analytical (draw conclusions and present recommendations).

The report body must include all details of the research in one coherent unit.

> When you write a research report using inductive structure, include these sections in this order in the report body:
>
> ☐ a well-reasoned introduction;
> ☐ thorough presentation, discussion, and summary of research findings; and
> ☐ conclusions and recommendations (analytical reports only).

The report introduction provides a context for understanding and interpreting the whole report.

Ensure that your introduction includes the following elements:

☐ Background of the problem being researched
☐ Statement of the research problem and purpose of the research
☐ Scope of the study
☐ Research procedures used
☐ Delimitations
☐ Limitations
☐ Definitions of terms (or reference to a glossary if many terms require defining).

As a researcher and report writer, your responsibilities are to:

- Collect raw data from secondary and primary sources;
- Reduce the raw data to sets of meaningful information (data analysis);
- Reduce the data sets to major findings (what the data reveal);
- Interpret the findings to produce conclusions and recommendations; and
- Report those findings, conclusions, and recommendations in a formal report.

In any research report, the presentation and discussion of findings make up the main section.

In the findings section of your research reports, make sure that you:

☐ Summarize your data visually (charts, graphs, and tables) when appropriate;
☐ Interpret the data for your readers, telling them what the data mean in relation to the research problem;
☐ Show similarities and differences among data groups and offered an explanation for the differences; and
☐ Use summary headings.

Conclusions, followed by recommendations, usually appear at the end of the report body. But some readers prefer having recommendations, followed by conclusions, at the beginning of the report body. Weather presented inductively or deductively, conclusions must flow logically from the findings.

> After writing the conclusions for your research report, use this checklist to evaluate effectiveness:
>
> ☐ All relevant data and analysis are presented before any conclusion is drawn.
> ☐ Each conclusion interprets findings, rather than restating them.
> ☐ Each conclusion is an objective statement supported by findings—even when it does not fit with your original expectations.
> ☐ Each conclusion is closely related to the report's stated problem and purpose.
> ☐ No conclusion introduces new information.

Recommendations are action statements based on the conclusions. Naturally, each recommendation must respond to the study's purpose. And your recommendations must be fitting to the individuals who will read and possibly act on them and to the organization the readers represent.

> Review your recommendations, looking for these attributes:
>
> ☐ Each recommendation is justified by a specific conclusion.
> ☐ Each recommendation begins with an action verb.
> ☐ Each recommendation includes a plan for implementing it (if needed).
> ☐ One or more recommendations involves further research on questions that arose during your study.

A report's supplementary parts contain related information that is helpful but not essential to understanding the findings, conclusions, and recommendations.

> For your research reports, consider the usefulness of these supplements.
>
> ☐ *Reference list.* If you cite secondary sources in the report body, then include a list of those sources immediately following the report body. This list enables readers to consult those sources if desired.
> ☐ *Glossary.* If your report contains a number of technical terms unfamiliar to some readers, add a glossary, listing each such word and its definition. If your report contains only a few terms needing clarification, omit the glossary and define those terms in the report's introduction.
> ☐ *Appendix.* Include materials that may be useful to some of your readers—such as data collection tools (questionnaires, interview guides, and so forth). Use a separate appendix for each type of helpful, nonessential information.
> ☐ *Index.* In most reports, the table of contents and clear section headings will enable readers to find specific topics. Add an index if you sense that readers may need additional help finding specific information.

The preliminary parts orientate readers to the report body; establish a context for understanding the research; and aid them in navigating the report. Wait until you complete the report body to draft the preliminaries. Then if you revise the report body, make corresponding changes to the preliminary pages. Few reports will include all the preliminaries described in this chapter. The title page, table of contents with list of illustrations, and executive summary are basic. Add other prelims as readers' needs dictate.

Maintain this order for the preliminary parts:

- ☐ *Cover or binder.* The cover or binder will protect report pages, especially if you expect a number of readers to handle the report now and in the future. Include the report title in full or abbreviated form.
- ☐ *Flyleaves.* Insert blank pages at the front and back if you want to connote formality, further protect content pages, or provide space for notetaking.
- ☐ *Title page.* Create a concise title that describes the report content. Include as much 5W information as conciseness allows. Make the title appealing but in keeping with the report's formality. Include these four items of information on your title page:
  - report title at top of the page in a display font;
  - person or agency for which the report was prepared, including contact information;
  - person or agency that prepared the report, with contact information; and
  - report completion date (month and year).
- ☐ *Transmittal message.* Use a personal style for this letter or memo, even if the report body is impersonal. You may opt to present the transmittal message separately. Choose from these content options:
  - review of the research problem, purpose, and methods;
  - highlights of major findings;
  - significant recommendations;
  - comments about the research experience; and
  - an offer to discuss the report or assist with future projects.
- ☐ *Authorization and acceptance messages.* Include these letters or memos to show secondary readers that your report was officially approved and accepted—unless these messages were exchanged orally or you referred to authorization in your transmittal message.

- ☐ *Contents.* Include a table of contents and list of visuals as an overview and navigation tool. List all report preliminaries, report body sections, and report supplements along with the page number on which each item begins. Outline numbering may be used to emphasize the organization of report content.

  If the report contains visuals, list them too. If fewer than four visuals, include them in the table of contents. When listing visuals separately, put them on the contents page if space permits. If only a few visuals are used, group tables and figures. Otherwise, list tables first; then, figures.
- ☐ *Preface.* Include details to generate interest in the report and relate precisely why the study was necessary and its importance. Omit the preface if you included that information elsewhere in the report.
- ☐ *Acknowledgments.* Use an acknowledgment page to recognize individuals who have assisted you with the project, or you can omit this item by mentioning them in the transmittal message. Write acknowledgments in the first person.
- ☐ *Executive summary.* Individual readers will use this synopsis or infographic to decide how much of the report to read, so give a comprehensive summation. Consider using deductive structure for the executive summary, even if the report body uses inductive structure.

Adapt report parts to your particular reporting situations. Know your readers and include only the parts that will assist them.

When working as a research team member, urge your collaborators to plan the project jointly as well as review questionnaires and such. Collect and interpret data individually; then come together to evaluate its adequacy before working independently to draft segments of the report body. All team members should read the final draft carefully before the report is finalized.

CHAPTER 5

Presenting an Oral Report

As you wrap up a written report, you may be expected to stand and deliver; that is, present the information orally to a select audience—often managers and executives in your organization or a client's. All effective presentations begin with planning, regardless of your audience.

Planning a Presentation[1]

Planning an oral report involves analyzing the context and choosing a delivery style, formality level, and structure. Planning also entails outlining your talk, preparing your presentation aids, and anticipating questions your audience may ask.

Analyze the Context

Start planning by examining your purpose; the psychological environment, or audience; and the physical environment. These factors make up the context.

> Ask yourself the following questions about your report and jot your answers:
>
> - What do I want to accomplish, and how do I want the audience to react?
> - Who is the audience, and what are their motives for attending my presentation?
> - When the audience does not know me, will someone introduce me or will I need to introduce myself?
> - About how many people will attend?
> - What does the audience know about my report subject, and what is their attitude toward that topic?

- What are participants expected to do with the information I give them?
- Where will the presentation be held, and what seating arrangements are possible?
- Do I need to arrange for presentation aids, such as a microphone, projector, screen, presenter's pen (combination remote control and laser pointer for use with a slideshow), or whiteboard?
- What are the potential distractions, such as noise, poor lighting, or overcrowding?
- Since "the show must go on," what will I do in case of an equipment malfunction, power outage, or a room that is too cold or too warm? Back-up plans help to eliminate surprises, which in turn boosts your confidence.
- How much time is allotted to my presentation?

Base the remaining planning decisions on your answers to these questions.

Choose a Delivery Style

Most experienced presenters use a combination of extemporaneous (seems conversational despite planning and rehearsal), scripted (reading a manuscript verbatim), and memorized (recitation of rote learning) delivery.

A fourth delivery style, impromptu (conversational and with little or no planning or rehearsal) is not recommended for a report presentation except when you are called upon unexpectedly in a meeting to give a quick update on a project. Even then, you can avoid being caught off guard: Anticipate topics that may be discussed in the meeting; listen to the discussion in case it moves into your area of expertise; and speak for a maximum of two minutes. To avoid rambling, restate your topic; state a key point or two and expand on each point; and tell listeners what you want them to remember.

Decide the Formality Level

Does the context call for a formal report (minimal verbal feedback from audience during presentation), informal report (encourages audience verbal feedback during presentation), or semiformal report (some parts formal, other parts informal)? As a general rule, the larger your audience, the more formal your presentation should be.

The formality level will largely determine how you handle questions and answers at the end of your oral report. Some speaking situations require that the speaker give the audience an opportunity to ask questions during the talk. At other times, the speaker may simply involve the audience by following a presentation with a question-and-answer session. At this point in the planning stage, set some ground rules for dealing with the audience's questions.

Decide on a Structure

Decide which basic structure you will use to organize your talk: direct (audience will readily understand and accept your report without background information and careful explanations) or indirect (audience will need background details and explanations to understand or accept your report, or both).

Continue planning by deciding which of the following organization plans will work best in your situation, or perhaps you will combine two or more of these arrangements.

- Chronological—organized by time units;
- Problem–solution—stated problem followed by proposed solution;
- Cause–effect—relationship between two or more factors;
- Spatial—organized by geographical units;
- Compare and contrast—similarities or differences between two or more entities;
- Topical—organized by subject.

Think of topical as the default structure. When none of the others seems to fit, organize your talk by topics. And you may find that a combination of two structures works well, such as cause–effect together with problem–solution.

Outlining Your Oral Report

Outlining your oral report is vital to prevent rambling; more specifically, to accomplishing your purpose and fulfilling the audiences desire or need for information.

In every case, be sure to include these four parts:

- *Strong opening.* Plan your first words to get audience attention, show relevance of your subject to the audience, and note the main topics you will cover.
- *Well-developed main points.* Divide your message into three to five key ideas; then, for each point, choose details that will support your purpose and lead the audience to take appropriate action. Think about *how* you will express the points of your talk so that you will use engaging language. Here are the techniques for doing so.
  - Think about the terms your subject involves. If the audience will be unfamiliar with these terms, you must either replace technical terms with common words or take time to define terms at the beginning of your presentation.
  - Talk about your subject from the audience's viewpoint. Put yourself in their place. Tell stories that exemplify and explain exactly what your audience needs or wants to know about your subject.
  - Use metaphors, similes, and analogies.
    - ☐ A metaphor makes an implicit, implied, or hidden comparison between two things that are unrelated but share some common characteristics. At the beginning of America's space race, John F. Kennedy spoke this

metaphor: "America has tossed its cap over the wall of space!"
- ☐ A simile makes a direct comparison—with the help of the words like or as—showing similarities between two different things. The author of *Proverbs* wrote this simile: "A lazy person is a pain to employers—like smoke in their eyes or vinegar that sets their teeth on edge."
- ☐ An analogy compares an unfamiliar idea or thing to a familiar, quite different, thing by way of explanation. Here is a time-worn analogy: "Life is like a race. The one who keeps running wins the race, and the one who stops to catch a breath loses."

○ Refer to people, not abstractions. Whenever you can, describe details, especially numerical data, in human terms. Contrast the presenter's words in the following examples:

Abstract terms: What you have is a mounting debt, as the city is assessed $1,000 a day—$365,000 a year—until you implement an acceptable plan.

Human terms: What could your organization do with an additional $365,000 every year? You could buy almost 400 personal computers; that's a computer for almost every classroom in every elementary school in Arcadia Township. You could expand your school-lunch program to feed every needy child in the township. You could extend your after-school programs to cover an additional 3,000 students.

○ Use rhetorical questions and follow the Rule of Three, as shown in the earlier human-terms example.
- ☐ A rhetorical question is one you ask without expecting an answer—as when the presenter asked, "What could your organization do with an additional $365,000 every year?"
- ☐ The Rule of Three is a communication technique that recognizes our ability to remember three items

better than four or seven or even one. By citing three possible uses of the additional funds, the presenter's message is strengthened along with the audience's takeaway.
    o Find thought-provoking facts and quotations related to your subject. Take time to search for appealing examples and quotes from historical or contemporary figures the audience is sure to recognize.
- *Purposeful transitions.* Write down how you will signal to the audience your move from Point A to Point B in your talk and from Point B to Point C, and so on.
- *Memorable conclusion.* What one idea do you want your audience to remember even if they forget everything else you say? If you present an analytical report, you will likely close with at least one recommendation. What will you do to make it stick long-term in participants' minds—not just for the next hour or the remainder of the day?

Preparing Presentation Aids

Base your choices of presentation aids largely on availability, cost, and time constraints. As you know, today's audiences generally expect visuals. You may choose to use direct viewing visuals, such as real objects and models, flip charts, and handouts. In addition, you will likely choose to use at least one projected visual, such as a slide deck, video clip or DVD, and one or more websites.

Prepare a Slide Deck

When you consider using a slide deck—especially for an informal presentation to a small audience—weigh its value against the need for audience interaction. Slide presentations can flatten discussion, sacrifice the richness of dialogue, and reduce audience involvement.

Presentation software options include the following products:

- Haiku Deck and Haiku Deck Zuru (www.haikudeck.com)
- Keynote for iOS (www.apple.com/ios/keynote) and Keynote 6.6.1 for Macintosh (www.apple.com/mac/keynote)
- Microsoft PowerPoint 2016 (products.office.com)
- SoftMaker's Presentations 2016 (www.softmaker.com)
- Google Presentations (www.google.com/slides/about)
- Prezi Business (prezi.com/business)
- Slidebean (slidebean.com)

Three of these products, Keynote, Microsoft PowerPoint, and Soft-Maker's Presentations, are applications for purchase and download. The others products are meant for online use in creating and projecting slides. The Google Presentations program is free. The Prezi Business application is available as a public account (publicly viewable, searchable, and reusable) or on three different subscription plans. Haiku and Slidebean, involve subscriptions.

If you use one slide deck for both your written and oral reports, refer to the content guidelines and design guidelines for slide deck format in Chapter 2.

When you plan and prepare slides for your oral report, keep the following ideas in mind:

- *Choose a design template or theme* provided in the presentation software or develop your own. Select a template that relates to your topic and fits the formality level of your presentation.
- *Avoid using the same few themes time after time.* For variety, you can download free templates from websites such as Google Slides, Presentations Pro, and Smile Templates.
- *Include your name and organization on your opening slide*, along with the title of your talk.
- *Avoid putting text over a patterned background unless the pattern is extremely subtle.* Even large text is hard to read against a bold, multicolored background. Consider using the pattern as a watermark or drawing a solid-color text box over the pattern for holding your text.[2]

- *Plan the right number of slides*—customarily one or two for each minute of your talk. More than that number could cloud more than clarify your message. Fewer than that number can lead to crowding too much information onto each slide. However, the trend is to display four to six simple, self-explanatory slides a minute, in rotation behind the presenter as he or she speaks.[3] The rationale: increased audience engagement and improved comprehension of content.
- *If including bullet points on your slides* (not recommended), *use a readable font size.* Think of size 40 to 44 for slide titles, 36 for subpoints, and 32 for supporting details. Use no text smaller than 24.
- *Follow the 7 × 7 rule for bullet points.* Put no more than seven lines of text on a slide and no more than seven words per line. (Use parallel, abbreviated sentences.) Thus, about one-fourth of each slide will be blank.
- *Consider replacing bullet points on a slide with one short, simple word in huge letters.* Make the word attractive and memorable by using a strong color and creative font. For a selection of creative fonts that you can download for free, visit PresentationPanda (presentationpanda.com/uncategorized/download-these-free-fonts-to-spice-up-your-presentations[4]).
- *Add images to your slides*, including charts and graphs, maps, photographs, and tables, recalling the guidelines in Chapter 3. Make each image large enough for the audience to see whatever details you want them to notice.
- *Prepare each image to focus on one main point.* Sometimes you may need to prepare more than one graphic rather than crowding too much data into one exhibit.
- *Choose harmonious colors and ensure sharp contrast between the slide background and content.* Select three colors—one for background, one for base, and one for accent. The background and base should be colors within a group on the color wheel (such as the warm colors red-orange and yellow or the cool colors blue-green and violet), while the accent color

should represent a shade furthest away from the background and base (for example, a blue to accent warm colors and an orange to accent cool colors).[5] The most reliable approach to presentation color is to use ColorBrewer (colorbrewer2.org) that is discussed in Chapter 3 (page 126).
- *Strictly limit animation, slide transitions, and sound effects.* If your oral report is lengthy, having one of these features occasionally could be useful to recapture audience attention. But too many special effects detract from, rather than enhance, your oral report.

An online presentation, or webinar—using WebEx, Citrix, or GoTo-Webinar, for example—calls for slightly different planning and preparation of your slide deck.

> Take these additional steps when planning a webinar:[6]
>
> - *Create a smashing cover, or title, slide.* Grab audience attention from the outset. Seeing your awareness of details on the first slide will tell the audience you are prepared to give them information they need or want or both.
> - *If your meeting software will not involve video conferencing, insert your photo near the beginning of your slide deck*, along with your name, organization, and job title (unless you are well known to the webinar participants). Thus the webinar audience can visualize you talking to them.
> - *Omit your image from the slides, if you will be seen on camera as you present.* Then remember to dress as you would for a face-to-face presentation and tidy those parts of your work space that will be seen on video.
> - *Plan more slides than you would when presenting face-to-face*—about four per minute in a webinar. Since the audience cannot literally focus on you, their attention may tend to wander. Additional slides will reduce that tendency.

- *Omit slides you would show for only a few seconds and* or text builds that rely on being synchronized with your spoken words.
- *If you will not be presenting on video, highlight what you want participants to look at on each slide.*
- *Create a special slide to display during question-and-answer time.* It may contain a relevant photo, the word Questions, or simply a large question mark. Dispense with this slide if you will use interactive presentation software, such as Zeetings (zeetings.com), Swipe (swipe.com), or OfficeMix (mix.office.com) for questions and answers. Audience questions, rather than a slide, will appear on the screen during the Q&A session.

Prepare a Handout

A face-to-face presentation or webinar can benefit from the use of audience handouts. These handouts can be your slide deck. (If so, include space for participants to jot their thoughts on how to apply the points of your message to their individual situations.) Another option is a handout that includes your slides plus your expanded notes. Expanded notes—which may include images and text not on the slides—have advantages for the audience (extra information) and for you (better than slides alone for keeping you on track as you speak). Therefore, become familiar with the software feature for creating notes along with your slide deck. In Keynote the feature is called Presenter Notes; in PowerPoint, Notes Pages; and in Prezi the feature is called Presenter View.

As part of your preparation, consider posting your handout in a file hosting service, such as Dropbox (dropbox.com), E-box (www.e-box.net), Mega (www.mega.nz), Sync.com (www.sync.com), or TeamDrive (www.teamdrive.com).[7] Then a few days before your oral report, notify the audience where the handout is stored. Individuals who want a handout to write on as you present can print your file and bring the printout with them to your talk. When compared with printing handouts, toting them to your presentation, and distributing them to the audience, this practice conserves effort, paper, printer ink, and time.

Dave Paradi at Think Outside the Slide offers an even greener (friendlier to the environment) option.[8] Start by saving your slide deck as a PDF file, one slide per page, selecting only the slides you want in your handout. Then use Adobe Acrobat Pro to enable Comments in the PDF file. Now, upload the PDF to one of the file hosting services. People who attend your oral report can download the files to a laptop, tablet, or smartphone. Tell audience members in advance to download your handout file as no paper handouts will be provided. At your presentation, show the web address so attendees can download the handout during the presentation—if Wi-Fi service is available.

Attendees can view and take notes on the handouts in the following ways:

- Print the handout in advance—preferably four slides to a page to save paper—using Adobe Acrobat Reader.
- Download the file to a laptop and use Acrobat Reader to add sticky notes.
- Use a PDF or book reader program to take notes on a smartphone or tablet.

Prepare for a Question-and-Answer Session

The first rule in managing a formal question-and-answer session is to allow a realistic amount of time for it, in light of your message content and the context in which it is given.

As an expert on your topic, you can anticipate specific questions. You can usually expect questions related to the most complex or controversial parts of your oral report. Additionally, you can prepare to answer those questions, using the impromptu delivery style described earlier. (In fact, some presenters have a slide in stand by for the top two or three questions they anticipate.)

Decide when and how you will take questions. Then the person who introduces you should announce this information after making the introduction. If you prefer, you certainly may provide this information; but do so after your strong opening.

You have several options for taking questions:

- Direct questions during your oral report.
- Direct questions at the end of your presentation.
- Questions via the Twitter backchannel (a secondary conversation about a presentation, presenter, or both that takes place online during an actual presentation).
- Questions online through an interactive presentation app, such as Zeetings. Besides audience questions and comments, an interactive presentation app combines slides, videos, audience polls, and Web content. While facilitating a presentation, the app can also collect and analyze data about audience reactions to the presenter's topic.[9]

Each option for questions is discussed fully later in the chapter. If you decide that the Twitter backchannel is appropriate for your Q&A, create a clear, short, unique hashtag early in your preparation. If fitting, generate interest in your talk by displaying the hashtag in every e-mail, poster, social media post, or tweet about your oral report.[10] In addition, consider using that Twitter account in advance to collect input from people who will attend your presentation. Ask them to share challenges they face that you can help resolve and suggestions for what you should cover or emphasize in your talk.

Whether using the Twitter backchannel or an interactive presentation app, the planning stage—when you are analyzing your audience very carefully—is a good time to decide whether to accept anonymous comments and questions (for a professional, mature audience) or only comments and questions that include the sender's name.[11]

Planning Team Oral Reports

Previous guidelines apply to the planning of a solo presentation. Since collaboration is standard practice in business settings, planning for team oral reports is a necessary skill.

Team presenters can benefit from the following pointers:

- *Assign responsibility for specific parts of the oral report to specific team members.* Try to assign primary responsibility for a part to the person most knowledgeable about it, and make speaking assignments roughly equal in length.
- *Strive to make each team member conversant with all parts of the report.*
- *For a team of relatively inexperienced presenters, plan for a distributed (divided) format.* Divide topics in the report outline, one or two to each person.
- For experienced presentation teams, consider using the merged (integrated) format. Members collaborate on a very detailed outline of points and examples; then they take turns presenting within each point.
- *Designate one team member to serve as coordinator.* This person introduces the presentation, team members, and topics, and may also summarize the report and moderate the question-and-answer session that follows.

After planning and organizing the content of your oral report, preparing your presentation aids, and thinking ahead to audience questions and your answers, you are ready to rehearse your oral report.

Rehearsing an Oral Report

Some of our society's most memorable public speakers—Abraham Lincoln, Winston Churchill, Martin Luther King, Jr.—were known to practice extensively before delivering a speech. In the business world, the late Steve Jobs, Apple's cofounder, was a world-famous presenter, who spent hours rehearsing. "To be more precise: many, many hours over many, many days."[12] A prominent consultant to high-level business presenters Nancy Duarte recommends 30 hours of rehearsal for an hour-long presentation.[13] Another writer suggested that you practice delivering your talk 7 to 10 times before your actual presentation.[14]

Practice your oral report until you are confident that you can handle all aspects with finesse. Rehearse not only the verbal content of the message but also your posture, gestures, and use of presentation aids. In addition, anticipate possible questions and rehearse appropriate answers.

If possible, rehearse before an audience—even if it is only one person, such as a helpful family member or coworker, who will provide honest feedback about the message content and your delivery style. When possible, rehearse in the room in which you will deliver your oral report.

If you cannot rehearse before an audience, make a video of your rehearsal so that you can do a critical self-analysis. As you evaluate your rehearsal, consider all planning aspects given previously and the following guidelines in this chapter. As you rehearse, do all the things you will do during your actual presentation, and time your presentation to be sure it fits into your allotted time.

Manage Your Notes

Blogger Matt Egan called attention to "a mania ... for speaking without notes, as if you need to be able to do so to be credible." Egan went on to say that being able to give a presentation with or without notes says nothing about your competence. He further advised that one way to give better presentations is to have notes with which you are comfortable.[15]

So, during rehearsal, experiment with different ways of managing your notes or manuscript. Some presenters use cards for extemporaneous talks; others prepare their notes on sheets of paper; still others use a handheld electronic device. Whatever method you prefer, you should practice so that your notes or manuscript are unobtrusive. Use the guidelines in Figure 5.1 to manage your presentation notes.

Manage Symptoms of Nervousness

Most people experience some level of nervousness, or speech anxiety, when they have to give a talk. (Surveys of the general public have repeatedly identified speaking before an audience as "the worst human fear."[16])

- If using a slide show, print your slides to use as notes. Arrange to have a speaker's stand on which to rest printouts.
  - Turning eyes away from the audience during an oral report to look at projected slides is NOT an option!
  - Add speaker's notes to each slide and print each slide and the corresponding notes on a page. The speaker's notes will not be projected for the audience to see.
  - Use Presenter View in PowerPoint to view your presentation with speaker notes on one computer (for example, your laptop) while your audience views the notes-free presentation on a different monitor (projected on a larger screen).
- If using note cards, record key points only. Exceptions: Since a strong opening is essential, you may record every word of it, especially if presenting causes anxiety. Likewise, you may record every word of your memorable closing, to ensure that you present it exactly as you planned it.
  - Do not use too many cards; try to limit yourself to one card for the opening, one for each main point in the body, and one for the closing.
  - Number these cards. Arrange them in numerical sequence with a rubber band around them. Remove the band just before your presentation.
  - Hold the cards or place them on the speaker's stand. (Holding the cards gives you more freedom to walk away from the speaker's stand during your oral report.) If you hold them, slip each card to the back of the deck as you complete its use. If you place the cards on the stand, put the used cards face down in a stack next to the deck.
  - Alternative 1: Staple cards in sequence inside a file folder and place the opened folder on the speaker's stand.
  - Alternative 2: Record all your notes on a single 5-by-8 card.
  - Alternative 3: Record key points of your talk in the Memo app on your phone. Adjust settings as needed to make your notes legible at a glance.
- Use letter-sized paper for a manuscript when you will use scripted (word-for-word) delivery style or if you want a confidence boost, when presenting extemporaneously. In the latter case, do not read the manuscript to the audience; only refer to it as needed. Ideally, you will be able to rest the pages on a speaker's stand so that your audience is not distracted by the rustling of paper.
  - Use a font size that is easy to read from an erect standing position.
  - Double-space the text and use 1.5-inch or 2-inch side margins; use only the top two-thirds of the page to help you maintain eye contact with your audience while also glancing at your notes.
  - Mark emphasis points in your manuscript pages using any combination of arrows, bold text, different colors, and underlining. Then use those cues as reminders to raise or lower your voice, slow down, pause, speed up, or smile.
  - Number the sheets and arrange them numerically, sliding each sheet unobtrusively to the side as you complete its use.
  - Alternative: When you will present extemporaneously, create a manuscript as suggested; but instead of printing it, open the file on your phone or tablet.

Figure 5.1 Guidelines for handling presentation notes

You may be familiar with common symptoms of speech anxiety: shaking, sweating, queasiness, dry mouth, rapid heartbeat, and squeaky voice.[17] (Fainting, hyperventilation, and vomiting are among the more severe symptoms.)

A small amount of tension before a presentation can be beneficial. Nervousness before an oral report can make you alert and prompt you to prepare thoroughly for your talk. But extreme nervousness may indicate that your focus is not where it should be. You may be placing attention on yourself and audience reaction to you, instead of attending to them, their needs, and how your message will meet those needs. The following list includes ways to overcome public-speaking anxiety or to make the anxiety work in your favor.

To overcome public-speaking anxiety:

- *Identify the cause of your anxiety.* Make a list of specific reasons why you feel anxious. Then make a matching list of ways you can deal with each fear.[18]
- *Justify your presentation.* Remind yourself that you have been asked to present because you possess information that others need or want—but do not have.
- *Bolster your self-confidence.* Make a list of all you know about the topic that your audience likely does not know and needs to know. Remind yourself of previous successful communication experiences, even minor ones. Eliminate problems that may have plagued your earlier presentations. Envision yourself (attired for the occasion) giving the presentation with confidence—from the first word of your strong opening to the last word of your memorable closing. Close your eyes and do a mental rehearsal of your oral report a few times before you deliver it.[19]
- *Trust your audience.* Most audiences are empathetic, receptive, and friendly. If you attract favorable attention with your opening words and show that you respect your audience's intelligence and needs, you stand an excellent chance

> of being respected in return. After all, the audience is not there to look at or judge you; it is present to hear what you have to say.
> - *Prepare fully for the presentation.* Prepare so thoroughly that you can vary your presentation to meet audience needs and can actually enjoy communicating important data to others. Think of the presentation as a conversation—an informed, animated one—on a topic that is important to you and your audience.
> - *Arrive early.* Become comfortable with the room and check seating arrangements and equipment that will influence your presentation. Chat with audience members who arrive early. Doing so will make you seem friendly, relaxed, confident—and credible. Then as you begin your presentation, not everyone in the audience will be a stranger.
> - *Use stress reduction techniques* just before and during your presentation.

Stress reduction techniques that speakers use successfully are shown in Figure 5.2.

In addition to controlling nervousness, effective speakers demonstrate control of the vocal and verbal aspects of speech.

Manage Vocal and Verbal Aspects

The vocal aspect of speech communication is the quality of sounds that come from your mouth; the verbal aspect relates to the clarity of words that come from your lips.

Vocal quality is controlled by three elements: inhalation, phonation, and resonation.

Inhalation

Inhalation is the process of taking air in through your mouth and nostrils for temporary storage in your lungs. That air is the fuel that powers speech

> **In private, a few minutes before assuming your presentation position:**
>
> - Stand tall (regardless of your actual height) as though you have just been declared champion and hold this power pose for two minutes. Studies by Harvard Business School psychologist Amy Cuddy showed that this technique decreases cortisol (the stress hormone) and increases testosterone (the assertiveness hormone).[20]
> - Breathe deeply and exhale slowly. This technique tends to relax the body and supplies the oxygen necessary for clear thinking. For more breathing exercises to calm and control anxiety, go to Write-Out-Loud (www.write-out-loud.com/ sitemap.html).
> - With arms hanging loosely at your sides, clench your fists, and then relax the fingers. Imagine and feel the tension flowing out of your body through the tips of your fingers.
> - Swallow a few times (without gulping air) and wiggle your jaw slightly to relax the muscles that control your throat and jaw.
> - If your mouth feels dry, sip water from a glass. Take the glass with you, placing it within reach but not in plain view of the audience.
>
> **Once you assume your presentation position:**
>
> - Pause before speaking a word. Sweep your eyes over the audience and smile. Note the participants who smile back at you, because they are the individuals to look at often (not exclusively) as you speak.
> - Look directly at one of the smiling participants and imagine conversing with that person.
> - Begin your planned opening with a confident tone. Acting confident (even if you are not) will establish rapport with your audience. Once you "connect" with the audience, your confidence will likely grow throughout your presentation.
> - Remember to smile often as you speak, unless the topic is so serious that a smile is inappropriate.

Figure 5.2 Anxiety reduction techniques

and supplies oxygen to your brain. When you breathe deeply, using your diaphragm (area between lower ribs and waistline), you take in a larger supply of fuel than you do when you breathe shallowly. Practice breathing exercises frequently to improve control of inhalation and exhalation. To find several effective inhalation (breathing) exercises, go to the Weil website (www.drweil.com).

Phonation

Sound is produced in the phonation phase. As you exhale, pushing the air out of your lungs, the air passes through your larynx, commonly called the voice box. The voice box has membranous surfaces called vocal folds.

Those folds vibrate as air passes over them, producing sound or vocal pitch. If the folds vibrate quickly, which occurs when the throat muscles are tense, the sound is high pitched. When the folds vibrate slowly, which occurs when the throat muscles are relaxed, the sound has a lower pitch. In general, a lower pitch is more pleasing to audiences than is a high pitch. Therefore, relaxing the vocal folds during speech is an important speaking skill to master. For useful phonation exercises, go to Voice-Over Voice Actor (www.voiceovervoiceactor.com).

Resonation

After passing through your voice box, the air enters the resonating cavities of your head. In this resonation phase, vocal timbre (quality) is determined. The cavities act as echoing chambers. If sound is permitted to resonate freely in the cavities, a rich, warm sound is produced. But if the cavities are constricted or closed, a strident or nasal sound is produced. To produce rich, pleasing sounds, try the exercises on the Voice Therapy page at Yeson Voice Center (www.yesonvc.net).

Articulation

Although you can create sound by inhalation, phonation, and resonation, you do not form words until the modification or articulation stage of speech. In this stage, you use your lips, teeth, tongue, and palate to form three kinds of sound:

- *Vowels.* Represented by the letters a, e, i, o, and u, a vowel is any sound that continues indefinitely as long as there is breath to support it (for example, a-a-a-a, e-e-e-e, and so on).
- *Diphthongs.* A diphthong is a sound made by combining two vowels, especially when it starts as one vowel sound and glides to another, like the oy sound in coin. In some diphthongs the vowels blend so rapidly they seem to produce one sound (for example, ei sounding like long i, as in height, and ie sounding like long e, as in pier).

- *Consonants.* A consonant is a sound other than a vowel or diphthong, many of which stop or interrupt themselves no matter how much breath is available (for example, k, p, and l).

Understandable speech results from precise articulation of all word components. One way to improve articulation is to practice pronouncing and enunciating difficult letter and word combinations. The tongue twisters you may recall from childhood were essentially articulation drills. For articulation exercises designed for presenters, visit the Diction Exercises page at Write-Out-Loud (www.write-out-loud.com/sitemap.htm).

The unique way that words are articulated by a group of people speaking the same language is called an accent. Thus, everybody speaks with an accent. Accents are a natural part of spoken languages and are usually classified as regional accents or foreign accents.[21]

Linguists have identified seven regional accents, or dialects, of American English speakers in North America (New England, New York City and Mid-Atlantic States, North, Midland, South, West, and Canada).[22] Because of regional accents, people who grew up in Indiana generally sound different from people who are from California. Because of foreign accents, a person who grew up speaking American English will sound different from someone from Rio de Janeiro who was raised speaking Portuguese and learned English as an adult. Similarly, someone raised in the United States may speak Spanish with an English accent.[23] A presenter's accent becomes a problem only when it detracts from his or her message or is unintelligible to an audience. In those cases, a person might consider accent reduction—also known as deaccentation, elocution, accent modification, or accent neutralization. In general, accent reduction is a method of learning a new accent. More specifically, accent reduction is the process of learning the phonology (sound system) of a language or dialect.[24]

Modifying a foreign accent often requires work with a speech-language trainer, either in person or online. Examples of speech-language trainers include the following organizations:

- Accent Reduction Institute (www.lessaccent.com)
- Accent Reduction Training Association (www.relaxandspeak. com/accent reduction/artamethod.html)

- ALTA (www.altalang.com)
- Testden (www.testden.com/index.htm)
- Voice Power Studios (www.voicepowerstudios.com)

Accent reduction training usually begins with an individual reading words, sentences, and paragraphs, and conversing as a trainer listens. Then the trainer sets goals based on the individual's needs, and individual or small-group training sessions ensue.[25]

The following exercises can be helpful in modifying an accent.[26]

To modify a regional accent:

- Listen to a clear speaker of the accent you want to acquire and repeat aloud after him or her.
- Record yourself reading, telling a story, or giving a presentation. Then review your recording, which will allow you to hear yourself as others hear you.
  - Listen for unclear vowel sounds, omitted final consonants, and metered speech (every word pronounced with equal intonation and stress).
  - Be sure to stress the correct syllable in multisyllabic words.
  - Make adjustments as needed and rerecord.
- Get a conversation partner; work with an ESL (English as a second language) tutor; join a chapter of Toastmasters International (www.toastmasters.org); or join your local organization of ProLiteracy Worldwide (proliteracy.org). Specify what you are working on—say, dropping word endings or selective replacement of r with ah—and ask to be corrected when you miss one.
- Ask your conversation partner or tutor for a list of 6 to 12 words that you pronounced in your existing accent. Next, ask another speaker to record those words for you. Then listen and repeat aloud, again and again, in your new accent.
- Speak slowly whenever you speak. Finish each word—including the final consonant—before starting the next

word. Practice speaking your new accent at least 15 minutes a day five days a week.
- Learn local expressions. Learn what words are used often in your region to describe things. A few examples follow.[21]
  - Is the evening meal called dinner or supper?
  - Do people in your region cut on the light or turn on the light?
  - Are rubber-soled sport shoes called sneakers or tennis shoes?
  - Is the first and last piece of bread in a loaf called the butt, crust, end, or heel?
  - Is a long cold-cut sandwich called a grinder, hoagie, sub, or submarine sandwich?
  - Would someone ask you to crack the window, open the window, or crack open the window?

To reduce a foreign accent:

- Watch YouTube channels devoted to accent reduction and American English pronunciation, such as Rachel's English (www.youtube.com/user/rachelsenglish). Listening to TED talks on a subject that interests you may also be helpful.
- Master the most pervasive sounds in the English language first: th, v, and w, r, and the many different pronunciations of the letter o.
- Use an online dictionary with sound. Look up words and listen to the pronunciation.
- Listen to something in English daily: an audio book, a film, a news program, songs, or TV shows.
- Listen to a podcast in English and read the text simultaneously. After each paragraph, record yourself reading the paragraph, using free online audio recording software, such as one of these programs.

- Ardour for Linux and Mac OS X (ardour.org/features.html)
- Audacity for Linux, Mac OS X, and Windows (audacity.en.softonic.com/download)
- GarageBand for iOS and Mac OS X (www.apple.com/ios/garageband)
- Presonus Studio One Free for Mac OS X and Windows (shop.presonus.com/products/studio-one-prods/Studio-One-Free).

Understanding the four elements of speech will help you realize that, through practice, you can control and improve the vocal and verbal qualities of speech. Through that control, you can improve the clarity of your oral reports and the ease of understanding them.

You can also improve oral reports by gaining greater control of your presentation aids.

Manage Your Presentation Aids

Presentation aids are audio and visual tools used to supplement your spoken message. A microphone, for example, improves your presentation in a large room. A large infographic poster helps you explain or dramatize data. A slide deck illustrates key points and links you to additional presentation aids on the web.

Use presentation aids to attract and hold attention, clarify meanings, emphasize or elaborate main ideas, or prove a point.

Using Presentation Aids Face-to-Face

Presentation aids are just that—aids. In a face-to-face oral report, you, as the presenter, are the center or focus. Choose only tools that enhance or extend your effectiveness. Then incorporate the aids smoothly into your oral report, leaving the audience largely oblivious to them.

The guidelines in Figure 5.3 will help you use a microphone and slide deck effectively. Follow these guidelines in both your rehearsal and actual report.

> **When using a microphone:**
> - Use your natural speaking voice.
> - Avoid having the mic too close to avoid extraneous noise.
>   - An appropriate distance for most mics is six inches from the speaker's mouth.
>   - Attach a lapel microphone to the inside of your lapel so your voice can be heard clearly whenever you turn your head.
> - Designate one person to signal you if the microphone volume is too loud or too soft or if a visual is not visible. Make necessary adjustments before your audience becomes distracted.
>
> **When using a slide deck:**
> - Remember that slides are meant to enrich your message, not become the message.
> - Display a slide only when you are ready to talk about it.
> - Do not block your audience's view of slides. Use a laser pointer or presenter's pen or walk to the screen and point with your index finger.
> - Speak to your audience, not to your slides. Face your audience as much as possible as you explain portions of the visual.
> - Do not remove a slide before the audience has had an opportunity to examine the contents. Do remove it when it is no longer relevant. If necessary, blank the screen briefly before advancing to the next slide. (In PowerPoint select Screen on the pop-up menu or tap "b" [for black] or "w" [for white] on the computer keyboard. Repeat the action when ready to display the slide.)
> - Make no reference to a slide once you have removed it from view. If you must show a slide again, do not click back through intervening slides to get to it. Instead display the slide list and select the one you want from the list. Return to your place in the deck the same way.
> - Following the last content slide, include a plain slide or image that will not distract the audience as you close your presentation and answer questions.

Figure 5.3 Guidelines for using selected presentation aids

Using Presentation Aids in a Webinar

Businesses have found that in many cases webinar presentations can be as effective as face-to-face ones. Naturally effectiveness is greatly influenced by the presenter's preparation. Use the techniques shown in Figure 5.4 to make the most of a webinar.

External factors, such as how you look and how you interact with your audience, will greatly affect your success as a presenter. These external factors can be described in one word: nonverbal. And nonverbal aspects are vitally important.

Take this action in your webinar	For this reason
Use a remote control (instead of the mouse or space bar) to advance slides, even though you are at your computer.	The remote will remind you of presenting face-to-face, increasing your awareness of your webinar audience "out there."
Use a timer app on your phone or a wristwatch to monitor the time.	Knowing that the presentation is on track helps you relax and attend to the audience.
When transmitting audio only, tell participants when you are going to be silent. Let them know, for example, if you will take a sip of water. If you display a slide you want them to read—a quotation, perhaps—introduce the slide with, "I'll let you read . . ."	Otherwise, participants may think they have lost the sound.
Use shorter pauses than you would face-to-face with the audience. Instead of long, dramatic pauses, insert tiny pauses between phrases and sentences.	Long pauses could make the audience think sound has been cut off.
Break for questions at the end of each section in your talk, with or without the benefit of the Twitter backchannel or interactive presentation app.	Participants—who will type their questions when they come to mind—will not have to wait too long to get answers.
If the webinar participants are not using the backchannel or interactive app (in which case questions will appear on everyone's computer screen automatically), have an assistant ask you the participants' questions.	Q&A will be smoother and more natural if you avoid monitoring questions on one screen and projecting answers from another.

Figure 5.4 Guidelines for presenting a webinar[28]

Manage Nonverbal Aspects

In any situation you will have 90 seconds (or less) to create a good first impression. And most of that impression will be formed on the basis of these nonverbal factors: your appearance, posture, eye contact, facial expressions, gestures, and mobility.

Appearance

The first impression that your audience forms of you—the type of person you are and what you have to offer them—is derived from your appearance. If you want to be thought of as a competent, professional person, you must present yourself as one. Basically, dress in such a way that people do not notice specific items that you are wearing but get an overall impression that you are well groomed.

For most formal presentations, men cannot go wrong wearing a suit, dress shirt, and tie, and women, a conservative suit or dress. In less formal settings, a man may safely wear a sports jacket and slacks; and a woman may wear a skirt or slacks, blouse, and scarf.

More importantly, though, look closely at the context of your talk. If you are presenting within your organization, dress according to the company's explicit or implied dress code. This could mean a man opting for khakis, button-down shirt, and loafers and women choosing slacks with a blouse and cardigan. If you will be at a trade show or conference, take into account the culture within the industry. Dress more casually when addressing people who work in artistic and technology fields; but wear dark, tailored garments when presenting to an audience in the finance arena.[29]

Another way to determine proper attire: How will the audience be dressed? Unless they will wear formal business dress, attire yourself slightly better; that is, more dressed up. If the audience is going to dress down, as many business people do these days, you, as a presenter, can too—but not as much. Opt for something on the smarter end of the dress-down scale.[30]

For additional help in deciding what to wear for a presentation, observe other presenters of your gender and make your own list of do's and don'ts. And ask a savvy associate for advice. Be sure your clothes are comfortable and that the colors complement you. In addition, wear a neat hairstyle that complements your features but draws no excessive attention to itself. Jewelry, if worn, should not be distracting. In all situations, avoid gaudiness and extremes.

Your posture works hand in hand with your attire in conveying that all-important first impression.

Posture

Your posture should suggest that you are in control of the presentation. Avoid slouching or rigidity as you stand or sit before your audience. Slouching connotes indifference or carelessness; rigidity indicates nervousness. In contrast, sitting or standing erectly tends to signify self-confidence, interest, alertness, readiness, and enthusiasm.

As you stand, place your feet 10 to 12 inches apart, with one slightly in front of the other (to reduce any tendency to sway from side to side). Balance your weight evenly on both feet; let your hands hang loosely at your sides; keep your spine erect, shoulders back, and stomach in. That position permits you to inhale and exhale properly for effective speaking. From that stance, you can also use your hands easily and naturally for gestures and move smoothly to a new position.

If you sit at a conference table with your audience, move comfortably to the back of the chair, permitting it to support your back and feeling the edge of the seat behind your knees. Place both feet flat on the floor, one slightly in front of the other, to keep yourself balanced and to prevent yourself from slouching or twisting in the chair.

Eye Contact

In most Western cultures, eye contact is considered essential for effective communication. Lack of such contact suggests discomfort, uncertainty, embarrassment, or even dishonesty. Through eye contact, you convey your interest in and concern about the audience. In addition, by maintaining that communication link with your audience, you can detect the reactions of individuals to your message. You will see enthusiasm, understanding, interest—or their opposites. When you note negative feedback, you have an opportunity to adjust your presentation to meet the needs of your audience. Eye contact will then tell you whether your adjustments are effective.

To make proper eye contact, you must look at individuals' eyes—not over their heads. Stick to a "Z" pattern for systematic but varied eye contact. (The top of the "Z" represents people in the back row; the bottom of the letter, people in the front row.)

- Start with a friendly or familiar face or the first person on your left in the back row; look in the eyes for a few seconds (finish a thought).

- Instead of eyeing the person seated next, skip a few people. (When you look directly at one person, the people around him or her feel included in your glance.)
- Continue to look and skip in a "Z" around the room. On finishing the "Z," return to an individual you skipped near the beginning.

In a very large audience, where individual eye contact may become impossible, divide the room into quadrants and look to each quadrant in turn, making sure to include people in the far corners. Everyone in that section will likely feel included in your eye contact.

Facial Expressions

Facial expressions convey emotions with remarkable accuracy. When you give an oral report, your facial expressions should suggest your enthusiasm for the material. Also, your expressions should show your interest in your listeners and your desire to communicate with them. Those feelings will be conveyed if you develop a positive mental attitude toward your report and your audience. In contrast, if you are nervous and unsure about your presentation, those feelings will likely be registered in your facial expressions. Therefore, the best way to control nonverbal facial communication is to be thoroughly prepared for and confident about your presentation. Some presenters mark their notes with reminders to pause occasionally and smile naturally, as though conversing with an acquaintance.

Gestures

Effective speakers do not remain stiffly in one position throughout an oral presentation. Use gestures—body movements—to complement your words. You probably use gestures spontaneously during interpersonal communication; try to achieve that same spontaneity in your more formal presentations. (But carefully avoid touching your face or head or fixing your hair.)

One way to improve gestures is to use them purposely in all oral communication situations. Another, is to use gestures deliberately while rehearsing your oral report, but do not think about gestures during the actual delivery. If you practice your presentation several times, concentrating on large, sweeping gestures, they will tend to become natural and provide appropriate emphasis during your talk. (Bigger audiences need larger gestures.)

Although some gesturing can improve your presentation, excessive body movement can become distracting. Use gestures purposefully to emphasize or clarify, not merely to release excess energy.

Guidelines for using arms and hands during a presentation are shown in Figure 5.5.[31]

Exceptions to these guidelines can be helpful if used only rarely: A clenched fist brought down on the lectern may be used to emphasize or to express anger; arms raised quickly, to express surprise; and an index finger pointed assertively at the floor, to convey urgency.

Two gestures to use habitually include raising fingers sequentially to enumerate and moving arms and hands to suggest size, shape, or motion. For more recommended gestures, including illustrations of them, see "20 Hand Gestures You Should Be Using" at Science of People (www.scienceofpeople.com).

If your audience is an international one, be aware that gestures have different connotations in different cultures. Some common gestures in

Keep hands in view at all times. Do not grasp the sides of the speaker's stand (lectern).
Start and end each gesture in the gesture neutral position; that is, with hands hanging loosely at your sides. Return to this position if you catch yourself making several unintentional gestures.
Confine gestures to what speech coaches (and baseball enthusiasts) *call the strike zone*; that is, between your shoulders and the top of your hips.
Hold only those objects, such as a presenter's pen, that can be used to enhance your oral report; put it down when not using it.
Avoid repetitive gestures, such as slicing the air, which become meaningless and distracting.
Use your whole hand, or the index and middle fingers together, to point at someone or something. Pointing with the index finger alone—especially at a person—may be seen as a rude gesture by some audience members, depending on their cultural background.
Keep palms open and turned up, a sign of trustworthiness.

Figure 5.5 Guidelines for using gestures

the United States that may be offensive in another culture are listed in Figure 5.6.[32]

Mobility

Purposeful walking during your oral report helps you hold audience attention and support your spoken message. Choose three spots in the presentation area to stand. (Guard against standing in front of your visuals.) Designate a central location to open your oral report.[33] Practice planting your feet on that spot and staying there for at least 30 seconds before walking to one of the other places. Then take two or three steps and plant your feet for another 30 seconds or more. Staying put for a minimum of 30 seconds each time guards against the appearance of pacing. Concentrating on just three places keeps you from wandering aimlessly.

Time your mobility to coincide with point-to-point transitions in your report, whether you talk or stop talking as you walk. Doing so emphasizes what you just said and signals a shift in topic. Walking to the center when you introduce or review your main message or theme equates your central idea and the center of the space.

To create closeness with the audience during your presentation, walk slowly toward them while talking softly. This move denotes the sharing of personal information. Finally, close your talk in the central location where you began.[34]

Besides rehearsing all aspects of your oral report, prepare to interact with the audience electronically.

Manage Background Conversations

As already noted, the backchannel is a secondary conversation about a presentation or presenter that takes place via Twitter during an oral report. These background conversations have become just another part of presenting and attending presentations. Interactive online presentation apps, such as OfficeMix, Swipe, and Zeetings, include features and advantages of the backchannel—in addition to many others—and may eventually replace the popular Twitter backchannel.

Action	Called	Meaning in the United States	Meanings in some other cultures
Raising left or right thumb	Thumbs-up	"I agree" or "I approve."	Highly offensive in Middle East; an insult in Bangladesh; number one in France, Germany, or Russia.
Forming "o" by bringing index finger and thumb together	Ok sign	"Everything is okay" (all right, fine, great, or perfect).	Obscene gesture in Arab countries, Brazil, and Germany; money in Japan; zero or useless in France.
Crooking an index finger	Come here sign	Used to ask a person, such as an audience member, to step forward.	Rude for beckoning a person in Asian cultures.
Raising left or right index and little fingers	Horn fingers (originally used by rock and heavy-metal band members)	"I approve"; "rock on"; "what's up?" In American Sign Language, "I love you."	"Your spouse is cheating on you" in some Mediterranean and Latin countries. A curse in some parts of Africa.
Raising left or right index and middle fingers	V sign or peace sign (Vietnam era) and victory sign (WWII era)	Peace	Insulting in Australia, Ireland, New Zealand, South Africa, and the United Kingdom, especially when back of hand is turned to audience.

Figure 5.6 Presentation gestures: Possible cross-cultural meanings

Today's presenters generally encourage audiences to transmit questions and feedback to them and to share comments with one another and other interested people outside the presentation room. However, not all presenters and audience members have agreed on the value of background conversations. Some people on both sides find it distracting, while others find it enriching.

It is easy to imagine that multiple conversations occurring at the same time could dilute focus on the presenter and his or her message. Furthermore, people post comments and questions anonymously in the Twitter backchannel, which naturally leaves room for a variety of unhelpful comments. (Some apps, such as Zeetings, allow the presenter or his or her assistant to select which questions to display and respond to.)

Background conversations allow audiences to discuss presentation topics with others in their field—a primary reason for attending presentations. In addition, background conversations allow a presenter's ideas to be discussed with interested people not in attendance, thus expanding audience size. Additionally, participants in background conversations have ready access to the web for fact-checking the presenter's information.

If you have not yet dealt with background conversations as a presenter, begin by realizing that audience members may not always return your eye contact as they look down to type on their handheld devices. Figure 5.7 shows ways to use background conversations effectively.[35]

During the planning stage, you planned how to handle Q&A as part of your oral report. As your presentation ends—even if you have answered questions throughout your talk—you are ready to implement that plan.

Manage Question-and-Answer Sessions

Think of the question-and-answer session as your grand finale—one more opportunity to show your confidence before an audience and competence on your topic.

Before your presentation begins, you (or the person who introduces you) should tell the audience how questions will be handled, in keeping with your Q&A plan. Although, the time allowed and the formality of the situation influences your management of a question-and-answer session, always be prepared to answer a question that cannot be forestalled. If

> **To use background conversations effectively:**
>
> - *As you begin, publicly welcome participants who will be interacting with you electronically* and let them know you will read what they write—and may read it aloud to the whole audience.
> - *Remind the audience that you will give a better presentation if they look up and make eye contact with you* when not communicating electronically.
> - *As a general rule, do not monitor background conversations while presenting.* Focus instead on delivering the talk you planned, prepared, and rehearsed. If there is a live display of the comments, ask the meeting planner or facilitator for control of it. Then turn off the display while you talk.
> - *Take background breaks.* Build breaks into your oral report to respond to spoken comments and questions as well as those posted electronically. (Display the questions posted electronically for attendees not following the background conversation.)
> - *Be aware of the data collected by the electronic medium* and use them for data visualization, forecasting, or data mining to uncover new information.
> - *Afterward, use the stream of background comments*—where you can see how the audience reacted moment by moment—*to evaluate your presentation.*

Figure 5.7 *Guidelines for managing background conversations*

the chief executive officer asks a question, for example, you may be wise to answer it when he or she asks, no matter what ground rules you have set.

Q&A for Informal Presentations

During informal presentations with lax time limits, you may permit or encourage participants to interrupt your presentation as questions arise. If you permit that questioning strategy, you must be able to redirect the discussion to your topic as soon as the question has been answered.

> The following techniques will help you resume the discussion after a question/comment break:
>
> - *Graciously remind the audience of the topic that was being discussed* before the diversion: Thank you for your comments. They were stimulated by the statement that customers want cardless ATMs. Let's return to that point briefly before we look at other services our customers requested.

- *Solicit other questions on the topic to assure the audience that relevant questions or comments are welcome*: Before we examine other options to expand customer services, does anyone have another question or comment about mobile deposit apps?
- *Summarize the discussion and show its relevance to the last point or the next one* to be discussed: You seem to agree that mobile deposit service is not your first choice. Let's look at other options suggested by our customers.
- *Politely stop a person who is monopolizing the question session*: You've asked some good questions. The last one is more closely related to a later topic that I want to cover. Let's hold that one for a while.

Q&A in Formal Presentations

For a formal presentation with no background conversation, you will usually ask the audience to hold their questions until the end. Presumably you reserved some of your allotted presentation time for questions.

But, what if no one asks a question? And how can you keep from losing audience attention as you answer questions? Also, what if you get a question you cannot answer? Likewise, what if you get more questions than you have time for? The techniques in Figure 5.8 will help you manage such problems that arise in formal question-and-answer sessions.

Technique	Reason to use it
Before your presentation, plant a question with an acquaintance in the audience. Advise the person to ask the planted question only if no one asks a question spontaneously.	Sometimes people are reluctant to ask questions. If someone asks your planted question, it may stimulate questions from other people.
Ask a question yourself. If the questioning begins slowly or lags, suggest a question by saying, "Some of you may be wondering why ..."	As you answer your own question, someone may be stimulated to ask another.

Acknowledge each question with a comment along the lines of "That's a good question" or "I often get that question."	Recognizing the questioner increases your rapport with the audience—and gives you an additional split second to formulate an answer.
Restate the question while looking at the person who asked it. But instead of repeating a short, simple question, just paraphrase it as part of your answer.	You help ensure that everyone heard the question, a basis for understanding your answer. You also ensure your grasp of the question and give the questioner an opportunity to edit the question before you begin answering.
Do not let one person monopolize the session. Politely suggest that you will continue the discussion later. Example: Let's discuss that over coffee. Then turn to receive a question from someone else.	Otherwise, you may quickly lose the attention of all but that person.
While answering, keep eye contact with the entire audience, not just the questioner.	Again, you want to keep the whole audience engaged until the end.
Give a direct answer and brief explanation.	Do so even if your oral report contained the answer.
When you finish an answer, look at the questioner and say something like, "Did I answer your question?"	You clear up any confusion before taking the next question or closing the session.
If you cannot answer a question during or after your presentation, consider three options: • Give a partial answer and suggest a source where the questioner could seek a complete answer. • Ask if anyone present can give a more complete answer. • Promise to provide an answer within a few days.	Much credibility is lost when a presenter gives a phony answer. Say some form of "I don't know" rather than giving a counterfeit response. Promise to provide an answer later only if you intend to follow through, and be sure to get the questioner's contact information.
If questions lag before the allotted time, thank the audience for their participation and interest and dismiss the group.	Most people appreciate the consideration of being given some free time rather than being held for a redundant discussion.
When the allotted time has elapsed, politely thank the audience for its participation and interest.	Offer to be available later (give time and place or your contact information) for further discussion. Do not hold an audience beyond the stated time.

Figure 5.8 Techniques for managing Q&A after a formal presentation

Special Considerations for a Team Oral Report

The previous guidelines have suggested that you will deliver your report alone. Oftentimes, though you will collaborate with others from the early planning stages through questions and answers. An effective team oral report is seamless—each segment supports the presentation's overall purpose and is linked to but does not repeat the material in the other segments.

> Use the following guidelines to help ensure a successful team effort:
>
> - *Rehearse all aspects of the oral report*—spoken parts, use of presentation aids, and seating arrangements—until the team achieves a smooth, comfortable performance.
> - *Time the total presentation, including introductions, speaker movements, and the question-and-answer session,* to be sure it conforms to the allotted time.
> - *As an individual completes a section of the report, that person introduces the next presenter and topic.* If the team is using a slide deck, a divider slide can accomplish that task and take attention away from the physical movements of the speakers as they change positions.
> - *While the current presenter stands before the audience, other team members are seated and quiet,* giving the presenter their full attention. That procedure permits the audience to focus on the current speaker and topic. The seating arrangement should permit a person to sit down gracefully when finished and allow the next presenter to take the speaking position smoothly. An exception, however, to this recommended seating arrangement occurs when the merged (integrated) format is used and team members take turns presenting within each point. In such cases, it is usually best for all presenters to remain standing throughout the presentation,
> - *Team members share responsibility for answering questions.* The team may choose to conduct the question-and-answer time in open-forum style or panel-moderator style.

- o Open-forum style means that audience members call on a particular team member before posing a question or throw out a question for anyone on the team to answer.
- o Panel-moderator style involves designating a team member to take and repeat each question, then to answer it or refer the question to the team member most qualified to answer it.
- *Tactfully step in to answer the question if you sense that a team member is hesitant or may be about to convey inaccurate information.* You can do so by interjecting a statement such as, "I've worked closely with this part of the project ..." Likewise, speak up if you can add important information to augment a teammate's answer.

Like individual reports, team reports, may be presented as webinars and may also involve background conversations.

Summary

Every effective oral report begins with careful planning and preparation, followed by thorough rehearsal.

Use this checklist to plan your next oral report:

- ☐ Analyze the context (purpose, audience, and physical environment). As you carefully consider each factor, jot notes for reference as you continue planning, preparing, and rehearsing.
- ☐ Choose from extemporaneous, memorized, and scripted delivery styles. You are encouraged to use extemporaneous mainly, while committing some parts to memory and reading other parts.
- ☐ Determine whether your oral report should be formal, informal, or some of both (semiformal).
- ☐ Decide which structure is most suitable for your talk: chronological, problem-solution, cause–effect, spatial,

compare and contrast, or topical. You may choose to combine two or more structures in one oral report.
- ☐ Outline your oral report, including four significant parts:
  - ○ A strong opening that gets audience attention, shows relevance of your talk, and lists the points you will cover.
  - ○ Three to five key points with well-developed details and engaging language, using analogies, metaphors, rhetorical questions, similes, and stories to relate information in human terms.
  - ○ Transitions that clearly signal your progression from point to point.
  - ○ An unforgettable conclusion that encapsulates your purpose for delivering the report.
- ☐ If you will use a slide deck, create one that will work hard in helping you accomplish your purpose. Upon drafting your slide deck, check off its attributes:
  - ○ Uses one eye-catching design template and one or two slides for each minute you will speak—more if necessary to keep each slide simple and content easy to grasp.
  - ○ Uses bullet points sparingly (7 × 7 rule); or forgoes bullet points in favor of images, each focused on a single idea.
  - ○ Demonstrates the aesthetic and psychological importance of color and involves sharp contrast between content and background colors.
  - ○ Severely limits the use of special audio and visual effects.

For a webinar slide deck, look for these additional attributes:
  - ○ Uses about four slides for each minute of your oral report, and highlights key points on each slide.
  - ○ Includes an extraordinary cover (title) slide and contains your photo early in the deck.
  - ○ Contains a slide with minimal content to display as you answer questions.

For an audience handout, consider using expanded notes in addition to your slides. Consider providing them electronically so the audience can jot notes.

> - o Plan for the question-and-answer time: Anticipate specific questions and prepare to answer them?
> - o Decide when and how to take questions, including the possibility of a background conversation during the oral report?
> - ☐ For team oral reports, use this planning checklist:
>   - o Assign responsibility for each report part to the team member most well-informed about that part.
>   - o Assure that every team member is generally familiar with all report parts.
>   - o Select one team member to serve as presentation moderator.
>   - – Decide on the On the basis of the team format: distributed format (less experienced and little time for rehearsal)
>   - – merged format (more experienced and more time for rehearsal).

Rehearsal makes the difference between a so-so presentation and a highly successful one. Practice your complete oral report until you feel comfortable with every facet—nervousness, notes, vocal and verbal factors, nonverbal aspects, mobility, presentation aids, background conversations, and even Q&A. If possible, rehearse once or twice before an audience.

> Using this list of do's and don'ts will help you recall what to rehearse in every oral report you make.
>
> - ☐ If nervousness is an issue, take steps to allay it:
>   - o Keep in mind that you are the expert on your subject and were asked to share that expertise with others.
>   - o Remember that the audience came to listen and learn, not to judge you or your skills.

- Use stress reduction techniques, such as striking a power pose, immediately before an oral report.
☐ As you rehearse, use prepared notes:
  - Use the type of notes that work best for you: slide printouts, index cards, smartphone screen, or a complete manuscript on full-sized sheets.
  - Use your notes in a way that does not distract the audience from your message.
☐ As you rehearse, be conscious of your voice and ask your rehearsal audience to comment on it:
  - Listen to your vocal quality, regulated by inhalation, phonation, and resonation
  - Check your verbal clarity resulting from articulation.
  - Use speech exercises available online for improving voice quality and clarity.
☐ As part of your rehearsal, practice nonverbal aspects of your oral report:
  - Maintain erect, relaxed posture, whether sitting or standing. (Imagine that you are attired as you will be for the actual event.)
  - Use the "Z" pattern, or other strategy, for eye contact with the audience.
  - Wear a pleasant, animated facial expression.
  - Avoid pacing aimlessly as you speak, but walk purposefully in the presentation space.
  - Avoid meaningless, repetitive gestures.
  - Use large, sweeping gestures to emphasize or clarify your message.
  - Be aware that most gestures have more than one meaning, depending on cultural background of the audience.
☐ Use all the audio and visual aids in rehearsal that you will use for the actual report:
  - Speak naturally into a microphone from a distance of about six inches.
  - Point out important details on slides. Avoid looking at your slides more than absolutely necessary.

- o Blank the screen if you display a slide before you are ready to discuss it.
- o Keep each slide visible long enough for the audience to examine its content.
- ☐ View a background conversation as a natural part of a business presentation, and take steps to use it to your advantage:
  - o Welcome participants in the electronic conversation, and remind them you will appreciate their occasional attempts to return your eye contact.
  - o Avoid monitoring background conversation while presenting, except in marketing presentations, for example, where your purpose is to assess customers' attitudes and turn prospects into customers. Take breaks to address comments and questions in the background conversation.
  - o Do mine the data generated by the background conversation and use it to your and your organization's advantage.
- ☐ Rehearse the question-and-answer portion of your formal and informal talks:
  - o Keep the audience on point, using the strategies included in the chapter and others that you read or devise on your own.
  - o Help get questioning started if necessary by having someone ask a planted question or by asking a question yourself.
  - o Restate each question while looking at the person who asked it.
  - o Avoid looking directly at the questioner while answering; instead, resume speaking to the whole audience.
  - o Keep one person from monopolizing the Q&A session.
  - o Never fake answers; have tactics in mind for handling questions that you are unable to answer at the moment.
  - o Thank your audience for their participation as Q&A ends.
- ☐ In general, rehearse team oral reports even more thoroughly than individual ones to make it flow smoothly:

- Practice moving from one presenter to another team member.
- Avoid detracting from another team member's talk; sit or stand still and listen as though the information is new to you.
- Share responsibility for answering questions, whether using open-forum or panel-moderator format.

Notes

Chapter 1

1. Clippinger (2016, 37–46).
2. "Texting Is Nearly Universal Among Young Adult Cell Phone Owners" (2012).
3. Kendrick (2013).
4. Smith and Giang (2014).
5. Shwom and Hirsch (1994).
6. Adapted from Writing Review Checklist in Shwom and Hirsch (1994).
7. Shwom and Snyder (2014, 102).
8. Wiens (2012).
9. Hoover (2013).
10. Common Grammatical Errors (2016).
11. Common Grammatical Errors (2016).
12. Compiled from Evans (2016); Shwom and Snyder (2014, 103); Vannest (n.d.); and Write Life Team (2013).
13. Singla (n.d.).
14. Adapted from Writing Review Checklist in Shwom and Hirsch (1994). Information in parentheses derived from Leybovich (2010); McMillan (n.d.), and "Writing Tips: Five Editing Principles" (n.d.).

Chapter 2

1. Shwom and Snyder (2014, 328).
2. Goudreau (2015).
3. Jovin (n.d.).
4. Galbornetti (2012).
5. Kyrnin (n.d.); Kyrnin (2016).
6. World Wide Web Consortium Schools for Web Design (n.d.).
7. World Wide Web Consortium Schools for Web Design (n.d.).
8. Guglieri (2015); Alred, Brusaw, and Oliu (2009); and World Wide Web Consortium Schools for Web Design (n.d.).
9. World Wide Web Consortium Schools for Web Design (n.d.); Alred, Brusaw, and Oliu (2009); and World Wide Web Consortium (n.d.).
10. World Wide Web Consortium Schools for Web Design (n.d.).
11. Shwom and Snyder (2014, 328).
12. Shwom and Snyder (2014, 359).
13. Shwom and Snyder (2014, 360 and 361).

14. Shwom and Snyder (2014, 359 and 360).
15. McMahon (2014).
16. Singhal and Anil (2015, 1).
17. Singhal and Anil (2015, 1).
18. Petrova (2015).
19. Balliett (2011); Office of National Statistics (n.d.); Yau (2011).
20. Smith (n.d.).
21. Dictionary.com (n.d.).
22. Beard (2014); "Using Neuroscience to Understand the Role of Direct Mail" (2015).
23. Beard (2014).
24. Kandler (2012).
25. "Newsletter Design Tips" (n.d.).
26. Kandler (2013a).
27. Kandler (2013b).
28. "Newsletter Design Tips" (n.d.).
29. Bear (n.d.).
30. Kandler (2013a).
31. "Newsletter Design Tips" (n.d.).
32. Kandler (2013b).
33. Kandler (2013a).
34. Kandler (2016).
35. Kandler (2012).
36. Kandler (2013b).
37. Kandler (2013b).
38. Kandler (2013a).
39. "Newsletter Design Tips" (n.d.).
40. Kandler (2015).
41. "Newsletter Design Tips" (n.d.).
42. Kandler (2015).
43. Kandler (2013).
44. Kandler (2013).
45. Kandler (2013).
46. Kandler (2016).
47. Kandler (2013c).
48. Kandler (2013c).

Chapter 3

1. Schweers (2013).
2. Lehrman (2013).

3. McCandless (2012).
4. Tufte (2001, 107–121).
5. Kienzler (1997, 172).
6. Kenrose (2016).
7. Valiela (2001).
8. Lin and Heer (2014).
9. Valiela (2001, 188).
10. Heer (2015).
11. Few (2012, 94).
12. Singh (2006).
13. Lin and Heer (2014).
14. Yau (2011b, 340).
15. Few (2012, xvii).
16. Few (2012, 9).
17. "Cultural Color" (2013).
18. Yau (2011b, 76–78).
19. Yau (2011b, 79).
20. Yau (2011b, 56–57).
21. Yau (2011b, 79).
22. Yau (2011b, 60–61).
23. Weber (2013).
24. Admin (2015a).
25. Admin (2015b).
26. Stevens (2016b); Stevens (2016a).
27. Few (2012, 275–276).
28. Few (2012, 276).
29. Few (2012, 94–95).
30. Iliinsky (2011).
31. Few (2012, 271–272).
32. Few (2012, 281–282); "Funnel Chart" (n.d.).
33. Few (2012, 272–275); "Radar (Spider) Chart" (n.d.).
34. Few (2012, 283–284); "Waterfall Chart" (n.d.).
35. "Statistical Maps: Best Practices" (n.d., 1).
36. "Statistical Maps: Best Practices" (n.d., 2–4).
37. Bloom (2015); Massanaro (2015).
38. Bloom (2015); "Using Images" (n.d.).
39. Burns and Lacoma (2016); Cox (2016); Stewart (2016).

Chapter 4

1. American Psychological Association (2010).

Chapter 5

1. Clippinger (2016, 46–64).
2. Schwertly (2014a).
3. Schwertly (2014c); Belknap (2015).
4. Noar (2016).
5. Schwertly (2014b).
6. Noar (2016)
7. Prinzlau (n.d.).
8. Paradi (n.d.).
9. "Zeetings Changes One-Way Presentations into Two-Way Conversations" (2015).
10. Stuurman (n.d.).
11. Moderating a Q&A Session (n.d.).
12. Gallo (2010, 179).
13. Kagan (2013).
14. "Speech Anxiety" (2008).
15. Egan (2014).
16. Genard (2015).
17. "Speech Anxiety" (2008).
18. "Overcoming Speech Anxiety" (n.d.).
19. "Overcoming Speech Anxiety" (n.d.).
20. Mullins and Jolicoeur (2015).
21. "Accent Modification" (2016).
22. Labov, Ash, and Boberg (n.d.).
23. "Accent Modification" (2016).
24. "Accent Reduction" (2011).
25. "Accent Modification" (2016).
26. Chuang (2013); Marshall (2009); Marshall (2014); Mozafarri (2013); Mutonono (2015); "How to Love Your Accent" (n.d.).
27. Karlan (2013).
28. Mitchell (n.d.).
29. "5 Tips on What to Wear" (2014).
30. "What to Wear at Your Next Business Presentation" (2014).
31. McGregor and Tan (2015); Genard (2015).
32. Gray (n.d.); "What Hand Gestures Mean in Different Countries" (n.d.).
33. Laskowski (2016).
34. Booth, Shames, and Desberg (2010, 167–82); Templeton and FitzGerald (1999, 139–53).
35. Mitchell (2009); Atkinson (2011).

References

"5 Tips on What to Wear." 2014. SlideGenius. www.slidegenius.com/blog/presentation-what-to-wear

"Accent Modification." 2016. American Speech-Language-Hearing Association. www.asha.org/public/speech/development/accent-modification (accessed September 16, 2016).

"Accent Reduction." 2011. *Wikipedia*. https://en.*wikipedia*.org/wiki/Accent_reduction

Admin. 2015a. "The Dos and Don'ts of Infographics: Create Infographics for Visual Content Marketing." Mabbly. www.mabbly.com/the-dos-and-donts-of-infographics

Admin. 2015b. "How to Improve Small Business Website User Experience." Mabbly. www.mabbly.com/how-to-improve-small-business-website-user-experience-2

Alred, G.J., C.T. Brusaw, and W.E. Oliu. 2009. *Handbook of Technical Writing*, 9th ed. New York City: St. Martin's Press.

"American Community Survey Statistics Give Communities Detailed Look at Income, Poverty, Health Insurance and Many Other Statistics." 2013. Commerce.gov (United States Department of Commerce). www.2010-2014.commerce.gov/blog/2013/09/19/american-community-survey-statistics-give-communities-detailed-look-income-poverty-h.html

American Psychological Association. 2010. *Publication Manual of the American Psychological Association*, 6th ed. Washington, DC: American Psychological Association.

"Annual Survey of Manufacturers and the Economic Census." 2016. U.S. Census Bureau. 2014 Multi-Sector Data Tables, Table 1. www.census.gov/data/tables/2014/econ/e-stats/2014-e-stats.html

Atkinson, C. 2011. "5 Ways to Use Twitter to Avoid a Backchannel Disaster." Mashable. www.mashable.com/2010/-3/-7/twitter-backchannel

Balliett, A. 2011. "The Do's and Don'ts of Infographic Design." *Smashing Magazine*. www.smashingmagazine.com/2011/the-dos-and-donts-of-infographic-design

Bear, J.H. n.d. "Reader's Cues: End Signs in Newsletter Design." About Tech. www.desktoppub.about.com/cs/intermediate/a/endsigns.htm (accessed September 22, 2016).

Beard, N. 2014. "Print Newsletters as Content Marketing Tactic: Pros, Cons, Examples and Best Practices." Top Rank Blog. www.toprankblog.com/2014/02/print-newsletters-content-marketing-tactic

Belknap, L. 2015. "Design Presentations with Consistent Color Schemes." Ethos3. www.ethos3.com/2015/01/design-presentations-with-consistent-color-schemes

Bloom, H. 2015. "15 Places to Find Free Stock Images Without Watermarks." Harry Vs. Internet. www.harryvsinternet.com/15-places-find-free-stock-images-without-watermarks

Booth, D., D. Shames, and P. Desberg. 2010. "Physical Grammar." In *Own the Room: Business Presentations That Persuade Engage and Get Results*. New York: McGraw-Hill.

Burns, E., and T. Lacoma. 2016. "Before You Resort to MS Paint or Piracy, Give These Free Image-Editing Tools a Shot." Digital Trends. www.digitaltrends.com/computing/best-free-photo-editing-software

Chuang, A. 2013. "Things I Did to Improve My English and Reduce My Accent." Good Characters. https://service.goodcharacters.com/blog/blog.php?id=175

"Climate Juneau—Alaska." 2016. U.S. Climate Data. www.usclimatedata.com/climate/juneau/alaska/united-states/usak0116

Clippinger, D. 2016. *Planning and Organizing Business Reports: Written, Oral, and Research-Based*. New York City: Business Expert Press.

"Common Grammatical Errors." 2016. IEEE Professional Communication Society. www.sites.ieee.org/pcs/communication-resources-for-engineers/grammar

Cox, A. 2016. "The Best Free Photo Editing Software 2016." Techradar. www.techradar.com/us/news/software/applications/best-free-photo-editing-software-10-top-image-editors-you-should-try-1135489

"Cultural Color: Cultural Meanings of Color and Color Symbolism." 2013. Empower Yourself with Color Psychology. www.empower-yourself-with-color-psychology.com

"Current Population Survey." 2014. United States Census Bureau. www.census.gov/hhes/www/socdemo/voting/publications/p20/2014/Table10.xls (accessed June 27, 2016).

Dean Runyan Associates. "West Virginia Travel Impacts, 2000–2014." 2015. www.deanrunyan.com/doc_library/WVImp.pdf

Dictionary.com. n.d. www.dictionary.com

"Digest of Education Statistics." 2016. Table 203.50. National Center for Education Statistics. www.nces.ed.gov/programs/digest/d15/tables/dt15_203.50.asp

"DoD Starbase 2015 Annual Report." 2016. DoD Starbase. www.dodstarbase.org

Dugdale, S. n.d. "Breathing Exercises." Write-Out-Loud. www.write-out-loud.com/sitemap.html (accessed August 12, 2016).

Egan, M. 2014. "10 Ways Anyone Can Give Better Presentations Using PowerPoint: Tips for Giving Better Presentations." PC Advisor. www.pcadvisor.co.uk/how-to/small-business/10-21ys-give-better-presentations-using-powerpoint-3584404

Evans, D. 2016. "Proofreading Practice (or How to Avoid Those Embarrassing Writing Errors)." GoodContentCo. www.goodcontentcompany.com

Few, S. 2012. *Show Me the Numbers: Designing Tables and Graphs to Enlighten.* Burlingame, CA: Analytics Press.

File, T. 2015. Who Votes? Congressional Elections and the American Electorate: 1978–2014, Population Characteristics. U.S. Census Bureau. www.census.gov/content/dam/Census/library/publications/2015/demo/p20-577.pdf

"Funnel Chart." n.d. Fusion Charts by InfoSoft Global Private Limited. www.fusioncharts.com/chart-primers/funnel-chart (accessed July 13, 2016).

Galbornetti, C. 2012. "10 Email Design Best Practices for a Mobile World." Target Marketing. www.targetmarketingmag.com/article/10-email-design-best-practices-mobile-email-smartphone-tablet-world/all

Gallo, C. 2010. *The Presentation Secrets of Steve Jobs: How to be Insanely Great in Front of Any Audience.* New York: McGraw Hill.

Genard, G. 2015a. "The 5 Key Body Language Techniques of Public Speaking." The Genard Method. www.genardmethod.com/blog/bid/144247/The-5-Key-Body-Language-Techniques-of-Public-Speaking

Genard, G. 2015b. "10 Causes of Speech Anxiety That Create Fear of Public Speaking." The Genard Method. www.genardmethod.com/blog/bid/169656/Top-10-Causes-of-Speech-Anxiety-and-How-to-Beat-Em

Goudreau, J. 2015. "17 Tips for Writing an Excellent Email Subject Line." Business Insider. www.businessinsider.com/how-to-write-an-email-subject-line-2015-1

Gray, M.D. n.d. "The Meaning of Hand Gestures in Different Countries." One How To. www.health.onehowto.com/article/the-meaning/of-hand/gestures-in-different-countries-1326 (accessed August 14, 2016).

Guglieri, C. 2015. "20 Steps to the Perfect Website Layout." Creative Blog. www.creativebloq.com/web-design/steps-perfect-website-layout-812625

Heer, J. 2015. "The Future of Data Visualization." You Tube. www.youtube.com/watch?v=vc1bq0qIKoA

Hoover, B. 2013. "Good Grammar Should Be Everyone's Business." *Harvard Business Review.* www.hbr.org/2013/03/good-grammar-should-be-everyon

"How to Love Your Accent." n.d. Wiki How to do Anything. www.wikihow.com/Lose-Your-Accent (accessed September 15, 2016).

Iliinsky, N. 2011. "Data Viz: You're Doin' It Wrong." You Tube (at Strata Ignite 2011). www.youtube.com/watch?v=i93iWza8sG8

Jovin, E. n.d. "Email Salutations." Syntaxis. www.syntaxis.com/book/email-etiquette/anatomy-of-an-email-message/email-salutations (accessed May 19, 2016).

Kagan, M. 2013. "7 Public Speaking Tips from the World's Best Speakers & Presenters." SlideShare HubSpot. blog.hubspot.com/blog/tabid/6307/bid/34274/7-Lessons-From-the-World-s-Most-Captivating-Presenters-SlideShare.aspx#sm.0002p3mqt1403djpxkv23wmrq5h5e

Kandler, D. 2012. "Tips to Make Your Company Newsletter More Cost Effective." Company Newsletters. www.companynewsletters.com/costeffect.htm

Kandler, D. 2013a. "How to Avoid the Most Common Company Newsletter Mistakes." *Company Newsletters*. www.companynewsletters.com/costeffect.htm

Kandler, D. 2013b. "Ten Tips to Make Sure Your Company Newsletter Gets Read, Not Tossed." *Company Newsletters*. www.companynewsletters.com/costeffect.htm

Kandler, D. 2013c. "Understanding Copyright Law Can Help You Avoid a Costly Lawsuit." *Company Newsletters*. www.companynewsletters.com/costeffect.htm

Kandler, D. 2015. "Tips on How to Take Great Photos for Your Company Newsletter." *Company Newsletters*. www.companynewsletters.com/costeffect.htm

Kandler, D. 2016. "The Easiest Way to Come Up with Newsletter Article Ideas, Topics." *Company Newsletters*. www.companynewsletters.com/costeffect.htm

Karlan, S. 2013. "The Ultimate Regional Vocabulary Throwdown." Buzzfeed. www.buzzfeed.com/skarlan/the-ultimate-regional-vocabulary-throwdown?-utm_term=.hePQAG6xa#.oexEZ97wg

Kendrick, J. 2013. "Texting in Business, Not a Good Idea." ZDNet. www.zdnet.com/article/texting-in-business-not-a-good-idea

Kenrose, S. 2016. "Misleading Graphs: Real Life Examples." Statistics How To. www.statisticshowto.com/misleading-graphs

Kienzler, D.S. 1997. "Visual Ethics." *Journal of Business Communication* 34, pp. 171–87.

Kuiper, S., and D. Clippinger. 2013. *Contemporary Business Reports*. 5th ed. Mason, OH: Cengage Learning.

Kyrnin, J. 2016. "How to Add a PDF Document to a Website." About Tech. www.webdesign.about.com/cs/beginninghtml/ht/htaddpdffile.htm

Kyrnin, J. n.d. "Best Practices for Using PDFs on Web Pages." About Tech. webdesign.about.com/od/pdf/a/pdfs_and_web_design_best_practices.htm (accessed July 26, 2016).

Labov, W., S. Ash, and C. Boberg. n.d. "Regional Dialects: Overview." The Atlas of North American English: Phonetics, Phonology and Sound Change. www.atlas.mouton-content.com (accessed September 16, 2016).

Laskowski, L. 2016. "Five Ways to Make Your Body Speak." Presentation-Pointers. www.presentation-pointers.com/showarticle/articleid/85

Lehrman, R.A. 2013. "The New Age of Algorithms: How It Affects the Way We Live." *Christian Science Monitor.* www.csmonitor.com/USA/Society/2013/0811/The-new-age-of-algorithms-How-it-affects-the-way-we-live

Leybovich, I. 2010. "Jargon, Buzzwords and other Bad Biz Writing." Industry Market Trends. www.news.thomasnet.com

Lin, S., and J. Heer. 2014. "The Right Colors Make Data Easier to Read." *Harvard Business Review.* www.hbr.org/2014/04/the-right-colors-make-data-easier-to-read

Marshall, L.B. 2009. "Accent Modification." Quick and Dirty Tips. www.quickanddirtytips.com

Marshall, L.B. 2014. "5 Ways to Reduce Your Accent." Quick and Dirty Tips. www.quickanddirtytips.com

Massanaro, G. 2015. "20 Sites to Get Free Stock Images for Commercial Use." Viralsweep. www.viralsweep.com/blog/free-stock-images-for-commercial-use

McCandless, D. 2012. "The Beauty of Data Visualization." YouTube, TED Talk. www.youtube.com/watch?v=pLqjQ55tz-U&feature=youtu.be

McGregor, J., and S. Tan. 2015. "What to Do with Your Hands When Speaking in Public." *The Washington Post.* www.washingtonpost.com/news/on-leadership/wp/2015/11/17/what-to-do-with-your-hands-when-speaking-in-public

McMahon, G. 2014. "Quit Decking Around: 7 Ways to Use PowerPoint." Make a Powerful Point. www.makeapowerfulpoint.com/2014/05/28/stop-decking-around-7-ways-use-powerpoint

McMillan, C. n.d. "5 Steps for Editing Your Own Writing." Themuse. www.themuse.com/advice/5-steps-for-editing-your-own-writing (accessed May 3, 2016).

Mitchell, O. n.d. "18 Tips on How to Conduct an Engaging Webinar." Speaking About Presenting. www.speakingaboutpresenting.com/presentation-skills/how-to-conduct-engaging-webinar (accessed March 2, 2016).

Mitchell, O. 2009. "8 Tips for Managing the Twitter Backchannel during Your Presentation." SocialTimes. www.socialtimes.com/8-tips-for-managing-the-twitter-backchannel-during-your-presentation

"Moderating a Q&A Session." n.d. Zeetings. about.zeetings.com/blog/moderating-a-qa-session (accessed August 19, 2016).

Mozaffari, C. 2013. "Five Ways to Reduce a Heavy Accent." Mr. Media Training. www.mrmediatraining.com/2013/10/30/five-ways-to-reduce-a-heavy-accent

Mullins, L., and L. Jolicoeur. 2015. "Helping Powerless Have "Presence": Amy Cuddy Expands on Hit TED Talk in New Book." The ARTery. www.wbur.org/artery/2015/12/23/amy-cuddy-ted-talk-book-presence

Mutonono, E. 2015. "Is It Possible to Get Rid of Your Accent?" Elena Mutonono Accent and Fluency Training. www.elenamutonono.com/2015/01/26/is-it-possible-to-get-rid-of-your-accent

"Newsletter Design Tips." n.d. PsPrint. www.psprint.com/resources/newsletter-design-tips (accessed September 2, 2016).

Noar, A. 2016. "These Webinar Presentation Tips Will Help You Create Your Best Webinar Ever!" Presentation Panda. www.presentationpanda.com/blog/webinar-presentation-tips

Office of National Statistics. n.d. "Infographic Guidelines." https://theidpblog.files.wordpress.com/2013/10/infographic-guidelines-v1-0.pdf (accessed July15, 2016).

"Overcoming Speech Anxiety: Top Ten Ways to Conquer Your Fear of Public Speaking." n.d. Oral Communication Program at the Center for Teaching and Learning, Stanford University. web.stanford.edu/dept/CTL/Oralcomm/Microsoft%20Word%20-%20OvercomingSpeechAnxiety.pdf (accessed August 8, 2016).

Paradi, D. n.d. "Going Green with Electronic Presentation Handouts That Attendees Can Take Notes on." Think Outside the Slide. www.thinkoutsidetheslide.com/going-green-with-electronic-presentation-handouts-that-attendees-can-take-notes-on (accessed August 8, 2016).

Petrova, J. 2015. "Cool Tools for Creating Infographics." Jeff Bullas. www.jeffbullas.com

Prinzlau, M. n.d. "Top 10 Secure Dropbox Alternatives." Cloudwards. www.cloudwards.net/top-10-secure-dropbox-alternatives (accessed August 22, 2016).

"Radar (Spider) Chart." n.d. FusionCharts by InfoSoft Global Private Limited. www.fusioncharts.com/chart-primers/radar-chart (accessed July 13, 2016).

Schweers, J. 2013. "UF Sets Up Team to Crunch 'Big Data." *Gainesville* (Florida) *Sun*. scene.gainesville.com/article/20131009/ARTICLES/131009583?Title=UF-sets-up-team-to-crunch-big-data

Schwertly, S. 2014a. "6 Presentation Design Do's and Don'ts." SlideShare. https://blog.slideshare.net/2014/04/07/presentation-design-dos-and-donts

Schwertly, S. 2014b. "The History of Color Psychology." Ethos3. www.ethos3.com/2014/06/the-history-of-color-psychology

Schwertly, S. 2014c. "The More Slides the Better." SlideShare. https://blog.slideshare.net/2014/02/10/the-more-slides-the-better

Shwom, B.H., and P. Hirsch. 1994. "Managing the Drafting Process, Creating a New Model for the Workplace." *The Bulletin of the Association for Business Communication* 57, no. 2, p. 1+. www.questia.com/read/1G1-15638059/managing-the-drafting-process-creating-a-new-model

Shwom, B., and L.G. Snyder. 2014. *Business Communication: Polishing Your Professional Presence*. 2nd ed. Boston, MA: Pearson.

Singh, S. 2006. "Impact of Color on Marketing." *Management Decision* 44, no. 6, pp. 783–89. DOI: dx.doi.org/10.1108/00251740610673332

Singhal, N., and A. Anil. 2015. "Infographics: The Artistic Way to Convey Information into Knowledge." *The International Journal of Science & Technoledge* 3, no. 2, p. 100. ProQuest database.

Singla, A. n.d. "8 Online Grammar and Punctuation Checker Tools for Error-Free Writing." Blogger Tips Tricks. www.bloggertipstricks.com (accessed April 24, 2016).

SmartDraw Software. n.d. "Flowchart Symbols." www.smartdraw.com/flowchart/flowchart-symbols.htm (accessed July 1, 2016).

SmartDraw Templates. n.d. "Venn Diagram—Comparing and Contrasting 3 Coffee Shops." www.smartdraw.com/venn-diagram (accessed June 24, 2016).

Smith, J., and V. Giang. 2014. "7 Rules of Texting Etiquette Every Professional Needs to Know." Business Insider. www.businessinsider.com

Smith, J. n.d. "10 Steps to Designing an Amazing Infographic." Fast Co. Design. www.fastcodesign.com/1670019/10-steps-to-designing-an-amazing-infographic (accessed August 12, 2016).

Society, the Individual, and Medicine. 2015. "Clinical Trials." www.med.uottawa.ca/SIM/data/Clinical_trials_e.htm

"Speech Anxiety." 2008. Speaking in the Disciplines, University of Pittsburgh. www.speaking.pitt.edu/student/public-speaking/speechanxiety.htm

"Statistical Maps: Best Practices." n.d. Neighbourhood Statistics. www.neighbourhood.statistics.gov.uk/HTMLDocs/images/Statistical%20Maps%20-%20Best%20Practice%20v5_tcm97-51126.pdf (accessed August 14, 2016).

Stevens, K. 2016a. "The 3 Calls to Actions Your Website Needs to Convert Traffic." Mabbly. www.mabbly.com/3-calls-actions-website-needs-convert-traffic

Stevens, K. 2016b. "How to Do SEO in a User Experience-Driven World." Mabbly. www.mabbly.com/seo-user-experience-driven-world

Stewart, C. 2016. "16 Essential Photo Editor Apps." Creative Bloq. www.creativebloq.com/software/best-photo-editor-51411752

Stuurman, P. n.d. "3 Step Plan for Using Twitter as a Backchannel." TweetBeam. wall.tweetbeam.com/events/twitter-backchannel.html (accessed August 23, 2016).

Templeton, M., and S.S. FitzGerald. 1999. "Nonverbal Techniques of Communication." In *Schaum's Quick Guide to Great Presentations*. New York City: McGraw-Hill.

"Texting Is Nearly Universal Among Young Adult Cell Phone Owners." 2012. Pew Research Center. www.pewresearch.org/daily-number/texting-is-nearly-universal-among-young-adult-cell-phone-owners

Tufte, E.R. 2001. *The Visual Display of Quantitative Information*, 2nd ed. Cheshire, CT: Graphics Press.

"Types of Thematic Maps." 2013. Centers for Disease Control and Prevention. www.cdc.gov/dhdsp/maps/gisx/resources/thematic-maps.html

"Using Neuroscience to Understand the Role of Direct Mail." 2015. Jigsaw. www.jigsawccs.co.uk/blog/2015/2/16/31/neuroscience_to_understand_the_role_of_direct_mail

"Using Images: Copyright & Fair Use." n.d. Using Images MIT Libraries. www.libguides.mit.edu/usingimages (accessed July 11, 2016).

Valiela, I. 2001. *Doing Science: Design, Analysis, and Communication of Scientific Research*. New York City: Oxford University Press.

Vannest, A. 2016. "5 Tips for Editing Your Own Work." Grammarly Blog. www.grammarly.com

"Waterfall Chart." n.d. FushionCharts by InfoSoft Global Private Limited. www.fusioncharts.com/charts/waterfall-charts (accessed July 13, 2016).

Weber, W. 2013. "What Is an Interactive Graphic?" Malofiej24. www.malofiejgraphics.com/what-is-an-interactive-information-graphic

"What Hand Gestures Mean in Different Countries." n.d. Busuu Blog. https://blog.busuu.com/what-hand-gestures-mean-in-different-countries (accessed August 14, 2016).

"What to Wear at Your Next Business Presentation." 2016. *Presentation Magazine*. www.presentationmagazine.com/what-to-wear-at-your-next-business-presentation-20886.htm

"What We Do." n.d. Women for Women International. www.womenforwomen.org/what-we-do (accessed June 28, 2016).

Wiens, K. 2012. "I Won't Hire People Who Use Poor Grammar. Here's Why." *Harvard Business Review*. https://hbr.org

World Wide Web Consortium. n.d. S.L. Henry, and L. McGee, eds. W3C. www.w3.org/standards/webdesign/accessibility (accessed June 3, 2016).

World Wide Web Consortium Schools for Web Design. n.d. W3Schools. www.w3schools.com/website/web_design.asp (accessed June 1, 2016).

Write Life Team, The. 2013. "25 Editing Tips for Tightening Your Copy." The Write Life. thewritelife.com

"Writing Tips: Five Editing Principles." n.d. University of Illinois at Urbana Writer's Workshop. www.cws.illinois.edu (accessed May 3, 2016).

Yau, N. 2011a. "The Do's and Don'ts of Infographic Design: Revisited." *Smashing Magazine*. www.smashingmagazine.com/2011/the-dos-and-donts-of-infographic-design-revisited

Yau, N. 2011b. *Visualize This: The Flowing Data Guide to Design, Visualization, and Statistics*. Indianapolis, IN: Wiley Publishing, Inc.

"Zeetings Changes One-Way Presentations into Two-Way Conversations." 2015. StreetInsider. www.marketwired.com/press-release/zeetings-changes-one-way-presentations-into-two-way-conversations-2047030.htm

Index

Acceptance message, 177, 178, 190
Acknowledgments, 182–183, 191
Adobe Illustrator, 98
Analogy, 197
Animation and interactivity, 99–100
Anxiety reduction techniques, 210
Appendix, 165–166, 189
Area graphs, 108–109
Authorization message, 177–178, 190

Balanced pie chart arrangement, 89–90
Bar graphs
  bilateral, 103, 104
  checklist, 132
  contrasting colors usage, 102
  data arrangement, 102
  labeling, 102
  length and width, 102
  multiple, 103
  pictograph, 103, 105
  segmented, 103, 104
  size and page location planning, 102
  uses, 101
  variations, 103–105
Bilateral bar graph, 103, 104
Bing static map, 123
Business research reports
  appendix, 165–170, 189
  collaborative research and writing, 185–186
  glossary, 165, 189
  index, 171, 189
  preliminary parts
    acceptance message, 177, 178, 190
    acknowledgments, 182–183, 191
    authorization message, 177–178, 190
    contents, 178–181, 191
    cover/binder, 172, 190
  executive summary, 183–185, 191
  flyleaves, 172, 190
  preface, 182, 191
  title page, 172–175, 190
  transmittal message, 175–177, 190
  reference list, 164, 189
  report body
    conclusions, 156–161, 188
    data interpretation, 144–146
    findings, 146–153, 187
    inductive structure, 137, 186
    introductory section, 138–144, 187
    recommendations, 161–163, 188
    report summary, 153–155

Call box, 65
CartoDB static map, 123
Chartjunk, 87
Choropleth map, 123
Collaborative report writing, 23–24, 27–28
Colloquialisms, 6–7
Conclusions, 156–161
Consonants, 212
Content lapses, 16
Content management system (CMS), 47
Contents, 178–181, 191
Contractions, 6
Contrast, 87–88
Corel Draw, 98

Data visualization
  animation and interactivity, 99–100
  area graphs, 108–109
  bar graphs, 101–104, 132
  business report, 129
  clarification, 83
  coherence, 86

250   INDEX

color associations, 96–97
credibility, 86
effective graphics
   balance, 89, 90, 130
   contrast, 87–88, 130
   simplicity, 86–87, 130
   unity, 88–89, 130
  ethical representation, 94
  graphic cues, 95–96
  graphing software, 97–99
  line chart, 82–83
  line graphs, 104–108, 133
  perceptual accuracy, 95–96
  photographs, 127–129, 134–135
  pie chart, 109–114, 133
  reinforcement, 83–84
  relationship charts, 115–118
  simplification, 83, 84
  SmartArt, 85
  statistical maps, 121–127, 134
  summary, 84–85
  tables, 118–121
  visual identification and placement
   data source, 90–91
   discussion, 92–93
   introductory statement, 91
   titles placement, 90
   visual display, 91–92
Decimal numbering system, 181
Diphthongs, 211
Distorted graphs, 94
Donut chart, 114
Dot map, 124

E-mail format, 36–38
Enhanced illustrations, 55
Enhanced pie charts, 113, 114
Executive summary, 55, 183–185, 191

Face-to-face oral report, 215–216
Factor relationship chart, 117–118
File transfer protocol (FTP), 47
Flowchart, 116–117, 133
Flyleaves, 172, 190

Fonts, 69
  default, 31–32
  spacing characteristics, 31
  styles and sizes, 30, 31
Formal table, 119
Format lapses, 16
Frequently occurring writing lapses (FOWLs)
  content lapses, 16
  format lapses, 16
  grammatical lapses, 17
  misplaced and dangling modifiers, 19–20
  mixed construction, 18
  nonparallel construction, 17–18
Funnel chart, 115

Glossary, 165, 189
Google Spreadsheets, 98–99
Google static map, 123
Grammatical lapses, 17
Graphing software
  Microsoft Excel, 97–98
  online graphics software, 98
Grouping and bulleting, 32–33

Headings, 33–35
HERE static map, 123
High–low (stock) chart, 107–108

Infographics format, 53–58
Informal table, 119, 120
Inkscape, 99

Letter format, 40–43
Line chart, 82–83
Line graphs
  accurate and nondistorting scales, 106–107
  bilateral line chart, 107, 108
  chart size planning, 106
  checklist, 133
  dimensions, 104–105
  frequency distribution, 105
  high–low (stock) chart, 107–108

labeling, 107
multiple-line chart, 107
standard plotting rules, 106

Manuscript format, 43–47
Mapbox static map, 123
MapQuest static map, 123
Mass Stats (Massachusetts statistics) map, 127
Mechanical lapses, 19–20
Memo format, 38–39
Metaphor, 196–197
Monospaced fonts, 31
Multiple-bar graph, 103

Nameplate, 65
Newsletter production, 77
  advantages, 58–59
  content guides, 65–66
  design guides, 64–65
  designing, 62–63
  disadvantages, 59
  do's and don'ts, 67–68
  hiring, 61–62
  marketing, 58
  not-for-profit organizations, 58
  template selection, 59–61
  visuals, 66–67, 78–79
Numbering, 32–33

Objectivity, 8–9, 25
Online graphics software, 98
Oral report presentation
  abstract terms, 197
  background conversations, 222, 224
  context analysis, 193–194
  delivery style selection, 194
  face-to-face oral report, 215–216
  formality level, 195
  handouts, 202–203
  human terms, 197–198
  memorable conclusion, 198
  nervousness management, 206, 208–209

nonverbal aspects
  appearance, 217–218
  eye contact, 219–220
  facial expressions, 220
  gestures, 220–223
  mobility, 222
  posture, 218–219
notes handling, 206, 207
purposeful transitions, 198
question-and-answer session, 203–204, 224–227
slide preparation
  attractive and memorable words, 200
  design template, 199
  harmonious color selection, 200–201
  images, 200
  name and organization, 199
  readable font size, 200
  right number of slides, 200
  software options, 198–199
  webinar, 201–202
strong opening, 196
structure decision, 195–196
team oral reports, 204–205, 228–229
vocal and verbal aspects
  articulation, 211–215
  inhalation, 209–210
  phonation, 210–211
  resonation, 211
webinar presentations, 216–217
well-developed main points, 196–197

Photographs
  checklist, 134–135
  license and credits, 128s
  online photo editors, 128–129
  online stock photos, 127
  photo editing, 128
  sense of reality, 127
Pictograph, 103, 105

Pie chart
  vs. bar charts, 111, 113
  checklist, 133
  2-D vs. 3-D, 110, 112
  enhanced, 113, 114
  labeling, 113
  segment balancing, 112–113
  segment values, 113
Preface, 182, 191
Public-speaking anxiety, 208–209

Question-and-answer session, 203–204

Reference list, 164–165, 189
Relationship charts
  factor relationship chart, 117–118
  flowchart, 116–117
Report formatting
  ALL-CAPS usage, 32
  bold and italics usage, 32
  E-mail format, 36–38, 71
  fonts, 69
    default, 31–32
    spacing characteristics, 31
    styles and sizes, 30, 31
  grouping and bulleting, 32–33, 69–70
  guidelines, 35–36
  headings, 33–35, 70
  infographics format, 53–58, 76–77
  letter format, 40–43, 71–73
  manuscript format, 43–47, 73–74
  memo format, 38–39, 71
  newsletter production (see Newsletter production)
  numbering, 32–33
  report deck format, 51–53, 75–76
  spacing, 29–30, 69
  web page format, 47–50, 74
Report writing style
  collaborative report writing, 23–24, 27–28
  drafts revising and editing, 13–15
  formality and informality
    colloquialisms, 6–7
    confidence, 9–10

  contractions, 6
  degrees of, 7, 25
  difference, 4
  echnical market information, 8
  first- and second-person pronouns, 5
  formal parts, 3
  format, 8
  names and titles, 5–6
  objectivity, 8–9, 25
  text messages, 4–5
  voice-to-text application, 5
proofing techniques, 27
report draft stages and steps
  near-final draft, 13, 26
  preliminary draft, 10–12, 25–26
  review draft, 11, 13, 26
report tone, 2–3, 25
thorough editing
  checklist, 22
  competitive training program, 23
  error finding techniques, 20–22
  frequently occurring writing lapses, 16–20

Segmented bar chart, 103, 104
Signalized Intersections map, 127
Simile, 197
Spacing, 29–30
Spelling lapses, 20
Spider web chart, 115
Standalone report, 55
Statistical map
  business themes, 120–122
  checklist, 134
  choropleth map, 123
  construction guides, 124–126
  dot map, 124
  geographic patterns, 123
  online mapmakers, 124
  sources, 123
  Static Map Maker site, 123
  symbols, 123–124
  variations, 126–127

Tableau, 99
Table of contents, 65

Tables
   checklist, 134
   construction guides and variations, 119–121
   formal table, 119–121
   informal table, 119, 120
Thematic map. *See* Statistical map
Tone, 2–3
Transmittal message, 175–177, 190
Typographical lapses, 19

Unbalanced pie chart arrangement, 89–90

Usage lapses, 20

Vowels, 211

Waterfall chart (misused), 115
Web Accessibility Initiative (WAI), 50, 74
Web-based report, 55
Webinar, 201–202
Web page format, 47–50

Yandex static map, 123

OTHER TITLES IN OUR CORPORATE COMMUNICATION COLLECTION

Debbie DuFrene, Stephen F. Austin State University, Editor

- *Managerial Communication for the Arabian Gulf* by Valerie Priscilla Goby, Catherine Nickerson, and Chrysi Rapanta
- *Technical Marketing Communication: A Guide to Writing, Design, and Delivery* by Emil B. Towner and Heidi L. Everett
- *Communication for Consultants* by Rita R. Owens
- *Zen and the Art of Business Communication: A Step-by-Step Guide to Improving Your Business Writing Skills* by Susan L. Luck
- *The Essential Guide to Business Communication for Finance Professionals* by Jason L. Snyder and Lisa A.C. Frank
- *Planning and Organizing Business Reports: Written, Oral, and Research-Based* by Dorinda Clippinger

Announcing the Business Expert Press Digital Library

Concise e-books business students need for classroom and research

This book can also be purchased in an e-book collection by your library as

- a one-time purchase,
- that is owned forever,
- allows for simultaneous readers,
- has no restrictions on printing, and
- can be downloaded as PDFs from within the library community.

Our digital library collections are a great solution to beat the rising cost of textbooks. E-books can be loaded into their course management systems or onto students' e-book readers.
The **Business Expert Press** digital libraries are very affordable, with no obligation to buy in future years. For more information, please visit **www.businessexpertpress.com/librarians**. To set up a trial in the United States, please email **sales@businessexpertpress.com**.

Printed by BoD in Norderstedt, Germany